ts

The Spanish Kitchen

OTHER BOOKS

The Sauce Book

Tha Masterchefs of Europe (editor)

Recipes from a Spanish Village

AA: Food and Drink of Spain

Self-Catering in Spain

Spanish Cooking

A Flavour of Andalusia

The Spanish Kitchen

PEPITA ARIS

CASSELL

A Cassell Book
First published in the UK as *The Spanishwoman's Kitchen* 1992
Revised and updated 1998

Cassell
Wellington House, 125 Strand
London WC2R 0BB

British Library Cataloguing-in-Publication Data
A catalogue record for this book is available from the British Library

ISBN 0 304 34954 2

Designed by Richard Carr
Edited by Caroline Ball
Illustrations by Sarah Symonds
Printed and bound in Great Britain by Mackays of Chatham

Contents

Introduction

OOD IS THE Spanish hobby – and has become mine. I inherited my mother's Spanish house some twenty years ago, at almost the same moment that I became the editor of a cookery magazine. How could I not run the two interests together? Driving across Spain at least twice a year, I travelled with a stack of index cards in my pocket: noting a recipe, a new or interesting use of an ingredient, commenting on the agriculture, and recording anything that struck me as unusual.

My first Spanish adventures were with my children. I remember a good-humoured waiter giving a long explanation of *sopa del rey*, its ingredients, its method, to a child of barely five. He ordered and enjoyed it. We also discovered the lamb ovens of Castile together. As adults they still speak of it with wonder. Later my husband went on to work for seven years in Madrid.

My house is in Andalusia, but Spain is a country of passionate regionalism. With a major collection of Spanish recipes behind me, plus some smaller Spanish books, I wanted to see more of other provinces. So I started to travel alone, kilometre on kilometre, in my tiny car; following introductions from kind friends, but also chasing the major Spanish food themes, and classic dishes, back to their most authentic source.

This is a picture of Spanish cuisine round the regions. I wanted to put on record what *cocido*, *paella* and *tostón* are really like, at their best and in their native places, to give a standard of comparison for travellers. They are unlikely to be equalled elsewhere. The book also reflects my pleasure in the Spanish hospitality I enjoyed.

As a good cook I know that ingredients are the key to fine cooking. So I have also looked hard at Spanish ingredients: there is almost nothing published about them – even in Spanish – so talking to the people who use them is the only way to learn.

The recipes I offer here are those I thought representative of the places I visited. They are not automatically the famous ones, which have started to appear in other books (including mine). Rather, it is a private collection of typical and interesting food that I thought would be enjoyed abroad, and give pleasure to foreigners as well as Spaniards. I believe they reflect the best offered by each province.

In my house in Andalusia, I am, for part of each year, a Spanish housewife. For the rest of the year I cook in London, and so have cooked these recipes in both places. I have therefore given you the original ingredients (now starting to appear in supermarkets abroad) and then, in order, the nearest substitutes. I hope you enjoy them.

Pepita Aris

Author, food journalist and broadcaster Pepita Aris has written five books about Spain and its food. These range from recipe collections like *Recipes from a Spanish Village* and *A Flavour of Andalusia* to guides for travellers, interested in eating well and authentically in Spain. She has owned a house in one of the prettiest villages of Andalusia for twenty years. Her husband, Stephen Aris, was the *Sunday Times* correspondent in Madrid. She was the editor of the magazines *Good Cooking* and *Robert Carrier's Kitchen* and was the founder-editor of *Taste* magazine.

ATLANTIC

Santiago de Compostela

Galicia

Miño

Oviedo

Asturias

León

Duero

Salamanca

PORTUGAL

Tajo

Cáceres

Extramadura

Guadiana

Santander

Cantabria

Bilbao

Bas(ou

Rio

Burgos

Old Castile

Segovia

Ávila

Madrid

Toledo

New Castile

La Mancha

Valdepeñas

Cordoba

Guadalquivir

Andalusia

Seville

Jerez de la Frontera

Granada

Malaga

Cadiz

FRANCE

Catalonia

Navarre

Tudela

Soria Zaragoza

Aragon Ebro Lérida Barcelona

Tarragona

Júcar

Levante

Valencia

Palma de Mallorca

Ibiza

The Balearic Islands

Mahón

Segura

Alicante

Murcia

ía

MEDITERRANEAN

N

W   E

S

The
Regions

Andalusia

EVERY IMAGE THAT IS SPAIN COMES FROM ANDALUSIA.
FLAMENCO AND BULLS. THE BROWN BARE HILLS OF
THE SIERRAS, TOPPED WITH THE SILHOUETTE OF THE
BULL THAT SO SPLENDIDLY ADVERTISES VETERANO
BRANDY. AND THE CONSTANT PLAY OF SUN AND
SHADE – SOL Y SOMBRE – REPEATED ACROSS
INNUMERABLE WHITE COURTYARDS.

WE WERE STANDING at the mouth of the Guadalquivir. Across the river the sand banks and pines of the Coto Doñana, Europe's major bird sanctuary, are silhouetted against a landscape of water. Beyond is Africa, a few short kilometres away and often visible across the Mediterranean. This is the way the Moors came in 711, up Spain's most navigable river. At Seville the valley is flat and fertile as far as the eye can see – until it reaches the uplands of the Sierra Morena to the north.

Andalusia is the huge underbelly of Spain. Wrapped by the Mediterranean, it stretches from Huelva on the Atlantic to Almería on the Costa del Sol. It is a land of tawny peaks and switchback roads, for the mountains within Andalusia are higher than those that define it. Three-quarters of Spain's grey-green olive trees grow here, and prosper where nothing else will.

In midsummer the sierras are bare and lifeless. The *pueblos blancos*, white villages, slip down their sides like a helping of cream. Approach one and the whiteness dazzles. By day they are silent, shuttered. No dogs bark. Streets are empty outside the social hours of the evening. In the *semana dura*, the hottest (hardest) week of summer, it can be 30°C/90°F at midnight. No wonder the day is broken by a *siesta*, and tasks are put off until *mañana*.

Despite the dust and heat, this is a land of water. It splashes from village fountains by day, and at night from house jugs on to pots of scarlet geraniums. And luxuriant orange and lemon trees crowd the valley bottoms and surround every small dwelling.

The Moors built the great cities which became Europe's cultural centres: Seville with its high Giralda; Cordoba with its courtyard of bitter orange and a mosque like a marble forest, with glades between the columns; and Granada, with the wonder of the Alhambra. Here, in patios smelling of myrtle, or under fretted arcades, to the noise of fountains, the Moors ate ices made with the snows of the Sierra Nevada.

The Moors planted the citrus fruit and the gentle almond. They cultivated sugar cane and rice and brought aubergines, mint and spinach. Their influence is still present in the architecture: enclosed patios and horseshoe arches; heavy grilles on windows; and street doors studded with the great nails called the *media naranja* (half orange).

Africa is still an influence in the kitchen. Many food words start with the Moorish *al*–, beginning with *almuerzo*, lunch. The Moors brought barbecued and skewered meat, like the charcoal-scented *churrascos* of Cordoba or the popular little kebabs, *pinchitos morunos*, flavoured with Arab cumin.

They brought the pestle and mortar whose cheerful clang is the prelude to an Andalusian meal. And with it came exquisite recipes, still in use, like *gazpacho* (see pages 14–15) and recipes with pounded nuts, like the chicken *pepitoria de gallina* or the almond sweetmeat *alfajores*. The Arabs loved saffron and cinnamon as flavourings for fish and meat. Now the presence of these spices marks the dishes as Spanish. They introduced pickled fish: delicate, vinegared *escabeches* (see page 114). And they started the habit of frying in olive oil.

Is it true Andalusia is the zone of frying? I asked. 'Yes, at home we eat three fried dishes a week, four stews. These things are never done in restaurants.' I conveyed the Madrid idea that the locals were crude cooks. An explosion resulted? 'How dare they say we cannot cook! We have the best climate, we have the best vegetables! Spain taught Europe the meaning of civilized cooking. In the time of the Moors we led the way!' I gently took note.

Rice, first planted by the Arabs, came to Andalusia in a big way in the hungry years after the Civil War, planted in former salt marshes on the Isla Mayor, near the mouth of the Guadalquivir. More grows here than in Valencia. Local dishes are the soupy rice *perrol*, with vegetables and perhaps rabbit and, for festival occasions, inevitably *paella*.

With water, the land is highly productive. Strawberries ripen in the coastal sands, asparagus flourishes in the inland valleys. Almería, once stark, has now disappeared under plastic tunnels and, from the hills, these gleam like marshes. The modern miracle of these *invernadores* gives three, even four, crops a year of green beans and tomatoes. Vegetables go away boxed to the whole of Europe.

In the white villages the pumpkin and the pepper, with the tomato, are staple fare. They go in the *olla* (stewpot) and give Andalusia its characteristic sauce. Chick peas – the potatoes of Spain – are stewed with the red *chorizo* sausage, or are eaten (as are potato crisps) as a fried snack with the evening drink.

Capers from the hillside, wild asparagus and fennel: everything is used. For this is gipsy country, refuge for the legendary Carmen, and a land of simple inventions. In *huevos a la flamenca*, for instance, baked in the little brown *cazuelitas*, eggs are swirled with coloured vegetables, prawns, sausages: any and everything that comes to hand! Another gipsy invention is *tortilla Sacromonte*, a creamy white omelette that now has brains or chicken livers in it, but once contained testicles. The most famous dish from the bullring is *rabo de toro*, oxtail cooked in sherry.

Tapas suits this society, a moment to unwind in a bar with morsels partnering drinks to stave off hunger: a few oval Jordan almonds (from *jardín*, a garden) or a saucer of olives; a chunk of Manchego cheese on bread, or slivers of raw, scarlet *serrano*. Two of Spain's greatest hams are produced locally, at Jabugo and Trevélez.

The southern coast is famed for its fish: boiled *gambas* (prawns) or *langostinos a la plancha*, big prawns cooked on the griddle. Fried battered rings of *calamares* (squid) are sold in every *tasca* (beach bar).

The wine to partner fish is a *copita* of *fino* from the sherry cathedrals of Jerez de la Frontera. Made in a *solera* system, huge tiers of barrels, where one year is filled from another, it is one of the world's finest white wines – and not just an aperitif locally.

If Andalusia has one dish, then it must be *gazpacho*, which carries overtones of the entire history of the province: Egypt then the Romans; the Arabs then the discovery of America which brought the tomato to Europe; the hungry years of the 1930s and '40s. All have had their influence, and are discernible in the many *gazpacho* variations.

Olive oil, too, is fundamental to this province, from the Phoenicians who first planted the trees in the time of biblical King Solomon, to the Arabs who transformed the way oil is used. Raw mountain hams and the fish of the coast are other significant foods. Andalusians are mocked for their sweet tooth; sweets, introduced by the Arabs but now made by nuns, end every festival meal. Festivals are another important part of Andaluz life, their rhythms pacing out the year. I decided to give each of these themes of the region particular study, or a special expedition. It is a pattern to be followed throughout the book.

But it is oranges and sunshine that are the enduring image of the south. The *siesta* is a symbol of a lifestyle, the sweating jug of iced red *sangría* on the table, chunks of orange and lemon gently bobbing in the wine. Andalusia offers the prospect of unwinding to a slower lifestyle, walking at a more measured pace, a place where all heavy tasks can wait until a sunny *mañana*.

GAZPACHO: THE FAMOUS CHILLED SOUP

Spain's most famous soup, icy in the summer heat. What is real *gazpacho* I asked. There was a general agreement that it was made from puréed bread and the raw vegetables of summer. In poorer times it was hot soup, too, lunch for agricultural labourers, served in olive-wood bowls.

And how do they make it so cold – here in the south? Ice is the modern answer, but *gazpacho* should never be a pink liquid, tinkling in a glass. Nor should it be served with ice cubes in it. It is an old recipe, with the chill of cold, cold stones, from standing all night on the cellar floor, *en la bodega* – a familiar word as it also means a wine store. Or it might be diluted with chilly water drawn from a deep well.

Where did it come from? Perhaps from the Arabs, perhaps from Roman times. It may simply be a way of using stale bread (from *caspa*, meaning 'bits' in Latin). Cucumber might be an old partner, for it has grown round the Mediterranean for centuries, but the essentials are garlic to give it interest, and vinegar which makes it refreshing. With them go salt and oil.

A strong counter-argument ran that it is Arab, because it is dependent – at least until the invention of blenders – on the smooth pounding of the pestle in the mortar. Olive oil, beaten until creamy, accounts for its slip-down texture.

And what should go in it? Agreement broke down. It depends who is making it. 'Your *gazpacho* is like your accent; it says where you come from.' In far-away Madrid (and many restaurants) it even contains mayonnaise. One woman included cumin – an Arab spice, I noted.

I remember reading an eighteenth-century traveller, named Richard Twiss, who admired a refreshing soup of bread, garlic, vinegar and oil, beaten till creamy with cold water. And this is probably the essence of it. Tomato, peppers, onions, cucumber, which are now so popular, are but pleasant extras.

Then the recipes. What a surprising diversity! *Gazpacho rojo* containing three or four puréed vegetables is much served, but the bright scarlet version (see page 118) was new to me. Herbs are rarer in the heat. But Huelva shares the Portuguese fondness for fresh coriander, and has a green version.

White *gazpachos* (see page 119) are older than the red ones. Malaga province is famed for its pounded almond and garlic version, garnished with the grapes that make the local dessert wine. And there are older, dried broad bean versions – and modern avocado ones.

Salmorejos are unquestionably Arab – and are very moreish. My favourite is a thick, pink, garlic-scented cream, with a garnish of chopped egg and raw ham (see page 120). It's a *gazpacho* without water. The modern version includes some tomato liquid, but the recipe has a longer history in Spain than tomatoes have, and older versions are still sometimes served.

A DAY BUYING OLIVE OIL

Close your eyes and try to imagine two million olive trees: the world's largest grove at Sierra de Segura. You can't see the extent of it, in a countryside broken by cliffs and gullies. Baena, near Cordoba, is more typical: the grid of grey-green trees against red soil is a pattern that stays on the retina.

Andres Núñez de Prado is the elder of two brothers who have 'an oil mill, not a factory'. In this D.O. (quality-controlled) area, they produce some of the finest virgin oil, sold in the square *frasco* bottle. The family moved here more than two centuries ago, though a tenth of the olive trees are older than this. But the trees are being replaced with smaller ones, because now olives for oil are handpicked. In late November the olives turn black and become sweet and full of oil. Green olives are younger, and these are intensely bitter when they are pickled for the table.

Lagrima is the finest grade of olive oil. The name means 'tears', and the oil has only 20 minutes to drip from the crushed olives. It is cloudy (unfiltered) and greenish and has the freshness of young fruit, almost appley. We eat it greedily on bread. 'The taste of oil is accentuated by light warming,' I was told.

The olives themselves are crushed by four rolling stones, great cones that leave them like crushed mulberries. This purple paste is moved to a woven mat and pressed. The flow of oil from it then separates in tanks by natural density: a cold-pressed oil. The equipment was modern, but to store the second grade oil they still used 200-year-old *tinajas*. These Ali Baba jars were buried up to their waists, so they would not dwarf the workers.

Southern dishes, in the old days, included a lot of olive oil for nutrition, for it contains all the vital amino acids. Now olive oil is in fashion once more, but for the healthy heart, for it is mono-unsaturated and cholesterol-lowering. I was amused to find it may also be an aphrodisiac for women, for it is high in ostreogen, the female hormone. And I always thought the effect of the south came from sunshine!

Olive oil is crucial for Spanish cooking: it is the perfect dressing, because it improves both the taste and texture of food. It makes sauces creamy (but is not as fattening as cream), for it remains in suspension when beaten with a liquid. It doesn't even separate when heated. But Spain's supreme culinary talent is for deep-frying. How do they manage food that is so pure and grease-less? The reason is that olive oil forms a thin dense crust round the food, so it absorbs less fat than it would be if fried in other oils. It is the superior oil for frying, and it doesn't go rancid at high temperatures, so you can deep-fry in it 20 times. Other oils should be thrown away before this.

I took away some useful tips, such as that smoking, too-hot oil can be tamed by adding a piece of potato. To clean oil for the next frying, put in a strip of lemon zest. And parsley chucked in at the end of frying will reduce the smell of frying around the house.

MOUNTAIN HAMS

I went to Trevélez because I heard their hams were cured in snow. Up the switchback road on the south side of Granada, climbing through the poor Alpujarras, whose Berber style of flat-roofed houses came from North Africa more than a millennium ago. Pass a tiny hamlet; an hour later pass it again, now 500 metres above it.

In the highest village of Andulusia the hams are made in a rather ordinary-looking commercial factory. The glory of the place is, rather, the Mulhacén, 3478 metres/11,401 feet, which commands the head of the valley: 'the ice lump in the heart of Andalusia'. So close to the Mediterranean it is unbelievable, a peak of snow-edged facets, cut like white diamond.

Do you bury the hams in snow? I asked. 'Of course not; they would be frozen, wouldn't they? They say they feed the pigs on vipers in the Sierra de Viboras (in Extremadura).' Did I believe that too? I demurred.

In the many ham shops of the village the raw hams hang, the lesser ranking ones from the white domestic pig, and the monarchs from the wild Iberian pig. The black trotters mark these *patas negras* and they hang on racks in a neat line, black ankles all in one direction. Irreverently, they reminded me of leggy chorus girls. We bought our ham, thick-sliced with a knife. It was not the black hoof (unobtainable here sliced) but the white pig, and we ate it in an Alpine-style picnic. It was soft and sweet.

The mountain site is important – hence the ham's name *serrano*, which means 'from the sierra'. For these hams are breeze-dried not freeze-dried, in the clean icy air, after a cure that for most hams is dry, though others are brined. In Jabugo, the most famous hams of all start buried in salt for 4–10 days, then are hung in airy, shuttered rooms upstairs for up to six months. When the weather turns warm the hams begin to sweat salt, which is permitted for a week. They are then moved to cool cellars and hang there for the six warm months, sometimes longer.

The finest raw hams come from Trevélez and Jabugo in Andalusia, and from Montánchez further west. Jabugo, in the hills of Aracena, is an anti-Mecca: a shrine to pigginess! These hams go to top restaurants, or as executive Christmas presents, long lean things, quilted in fat. Inside they are scarlet to a deep raw red, slightly dryish, but flecked with moisturizing fat. Unusually they are carved lengthways, with the grain of the meat. The results are somewhat chewy, with time to mull the flavour. Parma hams seem anaemic by comparison.

You can buy *jabugacitos* (red *chorizos* from the black pig). Other parts of pigs are cured too, the *caña* (loin), which is a prized *tapa*, and the cheaper *paletilla* (front shoulder). A new development of the 1990s is fresh black-pig steaks. They taste like venison.

The wild pigs run in the lower sierras. They are long, lean and dark with black hair, quite unlike the fat domestic porker. I have stalked them with a camera in the wooded Aracena, and around Grazalema, to the west. They scuffle in the undergrowth and loll under the holm oaks that supply their favourite food. Sadly, now only 5 per cent of hams come from the native pigs, compared to a third 30 years ago.

Quality is graded by what pigs eat. The best ham is *bellota* – fed on wild acorns. But only the *pienso,* a wild animal corralled and on a controlled diet for the last period of its life is accepted abroad. For Spain, rather than Germany or even France, is Europe's ham maker. Spaniards consume a whole ham a year per person – every man, woman and child.

When it comes to cooking, I find my neighbours highly practical. Hams on the bone are for *tapas* only. Like bacon, ham goes with everything, and ham bones are sold in ready-sawn rings for cooking. The Spanish stock cube?

ROMERÍA: THE VILLAGE PILGRIMAGE

I saw the Virgin go off in a taxi on May Day morning – along with half the village. She is smaller than my hand, crowned in gold like the child she holds, and enclosed for safety in a glass egg. Two bands with drums and bugles and a choir of women singing 'Hail Marys' escorted her to the edge of the village. The float she rode on was of shimmering silver, her halo standing high over the sheaves of pink and white carnations. Carved and gilded, the float was new, and had cost the village £25,000. Andalusia is devoted to its Virgins.

Forty sweating lads carried her from the church, with many rests and a few beers, to the village border. She was off, for a month, to her summer hermitage in the hills at Fuensanta. The hermitage is tiny, with a bell in a high white gable and two date palms which always fruit in summer. It used to be small and peaceful.

In the first week of June, the *romería* goes to fetch her home with all the splendour our village can muster. It takes two days: Saturday to go there, an all-night party, then Sunday back home again. This year the pilgrimage procession took three hours to pass.

A *burro* (donkey) in a hat and number-plates leads out the procession. Forty carts follow, the product of nights of decoration. Finest are the old gipsy wagons, with canvas over bowed frames. They are pulled by pairs of patient oxen whose tasselled head-dresses make me think of Cleopatra. Lorries next, with fancy awnings, family and celebrators singing and drinking in the back.

The horses travel in dozens. The Spanish ride the high saddle that the American cowboys adopted – and admire an elegant turn-out. The girls ride pillion, full skirts billowing backwards. Walking or riding, all wear local costume. It seems the village is full of beauties, with frilled flamenco skirts flouncing (spots are favoured) and elegant hair pinned high with blossom. The costume suits even the fuller figure.

A space has been cleared on the mountain, and 2000 people sit down to an all-night picnic. The working-men's unions (*cofradías*) organize every-thing, and each has its stand, a one-night hospitality house for 50–100 people. They do the same in Seville. There is supper – *paella* – then space is cleared for dancing.

From her hermitage, packed with lilies, the Virgin watches, a constant silent procession shuffling before her. Sunday is celebrated with a flamenco mass on the mountain. Then the great procession sets out again. Ensconced in the prettiest float, the Virgin rides back to Coín in triumph.

A BEACH PARTY: LITTLE AND GREAT FISH

It was Corpus Christi, the beginning of May, and a tearing Atlantic wind blew fine sand sidewards along the Malaga beaches. I went to grill sardines, on the first fire of the year, with an expert: curly-headed Juan Díaz, one of two fishermen brothers. Our fire was a plank and pieces of driftwood, all laid in one direction. Nothing like the wigwam fires of my scouting youth. But the wind roared through it, making it crackle and turning it swiftly to charcoal.

The sardines came from the market in the usual polystyrene box, the cheapest of fish. Newly caught, they were blue and green, and iridescent in the sunlight. He didn't bother to clean them.

The skewers were home-made from bamboo, with pointed tips. At the long handle end the cane was intact, but half of the rest was cut away to make a dagger. The sardines were efficiently stitched on, four or five to a prong. The handle then went in the sand, the fish parallel to the fire. They looked like galleons with top sails spread. Sizzling round the fire, they are one of the smells of a south-coast summer.

Malaga is also famous for minuscule *chanquetes*. Crisp-fried they are like threads of seaweed. Only the eyes mark them as animal. Threatened by extinction, they are protected, and anchovies or sardines, the size of matches, are battered and fried in their place. Every market here sorts fish meticulously by size, as an aid to perfect cooking. *Boquerones* – anchovies – are one of the best fish for frying. Their backs are green when newly caught, an inky black a few hours later. In Malaga the classic method is to stick the tails together first, to make 'fans' before frying.

To eat the best *pescaito frito*, fried mixed fish, one must go to Cadiz harbour. From this superb moon of enclosed water the fleets set sail for America, and Drake rode in, to burn the gathering Armada. And in the supporting hubbub in its port the fried fish take-away was first invented!

I had come to the Atlantic coast, with its tuna fisheries, to learn about big fish. The real surprise were the dogfish (with mouths like rottweilers) and shark: *cailón* (porbeagle), *pez martillo* (hammerhead) and *cazón*. This has very white flesh when cooked, and is known in English by the harmless name of tope. *Cailón* is a favourite, the medium-lean meat (for who would think of it as fish?) takes up a marinade and high spicing of vinegar and paprika in the local *adobado*. *Cailón en amarillo* is brilliant yellow with saffron. *Rosada* (literally 'pink') covers other nameless predators. Defeated and stripped of their rough skins, they look like great bones on the market slab.

THE NUN'S STORY: SPAIN'S SWEETMAKERS

Her name was Sister Sorena-María and she stood, a pleasant smiling face, behind a grille of iron. At table level a small open wicket gate allowed her to pass us the bags of pastries for which we had come. It was a closed convent in the Barrio de San Francisco below the town at Ronda.

'Go through the green gate, cross the patio to the door in the corner, then ring,' I was told, when looking for the nunnery. There – the only feature of an empty hall – was the *tornador*, a heavy revolving wooden door. This one had shelves upon it, for it was the means of communicating with the inside, sending letters and small presents. It was also the original means by which the nuns passed out sweets and pastries. For this is one of Andalusia's many orders where nuns live in *la clausura*. They never see an outside face. Nowadays, though, discipline is relaxed enough to allow a sister to speak to us through the grille.

Why should nuns be associated with baking? I asked. In Andalusia egg yolks are a traditional by-product of the sherry industry, where whites were used for clarifying the wine, and these were given to the convents for charity, sometimes in perpetuity. These yolks were then made into sweets and pastries for sale. In the nineteenth century, when many convents were stripped of their land, this often became their only source of income.

Less than 50 convents in Andalusia still make and sell pastries, some in houses reduced to half a dozen women. They are sold particularly at festivals like Easter and Christmas and some, like the *yemas* of San Leandro (round golden 'yolks'), made in Seville to a 400-year-old recipe, are famous all over Spain. Now 'fewer girls are called' and nunneries are closing. Ten years ago there were two convents in Ronda.

We discussed our small purchases: they were even called *dulces caseros* – home-baked goods. 'All made with love and no additives,' she joked, to traditional recipes. The nunnery sale list advertised *ganotes* (sweet potato cakes) and *mostachones*, S-shaped almond biscuits that pair to make a 'moustache'. But now they only cook things for which demand is steady: *roscones de vino* (small rings of a wine dough), *mantecados* (lardy cakes) and *polvorones*, little almond crumble cakes rolled up in paper, for they do indeed crumble all too easily. Some titbits still have Arab names, like *alfajores* (almond saddlebags) and *pestiños* (see page 202), little fritters drunk with honey, that date back to Arab frying pans. These nuns might not like the idea, but they are the direct successors of these harem bakers.

THE ANDALUSIAN RECIPES ARE:

Ensalada de alcauciles y pimientos rojos (Artichoke and red pepper salad),
see page 106.

Remojón (Salt cod and orange salad), see page 111.

Salmonetes en escabeche (Red mullet salad), see page 114.

Zoque (Red gazpacho), see page 118.

Ajo blanco con uvas de Málaga (White almond and garlic soup
with muscat grapes), see page 119.

Salmorejo cordobés (Chilled Cordoba tomato cream), see page 120.

Gazpachuelo (Warm potato soup, with eggs and vinegar), see page 122.

Fritura malagueña (Malaga mixed fried fish), see page 152.

Urta a la roteña (Fish with onion, brandy and tomato sauce from Rota),
see page 153.

Conejo en ajillo pastor (Rabbit with aromatics and saffron), see page 178.

Pestiños (Fritters in honey syrup), see page 202.

Soplillos de Granada (Granada almond meringues), see page 205.

Extremadura

PIGS AND SHEEP OUTNUMBER PEOPLE HERE.
IT WAS PROBABLY ALWAYS SO, IN THE COUNTRY
THAT TAKES ITS NAME FROM 'EXTREME' AND 'HARD'.
ON THE PORTUGUESE BORDER, IN THE MOST RURAL
PART OF SPAIN, THIS IS THE LAND OF THE
CONQUISTADORES, THE MEN WHO LEFT TO MAKE
FORTUNES IN SOUTH AMERICA.

THE PRICKLY PEARS are scarlet in November. They top the cactuses like a row of rifle targets, on all the rocky outcrops on the hill above Trujillo. Like the houses of the returning conquerors down below, they are conspicuous newcomers from America.

For this creamy-toned town, wrapped round a square like an arena, is the cradle of the *conquistadores*. Pizarro and Cortés, who conquered Mexico and Peru, Balboa, the first European to see the Pacific, Orellana, explorer of the Amazon, and Valdivia, founder of Santiago in Chile, all came from here. And there are palaces to prove it, chief among them that of Pizarro's brother on the main square. '¡Lo hice! I made it!' boast the buildings.

How could they bear to leave a land so beautiful? Sparse plain gives way to the open *charro*. The undulating hillside, whose name appears on local dishes, is dotted with little populations of holm oak and cork. In April and May it is knee-deep in flowers, pink, yellow, purple, but now the turf was close-cropped and the long acorns were falling, to feed turkeys as well as pigs.

Montánchez is pigsville. This slight hill is famous for one of the three best raw *serrano* hams in Spain. It seems every street has a 'home sale', and they make *chorizos* (paprika sausages) besides. It is an unusual equation that so poor a region should be such a consumer of meat, but pigs and sheep provide for themselves. There is not the soil to grow vegetables.

Extremeñan hospitality is famous throughout Spain. Plates are so generously heaped, you are advised to share them among three or four people. The dishes urged on me were of the humblest: 'Don't do without the fry-up of eggs, ham, sausage and pork.' *Migas* here are made with a magic touch. These breadcrumbs fried with streaky belly and dried peppers are an unexpected treat. And wonderful tomatoes appear in soups and salads with oregano, or stewed with peppers in the local chicken *pollo a lo Padre Pero*. A careful kitchen: figs here are cultivated, elsewhere wild.

In the north of Extremadura the lee of the Sierra de Gredos is famous for capturing sunshine. I drove past the slatted tobacco-drying barns, up the long valley of la Vera to Jarandilla. Here they make the best paprika in Spain. The new season's crop was just in (such a brilliant red!), heaped in sacks, and in three grades, sweet, piquant and *agridulce* – sweet and sour. It has, I learn, an exceptional amount of vitamin C. Perhaps this is why the population doesn't get scurvy on a pig diet?

Even fried eggs are served with paprika – and vinegar over the top. And paprika goes into the pork and the similar lamb *frite*. The flavours pair well with the cloudy *cañamero* wine, which has the appearance of beer but tastes of sherry.

Wild things are very conspicuous. Not just the storks, although half Spain's population breeds here and their great nests top the towers of Trujillo and Cáceres. Wild food is constantly on the menu. Frogs were abundant in November, their legs eaten crumbed and fried. Tench, barbel, trout and pike from the streams are eaten as *mojil de pez*, with wild mint and green garlic, or cold and vinegared as *escarapuche* (see page 115). And in the summer they eat lizards in Plasencia – caught with a loop of string and the help of a terrier. I also met a new way of barbecuing rabbit – *conejo a la teja*, in the curve of a roof pantile. 'It retains the heat so well,' I was told. The method was also good for sardines and pork belly, for terracotta absorbs some fat.

A restless place – loved by many who cannot stay – the country is marked by invisible routes. The Romans carried their silver bullion through, going north. And a vast migration of sheep passed twice-yearly, following the *cañadas*, to and from the summer pastures round Soria and the north. Sheep still winter here – but take the train north.

In spring there is *torta de Casar*, what the Spanish call a *señor queso* – a serious cheese. Made from ewes' milk (curdled with cardoon), it is soft, creamy, even runny, and good enough to challenge the French brie.

There are famous lamb dishes too, like *caldereta* (see page 198) made from young lamb and named after its cooking pot. Mutton is still cooked in old ways – *carnero verde* long simmered, then sauced with a green purée of parsley, mint and coriander. The latter is an unusual herb for Spain, only liked in the west, though common in Portugal.

Orange and lemon trees, and dishes with Mediterranean names, make visible the connection with the south. But the recipe are subtly changed.

Extremeñan *gazpacho* is bulky with chopped onion, and its variants like *cojondongo* contain eggs, and even pig's lights in winter.

Pilgrims are other travellers, to the great monasteries like Yuste and Guadalupe. The black Virgin of Guadalupe, with her exquisite pearly wardrobe, was a spiritual landmark for the *conquistadores* and the monastery at one time fed 1000 pilgrims a day with basic stews of chick peas or salt cod.

Equally famous, the monastery of Alcántara was sacked by a Napoleonic army, whose commander's wife sent their recipes to Escoffier. He made *faisán en la moda de Alcántara*, awash with port and truffles, the most desirable pheasant dish in Europe.

But it is back to pigs, to sum up the essence of the place. Eating pig is part of Catholic religion in Spain, and pigs have their own elaborate ritual in the *matanza* (slaughter). In this beautiful countryside, there is also a special relationship with nature. People are very aware food comes from the wild. From boyhood to old age shooting and trapping the abundant game is a way of life.

MATANZA, AND THE PIG THAT DIDN'T DIE

Rain stayed execution: too wet to make sausages. They need dry air to cure them, so my pig need not die. *Un auténtico rito*, I was assured, one of the great rituals of Spain. Indeed for centuries the death and eating of a pig was a Catholic rite, a demonstration that the participants were neither Arab nor Jewish.

Fewer families do it, in these factory days. Once the *matanza* season ran from St Martin's Day (after All Saints) to the end of March. Now it is just the coldest weather: *por Santa Catalina mata su cochino* – kill your piggy on St Catherine's Day (25 November).

I was in Cacéres for the slaughter – and it was postponed. My farmer-contact fed me beers and the red *chorizo* sausage, his round black eyes concerned on my behalf. But the wait meant days as a noviciate in the rituals of the wild *ibérico*.

The black pig has skin the colour of an elephant, and it dies on the table when its throat is slit. The blood spurts into the *gran cuenco*, a brown basin with a small base and wide rim. The light hair is the next to go, the body down into a straw fire, and then a scrub and wash.

I was shown the equipment, the table with its splayed legs used for slaughter and dismemberment and the *atrevesa*, a trough to hold the chopped meat or pieces for salting. Like a crib or manger, it was a hollowed half-log with sloping ends. Bigger ones are used, filled with rough salt, to cure the hams.

His moustache moved apologetically. 'Sorry. No death in this drizzle.' I eat *prueba de cerdo* (see page 189), delicious hot pork in paprika. We arrange to telephone again.

Another day: he is still jacketless, and in short sleeves, despite the drizzle. We discuss *chorizos*. The hams can be salted, the loin eaten fresh, or everything can be made into *chorizos*, which are then graded by their meat of origin. Ears and tails are invariably salted. Snouts go into stews. Ribs can be eaten fresh or are chopped (to my surprise) and are preserved in the major gut. *Cachelada*, a soup with the lungs etc and cumin, is made on the first day; very good it was too. I learn sausages are made on the second day. More *cañas* (beer), and *morcilla*. The blood sausage is magnificent here, cinnamon-flavoured, with blobs of fat like clotted cream.

Another day, and we contemplate the rain from shelter. His fingers appear from the left-hand pocket (where they had been so glued, I wondered if he were disabled). They flutter ... 'Maybe, *quizás.*' I go to telephone Julian *el carnicero* (butcher) in another town. After a three-day diet of pig (relieved only by bread and alcohol) I began to wonder about this pig thing. Pig palls!

In the end three pigs died. I have gutted an animal once, and it is best not described, except to observe how near death is to birth. Its legs splayed, the pig delivers its membraned packages, all of them useful. You can, they say, eat everything from a pig but its squeak.

The pigs hung in the garage, heads into margarine pots lest they drip, bellies splayed with a stick to get plenty of air. Their insides were like an eighteenth-century cabinet – neat, well-designed fittings. The caul and belly flaps (with teats) hung on washing lines to air. The latter goes to make pumpkin sausages further north. I helped the owners wash out the stomach and intestines into the ditch with a hose.

They make three sorts of sausages in Spain: dried with the red pepper that gives them their names, blood pudding or *morcilla*, with either onion or rice, and fresh *embutidos* or *longanizas*, so called because they have no links. The woman were reluctant, I found, to make *morcillas*. 'Blood is a messy job – for us, and to be sure to be clean. Oh yes, we like to eat them,' in answer to my question.

There was snow in the air, and in the crevices of the black sierra, on the day we finally made sausages, in a small kitchen made warm by a stove with a pipe through the ceiling. There was a faint oppressive smell of meat. The pig died yesterday and weighed 80 kg/175 lb, so we hoped to get 25 kg/55 lb of good *chorizos*. The meat was hand-chopped first. Barely 5 per cent fat, each kilo was flavoured with 3 garlic cloves, 27 g/1 oz each of salt and paprika (half *picante*, half sweet) and made into balls, ready for the mincer.

Three women is the natural team for sausage-making, and I joined Julian's wife, her mother and daughter. The youngest wound a massive mincer. Mother fitted the casing on to its solid spout, and pricked the sausage as it formed, and granny tied them. The intestines lay in a bucket under water, 45–60 cm/18–24 in long. Loop and knot at the bottom, then fingerhold it on to the machine. The meat spurted into the skin which swelled, a gentle rhythm as the handle turns.

A good reef knot, granny tied, not a granny, starting in the middle, for this was solid meat, which cannot be squeezed. A quick flip of knife to remove the ends and a new string of six sausages went down into the bucket. The bigger intestine of the pig made fatter sausages: into a different bowl, for they have a different drying time.

We carried six huge bowls and trays into the back kitchen behind the cow byre, where the windows were open on to the mountains. Ceiling hooks were hung with extra strings and wooden poles posted through the loops. We draped our strings of sausage. As they dry the ends are tied in loops.

'Drying takes a week,' I was told, 'if it doesn't rain.' They shrink and turn bright scarlet. 'If it rains we light the fire – a wood oven in the wall. 'Sometimes we conserve them in oil.' We rested, and ate bread and *chorizo* from the previous batch as night closed in.

GAME: A PASSIONATE HUNTER

'We have to be careful not to let the children go out on Sunday into the rough grass' – I was admiring the parkland so close to the city – 'because of the guns.' Over three-quarters of Spain is hunting country, I discovered – the rest is city! Even in the suburbs of Madrid you can hear the noise of gunshot.

Spain has some of the best hunting country in Europe. *Caza mayor*, big game, is plentiful in most mountains – red deer, boar and others; wolves and bears are protected. But it is *caza menor*, small game, that is the common sport. It needs countryside and Spain still has it. On the main migration routes south, birds come through in great numbers: 'I once saw a band of *paloma torcaz* (pigeon) passing over, 4 kilometres wide. And it took three hours to pass!' I was told. Spain also combines the variety of Africa with that of Europe.

Dr Alvaro Lozano is out every weekend, Saturday or Sunday. He has been shooting partridges since he was eight years old, and learned it from his father: 'a living thing' he wants to see passed on. 'There are very few bad things about hunting. You get to know a lot of people, like the shepherds. I walk 40 kilometres/25 miles in a day with a dog. From dawn to 2–3 pm, perhaps six hours, with a *taco* (a little something) – a *bocadillo* and wine.

He launched into a passionate defence. 'Hunters are preservers, not killers – *cazadores no matadores*. Ecologists understand this. But lots of people come who don't understand: they don't differentiate. *Caza* is an art, like a profession.' He will go out for something and select it. 'A piece is a trophy, a record of success. Others will take a bird on a partridge hunt, even if it is not a partridge. They get in a great wall and shoot everything that comes over, big and little.' He wiped a trembling moustache.

'In Spain there are 4 million partridges, 10 million quail, 7 million rabbits. Partridge is good in October, but wood pigeons, *palomas*, are there all the year. They're now cross-breeding with European pigeons. Turtle dove is just midsummer.

'Quail are summer birds. There is a short season for birds which breed here – 15–20 days, then they are on to Africa. But the wild bird is far superior to the farmed one. The Spanish red-leg partridge is not found elsewhere.' I demurred but he insisted that it is now cross-breeding. 'They fly in vast clouds, on the way to Africa. About a third of the birds that pass over Spain are killed: the rest are for reproduction. We kill about a million partridges, but not more. The *fincas* (there are 27,000 private shooting clubs in Spain, as well as vast national parks) count the number of dead to keep control.

'Starlings used to be taken with a line decoy. You can shoot 400 a day with a bait like this. It's not a sport, but it's been done like this for centuries. Two or three men and a dog can get 140 without a trap.'

I asked about hanging. 'In November the temperature is still high at midday, and a pheasant can easily get tainted in 5 hours. But they might hang one or two days in winter. In summer it's in the 40s (over 100°F) and you can't even leave turtle doves a day. We carry them in canvas bags – there is the danger of flies. You must get them into the fridge, and into the freezer in 2–3 days.' Normally he sold the carcasses. But at home the men cleaned them, the maid cooked them.

What did he like best to eat? 'Thrushes in rice, but turtle dove is even more exquisite and wild quail also wonderful stewed. Woodcock – it's more from the north – stuffed with own innards. Hare – find it in La Mancha and Extremadura – is good with chocolate, and rabbit, with either garlic or tomato: you should eat it with thyme, oregano and rosemary, the natural herbs, picked at the same time. It's smaller and slightly darker than tame ones – like boar is to pig, harder flesh and stronger.'

Acuática, duck hunting, is a special branch. Out came the photographs, himself in hunting waders with braces, car bonnets covered with ducks – green-headed, red-headed, striped-winged – 20 years of successes recorded under plastic covers. A good day was when three or four people shot 70 ducks one day, 20 on another. He watches the temperatures across Europe, and so knows when the ducks will come. But others rely on barometers!

'Aquatics are very varied: there are ducks for winter and ducks for summer. There are mallards in all the lakes of Spain. We hunt them in October, standing in water up to the armpits, hidden in reeds. Pigeon come later, when it is cold in Europe. There are shovellers in winter too.

'Ducks are very serious sport, and few people specialize in it. You must distinguish them in flight. Once I was waiting when a flight of 100 descended – *cosa impresionante*, a marvel! We watched without shooting for 1½ hours – it would have been a massacre – and they wheeled and then left, little by little.' A portrait of a happy man!

THE EXTREMADURAN RECIPES ARE:

Escarapuche (Cold trout in vinegar with chopped salad), see page 115.

Sopa de tomate con higos (Tomato soup with fresh figs), see page 125.

Pato con aceitunas a la antigua (Duck with olives the old-fashioned way), see page 174.

Liebre guisada (Hare in red wine), see page 180.

Costillas con níscalos (Pork ribs with wild mushrooms), see page 185.

Prueba de cerdo (Fried pork with paprika and vinegar), see page 189.

Caldereta extremeña (Extremaduran lamb stew), see page 198.

New Castile and La Mancha

SOUTH OF MADRID, LA MANCHA FORMS THE
GREATER PART OF THE CASTILIAN PLATEAU. THE
HOTTEST AND DRIEST PART OF SPAIN, THE REGION IS
SO BACKWARD THAT WHEN CERVANTES WANTED TO
BRING A SMILE TO THE LIPS, HE CHOSE IT FOR HIS
GOOD KNIGHT, DON QUIXOTE DE LA MANCHA.

JOINED THE TRAIN at Chamartín, Madrid's main station. It is like an airport. Distant places flash up on the indicators, with their gates, then roll away. All tickets bookable and every ticket guarantees a seat. Outside, the platforms are low-slung for Continental trains. Oh, the glamour of those long-distance engines, with great headlights, and the carriages with flights of steps up into them! A period of frenzied activity followed, as old ladies with cardboard boxes (fortified with rubber ties) were shoehorned by half the family into their compartments.

'Only 20 minutes late,' said my companions with approval, as the engine started to take the weight. In our compartment three jolly chaps settled down to play cards, then there's me and a granny, and a couple of mums with small children. Out came colouring books and new crayons. We knew we had ten hours to reach the south!

La Mancha means 'bone dry', from *manxa*, the Arabic for parched earth, for this elevated plain is not irrigated. Cereals, vines and olives grow here, fields of saffron and a vast production of sunflowers. The river Tajo lies south of Madrid, with Toledo and the summer palace of Aranjuez in the last green valley. Then the plains go on for ever. There are six or seven market towns, and fewer cities, at the plain's four corners.

In summer the sun's heat obliterates all thought but of shade and water. La Mancha survives under a sky of molten metal, shimmering and apparently uninhabited. But in March rain hangs in the air. There is a sense of space and far distant horizons. Cyclists in racing colours, a fast-moving bunch like horses on the Irish Curragh, sweep past the train – the *rápido* does not live up to its name and proceeds at a stately pace.

The pruned vines look like rows of black stopcocks, close to the earth. This is the wine lake of Spain, Europe's biggest and poorest vineyard. It produces rough yellow wine: as someone said of Madrid's river in summer, 'contributed by mules'. Hour after hour the train rattles across it. Every field has a small white building and water wheel, with an attendant almond tree. Spring is late here, icy like Britain's, and they are covered in deep-pink blossom. There really are windmills in La Mancha, clustering on the slightest ridge.

Castile is a region of poor man's food. I can see why. Simple hearty garlic soups, beans with cardoon, lentils with rice, and meals with chick peas or potatoes plus items from the *tocinería* (pork shop). But it has some of Spain's best-known dishes: *garbanzos con chorizo*, chick peas with spicy red sausage that so perfectly flavours them; *potaje* (chick peas with spinach and salt cod), eaten particularly in Lent; and *pisto* (see page 109). *Olla podrida* is an everyday pot with chick peas and humble things from a pig, rather than solid meat, like Madrid's *cocido* (see page 37). *Tortilla* was invented in New Castile, a dense egg cake quite unlike a French omelette. And eggs go into everything. *Mojete* (which just means moist) is another tomato mixture, this time with fried potatoes and garlic, to which a poached egg is added 'for charity'.

They like strong flavours here, to combat the climate: raw tastes against winter cold and summer furnace. Cumin, from Arab times, is backed up by thyme in unheard-of quantities. Cumin goes into *sopa castellana*, into the local *gazpacho* and on to tomato or red pepper salads. It is noticeable in the tomato-sauced beans, *judias a lo tío Lucas*. Another strong flavour is that of toast: toasted bread (which can dominate a dish), but often cinders or the grill. *Tiznao*, fish started in the ashes, then finished in pepper sauce, is the most elegant example.

Escabeches – also Arab – are marinated foods, cooked in wine and vinegar. Most famous is the red-legged partridge, which breeds here. And all the village fairs sell aubergines pickled with hot peppers from Almagro.

Partly cereal country, there are ancient bread-thickened dishes like *gazpacho manchego*. The country recipe is nothing like the tourist dish. Large flat pieces of unleavened dough become fried pizzas. On a good day, a stew of rabbit or pigeon would be cooked separately, and broken crusts added to the gravy. The meat was then served on another crust. Some days no game was caught.

Saffron is grown in both Castiles, while Toledo is celebrated for inventing marzipan some 800 years ago. Better wines are made at Valdepeñas. When driving you know you have reached it by the vast Ali Baba jars beside the road. These *tinajas* are still used for wine-making.

La Mancha also makes the most famous cheese in the country, from the milk of *manchega* ewes, that cross it twice a year, to reach winter or summer grazing. Much copied, Manchego is the Castilian cheddar, sold at all ages. It may be soft, mild and dull, or *curado*, sharp and crumbly, sometimes in a gold rind, sometimes a black one, with braid marks on it. The taste of aged Manchego cheese (*añejo*) is haunting and addictive, reminiscent of good parmesan. It is more expensive, though, for parmesan is made from cows' milk, and Manchego from ewes'. Look out also for *páramo de Guzmán*, Manchego-style cheese preserved in olive oil.

There are three things for which La Mancha is world-famous, was my increasingly sleepy reflection. The cheese, of course; that gangling, good-hearted, self-deluding knight, Don Quixote; and saffron, the royal spice, valued and coloured like gold. These would need further investigation. Out came the cheese and ham *bocadillos*, then our compartment settled down to snooze.

IN SEARCH OF DON QUIXOTE

I saw what Cervantes saw, with a shock of recognition. Driving north across the plain, featureless in the dusk, towards Consuegro, the castle was silhouetted against the evening sky. And to its left, along the ridge, were six giant figures. The famous windmills of Don Quixote! But at this distance all scale was missing. They looked like giants with lances.

Windmills, I discovered, were introduced from Holland about 20 years before Cervantes began his epic book. No wonder his hero found them striking! Was Don Quixote, then, an early Luddite, battling against the machines? Now it would be the electricity pylons. Built like figures, with the profile of a hat, broad shoulders and legs, a row marches across the plain north of Toledo. He would have fared much worse.

Don Quixote opens with food: 'His habitual diet consisted of a stew, more beef than mutton, hash most nights, *duelos y quebrantos* (sorrow and suffering) on Saturdays, lentils on Fridays and a young pigeon as a Sunday treat. This took three-quarters of his income.' The puzzle is: what are *duelos y quebrantos*? 'Boiling bones' says J. M. Cohen in the Penguin translation. This is not what's served now in La Mancha. Eggs are involved, for certain. I've been offered eggs with *chorizo*, the red of the sausage, I was told, signifying 'wounds' – *duelos*.

In the end I found an academic who had given it a corner of his mind. The phrase means the same as 'scraping the barrel'. And finally to Calderón de la Barca (in the 1650s), who writes of *huevos y torreznos bastan que son duelos y quebrantos*. We are back to eggs and bacon!

Torreznos are very typical of Castile and essential fare at *la matanza*. Fingers of cured streaky pork belly become crisp, light (like empty sponge) and fatless, by first dry-frying then applying high heat. Better-tasting and better for you than English crackling.

SAFFRON: OCTOBER GOLD

Flying fingers pull the scarlet stamens from the centre of each crocus. It is like sewing with fine silk: meticulous repetition. I wonder they do not get cramp, from so intense and seasonal an occupation.

The purple *rosas* are tipped upon the kitchen table and three stamens and a pistol must be plucked from each one. When they are heated during cooking, they produce a heavy aromatic scent, an aromatic oil and a water-soluble colour. But at this stage a good day's work is 50–70 g/2–3 oz plucked and a week to get a pound! 160,000 blossoms are needed for a kilo.

Last of all comes *el tueste*, the toasting. Only older women are trusted to do it. To dry the stamens, they are put on a sieve over a pan of charcoal. Moments when weeks of labour are at risk. No wonder this is the world's most expensive spice!

Mancha *selecto* is the world's best saffron: deep-red stamens, as long as the first joint of your thumb, packed and date-stamped. Lesser types, like sierra saffron, have shorter stamens and a quantity of white and yellow flower parts. They also have a bitterer flavour.

The festival in Consuegro is the cheerful public side of muscle-aching labour. It starts on the Friday with a *chupinazo*, when sweets are scattered to the children in the Plaza de España. Here, too, there is dancing by the local girls in dark red skirts and black aprons. There are bull fights and the election of a beauty queen. In her gold and scarlet sash and sixteenth-century costume, she is called La Dulcinea after Don Quixote's enamorata. There are saffron-plucking races between the girls from different villages, and even a children's competition.

Saffron by weight costs more than gold, but little enough of the latter sticks to the hands of those who produce it. Landless labourers plant the bulbs on rented land, as an insurance policy. Anywhere suitable: round the grapes, or where winter wheat will grow later. Always the poorest, I was told, and always the same families. Some years they don't want to do it.

The flowers of *Crocus sativus* appear overnight, round Santa Teresa's Day, 15 October. In a landscape burnt brown by the sun, they are more like purple rugs than carpets. They must be hand-picked the same day, so it is out at dawn, for perhaps 19 hours of stooping. Not surprisingly the crop has dropped by half since the 1930s!

The Arabs worked out the secret of saffron cultivation more than 1000 years ago and gave the spice the name yellow, *za'fran*, though the Romans brought it to Spain. Now it grows in Aragon, Murcia and Old Castile. The best quality is from Manchuela, from Cuenca south to Albacete.

Saffron has been exported since the 1400s, when adulteration was also a problem. In Spain the substitutes are safflower (the yellow *cártamo*) and packets of dye labelled *colorante*, which contain tartrazine.

A 0.125 g pinch of stamens serves 4–8, about 30 stamens or ½ teaspoon by eye. Italian packets of powder (usually 0.1 g) serve about the same. Some recipes call for 50 strands; this equates to about 0.25g or 1 teaspoon. Stamens are crushed in a mortar though fingers are easier and are soaked for five minutes.

In Consuegro the local recipes seemed modest: yellow potatoes (4 packets!), rice with saffron, *cocido con garbanzos* (chick peas in golden broth), a sweet saffron sponge cake. Indeed saffron seemed to go into most things. It adds substance and subtlety; something that wasn't quite there before. Like enriching the dark velvet quality of a shadow.

THE RECIPES FROM
NEW CASTILE AND LA MANCHA ARE:

Tortilla de patatas con azafrán (Potato cake with eggs and saffron),
see page 99.

Pisto Semana Santa (Peppers, tomatoes and onion with tuna), see page 109.

Sopa de la abuela castellana (Granny's garlic and bread soup), see page 123.

Crema de Aranjuez (Aranjuez cream of asparagus soup), see page 126.

Pollo con salsa de ajos (Chicken with saffron and garlic sauce), see page 165.

Perdices estofadas (Partridges in wine and vinegar), see page 175

Alajú (Arab honey and nut sweetmeat), see page 211

Madrid

AT THE HIGH CENTRE OF THE COUNTRY, MADRID
WAS THE OBVIOUS CAPITAL WHEN THE COUNTRY
UNITED 500 YEARS AGO. A CITY OF BROAD AVENUES
AND SPACIOUS PLAZAS, IT MUST BE A PLEASANT PLACE
TO LIVE IN, DESPITE EXTREMES OF WEATHER, FOR
THE GUADARRAMA MOUNTAINS ARE VISIBLE FROM
CITY OFFICES.

MADRID IN MARCH. No leaves, yet, on the trees in the Paseo de Castellana, the avenue which bisects the city. But the Metro posters are all of beauties in wedding dresses. The sun has banished overcoats, and dark-stockinged legs are visible everywhere. It seems a pity I am not a fellow.

Fashionable eating, I soon discover, is in the *casas regionales*, many round the Plaza Santa Ana. Every region has an authentic restaurant here. Botín's, the oldest restaurant in the world, and Lhardy's (a bar, restaurant and charcuterie all in one) are beloved institutions, and there are Michelin-starred restaurants, too, notable Zalacaín, which has Navarre connections. It is also a fine city for food shopping, as I was to discover.

It is the hours that are so punishing. 'I have never had more than five hours sleep a night, and I have never had a siesta,' said one *madrileño*. Madrid has the most robust nightlife (and appalling hours) in Europe, with restaurants opening at 10 p.m., smart to arrive at 11. How can executives dance till three on a Friday night? – but they do. The rush hour is often around 3 a.m.

I ask about Madrid food. A *la madrileña* used to mean short-order food, I discover, restaurant dishes, cooked to order, whereas all the old ones were all-day affairs. 'Oh yes, Madrid has its official dishes – *cocido* and *callos* (boiled meats, and tripe with various sausages) – but they're drawn from the countryside. Grannies might cook them.' The implication was they are not for us. *Cocido*, though, remains a totemic dish, a national number with regional variations and several derived dishes. It was something I had to pursue further.

The famous quote about Madrid is 'Nueve meses invierno, tres infierno': nine months winter, three months hell. In December the Puerto de Somosierra (the mountain pass just north of the city) may be closed by snow, and chill grips the city. But the lights twinkle in the Calle Serrano, and Velázquez, as they do in London's Regent Street and New York's Fifth Avenue, and luxuries appear in food shop windows.

Behind the glass, next to the door, I saw bottles of Vega de Sicilia, Spain's most expensive and difficult-to-obtain red wine – just two or three of them, in a place where you cannot miss them. There are big baskets of glacé fruit everywhere, and El Riojana, in the Calle Mayor, has tarta de Mondoñedo (Spain's answer to treacle tart) covered with candied fruit. And every ultramarinos (specialist grocer) sells the Twelfth Night cake, roscón de reyes, a yeast ring cake with one hidden bean inside.

Hams, not turkeys, come into their own. El Corte Inglés and the Museo del Jamón (shops, despite their names) have impressive displays. King of the mountain, the lean black-footed Jabugo serrano commands about £30 per kilo, down to the Extrameño rounded golden blanco (white pig) and still cheaper hams from Murcia. At 6–7 kilos each, these are no cheap purchase. Many end up as executive Christmas presents, or something to buy if you win El Gordo (literally 'the fat one'), the Christmas lottery with prizes as big as those in Britain.

MARKETING IN MADRID

You can cross Madrid in half an hour by Metro, yet everyone owns car. And they use it: to go five minutes to a bar. There is nowhere to park – temporarily or permanently. Complaints (and scrapes) are constant.

I was met by Jaime in a green buggy with no doorlocks and a Palma de Mallorca number plate. 'The Madrid police process 25,000 infractions a year,' he explained. 'With these it will be a while till they get round to me.'

Our market tour starts with one that has no food, a fine 1930s building near the Rastro, of soaring concrete in the Fascist style. Built for fish, it now houses antique booths. The fish have moved to Mercamadrid and fish shops are first on our list, to reach them early in the morning. The Casa Francisca in the Calle Bailén he thought the best for cod, La Marquinesa best for fresh tuna and Pescaderías Coruñesas for shellfish.

The Pescadería Pardiñas at Calle de Alcalá 131 shone white, the tiles reflecting the morning light. Here we hoped to find gallo (Madrid's answer to plaice). Fish is so fresh in the capital (despite an 8-hour drive from the sea) that one popular local dish is called mata mulo – the mule killer. The speed getting to Madrid did the animal in!

There are mussels, five sizes and varieties of prawns, and the beautiful, eccentric barnacles called percebes (see page 47) at around £40 per kilo. The salmon-trout, *reo*, looks more like a carp, short, stubby, brown. There is *bonito* in a great joint like a lamb saddle and swordfish, *pez espada*, grey-pink round a central bone.

'You can buy foreign produce like South American swordfish. It's cheap, like sardines ...' Jaime was back from solving our parking problem and information flowed out of him like bullets '... and big prawns from Thailand with red and pink rings, but I don't advise it. The best anchovies come from L'Escala.' Then the amounts of fish needed for *paella*: I remember there was 1 kilo of rock fish for the stock, and crabs to go on top, but I was unable to take in so much advice.

Back to the buggy and we whirl through Madrid, to the Mercado de la Paz in the Barrio Salamanca. Madrid buys splendid beef from Galicia and the Basque country. The famous veal producers are at Ávila. Jaime didn't like it: 'Insipid!' Better pink veal (the popular taste) to milk-fed. The market sells veal haunches for roasting, labelled with their age: one year or two years. 95 per cent of the beef in Spain is not hung, and is the equivalent of British pink or grey veal. Like the hams, the labels say what the animal ate, to indicate the quality. *Lomo cebón* is veal loin fed on barley.

Walking across the street, the Frutas Vazquez (Calle Ayala 11) was as pretty as a doll's house, the shop-front folded back on either side, with flanking shelves. Dramatic crookneck squash, pumpkin, pineapples in baskets and asparagus 60 cm/2 ft high framed the door. And the shop apron was full of good things: ginger in flat hands and new potatoes from Almería. The very best from the regions: *cogollos* (lettuce hearts) from Tudela and spicy pointed peppers, *pimiento de piquillo*, and fresh bouquets garnis with a dozen herbs tied up with string, for 50p.

Spring fruit is quite different in Spain: wild strawberries, and raspberries from Segovia. There were chanterelles and enchanting *cardillos*, tiny hearts of curling stalks, purplish on the outside and part of the artichoke family. I bought a bag of white *criadillas*, summer truffles, from Cáceres.

We stop for a beer at Cervecería Alemana in the Plaza Santa Ana, a favourite with Ernest Hemingway, then work through the backstreets, past La Casa de la Abuela, a *tapas* bar famous for prawns. I comment on the pink heads on the floor. 'They couldn't sweep it, or the place would seem unpopular,' was the answer. Up the Calle Victoria where the bullfighters drink, and along Echegaray. We look into Los Gabrieles. Huge tile pictures frame the walls. One is a pastiche on Velázquez's *Los Borrachos*, the drunkards. Others advertise wine, or biscuits for Galletas Olibet. Then into a dark brown cavern, stacked with sherry butts, to drink *fino* and eat *mojama*. This is cured tuna and a speciality of the south and east coasts. It looks like dried beef and comes from the back, sun dried and sea-washed.

Madrid's best pastry shop is Antiqua Postería de Pozo at Calle del Pozo 8. Puff pastry is their forte, salmon pies, and desserts with the favourite squash jam, *cabello de ángel*. *Bartillos* are triangles filled with almond custard, then deep-fried.

Back at the Mercado de la Cebada, near where we started, there were problems (again) with the parking. Jaime disappeared for hours and I inspected the Galician charcuterie: dark sheets of fat, paprika-dusted pork belly and *cecina* (beef ham) from León. 'It fed the conquerors of America.' Jaime has reappeared again.

Even food, it seems, is subject to politics. The Franco era kept the shutters down for 30 years – nothing from outside. One woman told me, 'People were asking: What is a raspberry? In 1980 broccoli hardly existed.' Today the market is flooded with small, sweet Canary bananas and *ajetes*. This green sprouting garlic, much the same size as spring onions, has a mild flavour and is favourite with eggs.

Back to my Metro station, we divide the shopping and I try to pay for mine. 'Don't give me money, especially here! Someone might see you!'

COCIDO: CAPITAL FARE

'As a young bride I could not believe that people eat so much,' said Denyse Casuso, when I asked about *cocido madrileño*. 'When it came out, I looked at all these platters, and thought: what can I eat? Then there was often a second course of steak with chips. Then they would ask if anyone was hungry? Would any one like a fried egg? – and some did!'

In the national dish several courses come from the slow-simmering pot, where many meats make a slow exchange of flavours. The broth, *caldo*, is served first as soup with rice or pasta cooked in it. (It is also a favourite item in other Spanish recipes.) 'The chick peas were cooked with the meats, but they were put in a bag, so they could be served in a separate dish. My mother-in-law served green beans and tomato sauce too. Then there were the meats, all carved: beef, chicken, cooked *serrano*, black pudding, *chorizos*, pork belly – all together. The last dish was carrots, turnips, leek, potatoes – all the vegetables – but all the plates came out together.

'The *chorizo* and *morcilla* (black pudding) were cooked in the main pot, to colour the *caldo* pink, added just at the end. *Morcillo* breaks up if cooked longer then five minutes. The whole thing must be cooked slowly, in the traditional way. Not in a pressure cooker.' A second casserole held the vegetables: chard, drumhead cabbage, green beans or cardoons. This was to keep the taint of cabbage away from the pure meat broth.

The joke is that when that doughty queen, Isabella the Catholic, expelled the Jews in 1492, Spain adopted their most-Jewish dish. *Cocido* is the direct descendant of the chick pea *adafina*, left to simmer all the sabbath. There are other similarities, too. In wealthy households fried meatballs are still added towards the end of cooking. (In the poorer south these are made of bread and chicken livers.) Called *pelotas*, they are the symbolic traces of the Jewish hard-boiled eggs. I have also met strips of omelette as a garnish.

Of course the Christians set about 'converting' their adopted casserole. Pork and sausages went in at this point, and its consequent meat content made it an aristocratic dish. Nowadays the favoured sausages for *cocido* are *chorizos* from Cantimpalo (in Segovia).

With local changes, *cocido* is still made in every region of Spain. Its vegetable content increases away from the capital. And as a consequence it has slipped down the social scale. The Basques use red beans instead of chick peas, in Galicia turnip leaves go in, and in the contrary Maragatería (León) everything goes on the table in the reverse order, ending up with soup! The south likes its *pucheros* much sweeter, with pumpkin and even pears. And in Catalonia the soup becomes *escudella* with noodles and the *carn d'olla* (meats of the pot) becomes one huge dumpling.

Like our Sunday roast, meat from the *cocido* goes on to make a hash on Monday. In Spain this is called *ropa vieja* (old clothes) with yesterday's meat and chick peas reheated in a tomato sauce.

THE MADRID RECIPES ARE:

Aceitunas aliñadas (Marinated olives), see page 96.

Torta de gambas (Prawn-glazed loaf), see page 100.

Tigres (Stuffed crumbed mussels), see page 101.

Surtido de verduras rellenas (Stuffed vegetable selection), see page 138.

Merluza de Mama (Hake with two mayonnaises and a soup course), see page 150.

Besugo al horno (Baked whole fish with lemon and potatoes), see page 156.

Redondo de ternera mechada (Pot-roast beef larded with ham), see page 194.

Chuletas de cordero con pimientos asados (Lamb cutlets with soft red peppers), see page 197.

Old Castile and Rioja

THE HEART OF SPAIN, BOTH PHYSICALLY AND
EMOTIONALLY, CASTILE IS THE HIGH TABLELAND AT
THE CENTRE OF THE COUNTRY. THE LANGUAGE
(WHICH IS CALLED CASTILIAN) AND THE STRENGTH
TO BATTLE BACK AGAINST THE INVADING MOORS
WERE BOTH FORGED IN CASTILE. A LINE OF CASTLES,
EXTENDING ACROSS WHAT IS NOW WHEATLAND,
MARKS EACH SURGE TOWARDS THE SOUTH.

I ENTERED CASTILE BY the back door, driving up the Valle de Jerte. It's the south-western corner of the province, coming round the Sierra de Gredos, the mountain rim west of Madrid. The road weaves and climbs to the Castilian plateau, through a sea of cherry trees. The leaves were golden in October. On to the Puerto de Tornavacas and over the top, to meet the first castle.

El Barco de Ávila is a small town, with a tiny, shabby square. It is famed across Spain for its round white kidney beans. In the autumn sun, the cartridge belts hung up along the high street, and the sausage skins, dried *tripas*, fluttered brown like massed condoms. I bought the *judías* (beans) and the local paprika, a deep, deep red. What prodigality, to see a whole sack of such a spice!

Despite the presence of historic cities – Ávila, Segovia, Salamanca – this is a poor region. Stewed beans and peas, not meat, are daily fare – lentils on Monday, chick peas on Tuesday and beans on Wednesday. Lentils were eaten with chicken giblets and fried *chorizo* (paprika sausage) or pig's ear. Beans were cooked with *chorizo* and *tocino* (pork belly), 'but less now everyone is down on pork, for health reasons.' Bay and parsley are added; some use cumin. Garlic is the flavouring *par excellence*. 'And 14 December, the feast of St John of the Cross, is the day to eat *garbanzos*. In Arévalo, huge cauldrons are set up in the monumental market place.'

There is, however, no lack of meat, just of money. The wide valley of

Amblés rears the best veal in Spain. I was more conscious of the sausage factories and the smell of piggeries.

Light snow was in the air as I stood by the walls of Ávila: 88 perfect turrets, and part of the second line of fortifications, which included Segovia and Salamanca. Fur tippets were in fashion, I noticed, and pony coats, in the highest city in Spain. Santa Teresa is an ever-present figure, for from Ávila she reorganized the convents which once held one in ten of Spain's women.

The heartbeat of history pulses near the surface here, as successive lines of castles mark the fight against the Moors. It is impossible to ignore them, or get away from the fighting presence of Queen Isabella, *la Católica*. Born in one castle, at Madrigal de las Altas Torres, she died in another, at La Mota. Fighting a battle here, giving birth there (wherever she happened to be stationed), she had her way just as effectively as Santa Teresa. Spain certainly has a tradition of strong women!

North of here, in León, the Tierra de Campos is the granary of Spain, round Carrios de los Condes, with its red brick villages, and south towards Zamora. The wind blows through the seas of frozen wheat in winter and the sun crushes it in summer. They grow the best wheat in the country here and still make the large *hogaza*, the *pan de padre nuestro*, 'our daily bread'.

Ancha es Castilla goes the saying – Castile is wide: there is room for people to be themselves. Driving westwards at sunset across its open, undulating vastness, space and time blend and it seems that, by driving fast enough, one could catch the night and stay permanently suspended in that blood-red light.

The great plain is framed in the north by the Cantabrian mountains and, to the south, by the Sierra de Gredos and the Guadarrama range that shelters Madrid. The east, too, is high, so the plain tips west. This is *tierra del vino*, with four major wine areas; three lie along the Duero. Spain's single most expensive wine, Vega de Sicilia, is produced at La Ribera del Duero, as are good whites. Rioja lies well to the east, immediately south of the Basque country and, in the higher, cooler Rioja Alta, produces wines with the possibility of great maturation. A *la riojana*, I find, does not mean a dish with red wine, but one with red peppers. Lodosa holds a pepper fair. It was something I intended to find out more about.

South of Rioja is the Meseta, where fortunes were made from sheep and are recorded in stone, in cities such as Burgos and Soria. Sheep, which wintered in the south, walked north in summer, to graze the higher plateaus, a massive shift of animals, twice a year. Lamb stars at the September wine fairs, where *chuletas de cordero*, diminutive lamb cutlets (four, even five, to a portion) are grilled over vine-prunings, *al sarmiento*. But the culinary glory of Castile is *lechazo*, milk-fed lamb, roast in the traditional beehive oven. It's a dish unchallenged anywhere in the world, and is copied across Spain as Easter fare. From Aranda del Duero southward is lamb country, and I feasted in some of the famous places: more about this later.

Not be outdone, pigs hold their own, for the necessary supply of hams and sausages. In Castile I succeeded in celebrating the *matanza* (slaughter) with five hours of hard eating and drinking – as opposed to the messy business with knives and aprons!

The plateau is icy in winter, an aid to good sausages, like *chorizos* with oregano, the Burgos *morcillas* with blood and rice, and the ugly but delicious *botillo* from the Bierzo. Salamanca also has a *farinato* (a bread sausage with paprika) – they consider it a mid-morning snack – and *hornazo*, a pie with a mass of meats inside: *chorizos* and ham, pork belly and birds, topped with criss-cross pastry. Pig and goat, as well as lamb, are cooked in the round ovens. There are also good stews, some with lamb, and in the little *tascas* (bars) they serve *conejo al ajillo*, rabbit with garlic.

Spanish respect for ingredients includes every part of the animal. Offal is *tapas* bar fare here. The tiny lamb's feet really moved me, their porcelain toes like those of Nicolette in the French fairy story about Prince Aucassin: 'the whiteness of her feet shamed the daisies as she passed.' I ate 16 in one plate-ful! They tasted as smooth as custard and the pearly toes left on the plate were like children's loose teeth, left for the fairies.

At Guadalajara, on the way to Madrid airport, I ate the local delicacy, *zarajos*. An entire lamb's intestines, it was wrapped round two sticks, like a ball of wool for knitting. It was grilled until crisp outside but remained succulent within. These inside things are delicious! As the traveller Richard Ford said of cat-stewed-for-rabbit: 'It is only knowing that hurts.'

Tucked into the northern rim of mountains to the west is the ancient kingdom of León. With the mountains of the Bierzo behind it, game such as red deer – *ciervo* – is abundant. There are also hundreds of miles of trout streams, and the fish end up in the local red wine. Frogs' legs are eaten battered in La Bañeza, with garlic in Zamora, and the Herrera del Pisuerga is famous for its crayfish festival. Game birds pass south over much of Castile, to winter away from Europe. 'It rains *codornices* (quail) in season,' I was told more than once. The stewed partridges (see page 175) are a favourite.

Unlike New Castile there is a longstanding tradition of little cakes in this part of the plateau, like the golden, sugar-rich, round *yemas* (the size of a bantam's yolk) in Ávila, *mantecados* (small square sponges) in Astorga, and one in León called *polvorones* (crumble cakes) 'Jesus, they're exquisite! May I choke on them!'

ROAST LAMB, SUCKING PIG AND ARAB OVENS

Sepúlveda is stretched along the ridge, a small town north-east of Segovia. Easy to see, difficult to reach, as this means snaking round the valleys. The site is so narrow the town can barely manage a main square, houses stacked on stepped streets or squeezed out along the promontories. It is famous for its *asadores*, lamb ovens. My children were at baby ages (round five) when they ate their first roast *lechazo*. They still speak of it with wonder 15 years later.

The ovens are on Arab models. I have just such a one in my orchard, further south. Built for a private house, it is bigger than a wheelbarrow inside – rings of brick rising in a low domed ceiling with a small door for putting in wood and baking. It needs time, and much wood, to heat it.

Sucking lamb, from the surrounding hills where the ewes sup on thyme and rosemary, is the speciality in Sepúlveda. A leg to a single portion, it has an unmatched flavour.

The west of Castile is equally famous for its ovens but here they roast sucking pig instead of lamb. Where was the line? Arévalo and Segovia were piglet country. On, then, to Arévalo, to eat the rival *tostón*, hoping for a recipe. 'We get them from the baker. We ring up and tell him what time we want to eat and he delivers them hot.' Some take-away!

I went to visit my lunch cooking. The smell of roast meat wafted down the street, as we walked into a wood shed. The baker opened a small iron door and there, on a revolving turntable, were 30 little piglets. Golden skinned and fatless, they are cooked split-and-flat, each in an earthenware dish. Head and tail up, legs splayed, they meet their apotheosis in cheerful abandon, as though they were sky-diving.

The cooking process is slow, with nothing in the way of secret herbs or spices. What was the recipe, I asked? The wood, the baker said. 'Holm oak; the mothers from which they come; the age at which they are killed' – 15–20 days old. 'And four generations of experience!' Such things are wedding fare here. The golden skin is ceremonially carved with sharp blows from the side of a plate. I have the shoulder-blade of that piglet still; in size and shape it matches my car key.

RIOJA RED PEPPERS

La Guardia, on the hill, looks out over Rioja, a balcony to view the vineyards. Scrubby, ground-hugging vines, sprawling on small hills, have an uncared-for air to those accustomed to the neat vineyards of France or Germany.

Our journey up here took us past walls bearing famous names. Viña Ardanza going through Haro, Marqués de Cáceres in Cenicero and Marqués de Riscal (and a fine group of conker trees) in El Ciego. I was reminded of my grandfather's story of a French general who made his troops present arms to the vineyards of his favourite burgundy.

La Guardia also has the most colourful medieval portal in Europe. Its saints seem freshly painted, for the citizens built a porch with an outside door, which saved the stonework from the weather. But in late September the colour was in the streets: bright with peppers. Scarlet, long and pointed, they were festooned from every balcony. Against the walls were also silver necklaces of foil balls. 'Those are prunes, drying for Christmas,' I was told.

As I had discovered with surprise, *a la riojana* means a dish with peppers, rather than one with wine – potatoes with peppers, for instance, or with *chorizo* sausage, which is flavoured by them. The nation is pepper-proud, and the subtle use of peppers and tomatoes distinguishes Spanish cooking. Tomato plays the cello role in sauces: not dominant and scarlet, as it is in Italy. Here it just conveys the pepper, sweetness balancing the heat, with an occasional addition of vinegar to make a sauce more spicy.

Columbus went to the Americas to discover a cheaper source of pepper, and chilli peppers were the most immediate gain. Spain has three main dried ones. The heart-shaped *choriceros* go into old dishes like *chilindrón* (see page 199) and *bacalao a la vizcaína*. The red hue of these dishes was once soaked, pulped pepper (up to two per person), not tomato as it is now. But *choriceros* are most associated with the sausages – *chorizos* – to which they lend their name, colour and piquancy. Oregano is a frequent partner in *chorizo* sausages across the country.

Ñoras, small squat balls, are favoured for rice dishes in Alicante and Murcia. Their Catalan name is *romesco* and in Catalonia they make their greatest sauces (see page 160), in association with the local hot *bitxo* chillies. *Guindilla* is the one national hot chilli, slim and pointed. Spain also has three paprikas, sweet, sharp and *agridulce*. The best comes from Jarandilla in the Sierra de Gredos. Paprika is now Spain's basic pepper.

But here the famous pepper is *pimiento de piquillo*. It even has D.O. (*Denominación de Origen*) status, like wine. It's name means beak-pepper, and it is thin-skinned, wonderfully spicy and famous stuffed.

THE PIG FEAST

The squealing had stopped when I arrived, for pigs die at dawn. We were in a vast hall in Burgo de Osma, not to witness the sacrifice, but to celebrate *la matanza*. The bibs round every neck, said Virrey Palafox, *la catedral de buen comer* – the cathedral of good eating.

We started with a toast to the Virgen de Pilar. I envy Spanish capacity to be merry before ever the drinking starts. The band in fringed velvet breeches processed, and the trail of music started big hips swinging and a little burst of dancing. We sang to *la fiesta de San Fermín* and 20 people down one side of the table swing together. Two lines of chorus, each with one long-held note, and it melted 30 seconds later.

A scurry of waitresses and the arrival of the first course: cured meat from last year's pig – and six more dishes. Two were from our porkers, *torreznos*, crisp pork belly strips cooked almost to crackling, and brain pudding with gravy. It was the last dish I finished. I was growing wiser.

Next a salad of chicory, a few strawberries on top and boiled pig's ear. I was so glad that I tried it: membrane with a delicate texture. More bottles of *rosado* and ties were loosened. Expansive, pink and sweaty, we were starting to resemble Walt Disney's pigs in clothing.

A squealing like burst bagpipes announces the arrival, at our table, of the band. Dressed in black velvet, there were two oboes and big and little drums. They played old tunes, with many repetitions, so everyone knew when to sing *Olé* at the right moment. Then bravura blowing from the oboe. All on one breath, phrase after phrase, cymbals banged and clicking drumsticks marked off the moments, lungs busting and crowd clapping.

The hot starters, next, were more ambitious cooking: pig's tongue in white wine with peppercorns, brains with oyster mushrooms, and pig's tail with carrots. Stewed trotters in the slight red juice from *choricero* peppers were cooked to a succulent jelly; Spain values a range of textures. My attention must have wandered at this point, for I missed the grilled spare ribs entirely. It was because my neighbours had a side order of meatballs and grilled salmon.

A *jota de ragón* started down the table and the clatter lessened. A large blonde lady singing, in quarter-tones and with Arab sorrow, of past loves. Just discernible, her young child sang with her, a high echo of the mother's *basso*, matching the line exactly.

Next, a few dishes without meat. Feeling a trifle full, there were flapping bibs and general calling for *sorbete*. It came: short glasses of iced *cava*, Spain's champagne-style wine. 'Drink this, to clean the system.' Indigestion pills came out of handbags. Down the table were shouts of *Mandales la botella* – pass the bottle. Tantara: a hunting horn came from someone's pocket.

The start of the main course meant serious pig-eating – a roast loin that had been marinated for a week, a roast leg with raisins (see page 191) and, high point, the roast suckling pig, *cochinillo asado*. So small, so succulent and wonderful! A gold skin like a net of grilled sugar enveloped meat without fat, tender and creamy. What could follow? Pork fillet, roast wrapped in raw ham, and served with tiny vegetables.

More wine, more drinks, puddings, an orange sorbet in the fruit shell and little cakes. Counting up, in four hours we had eaten 30 dishes. Dancing – and drinking – started in earnest. Before next year I must, must, must learn to dance a good *paso doble*!

THE RECIPES FROM
OLD CASTILE AND RIOJA ARE:

Judías del Barco de Ávila (White bean pot), see page 135.

Revuelto de ajetes o puerros (Cold scrambled egg with leeks and mayonnaise), see page 139.

Pimientos rellenos de merluza (Red peppers stuffed with hake or cod), see page 145.

Menestra de pollo (Cauliflower, artichoke and chicken hotpot), see page 164.

Calderillo bejerano (Potato, green pepper and rib stew), see page 186.

Jamón asado con pasas (Roast pork with red wine and raisin sauce), see page 191.

Menestra de ternera (Veal with new vegetables), see page 192.

Carne con chocolate (Beef stew with chocolate), see page 193.

Galicia

EUROPE'S WESTERN CORNER, THE STORMY ATLANTIC
SWEEPS GALICIA ON TWO SIDES. AMERICA NEXT STOP!
GREEN, WET AND MISTY, THE NORTHERN COAST IS
THE CELTIC FRINGE OF SPAIN. IT HAS MORE IN
COMMON WITH WALES OR SCOTLAND THAN THE
SUNNY MEDITERRANEAN BEACHES.

ROCKING IN THE wind, like upturned green skirts, the cabbages identify the place as Galicia. Hundreds of them, waist high, in every cottage patch and village field. And every homestead has its *horreo* outside. They look like coffin-houses. Grey and stone-roofed, with a cross at one end and slatted sides, they are lichened by wet weather. These long store-cupboards are used for storing vegetables, maize for the poultry (secure from rats) and the local soft cheeses.

I was driving south from Santiago out of the wind in the valley behind the coast: down the E1, Europe's first highway. It crosses broad, calm rivers which emerge on the unseen coast as deep fiords. There are trout, salmon and lamprey (to which salmon is host) in those brown waters. It was December and I passed stands of brown maize, still in the husk, and bright orange osier branches, from which two-handled baskets are made. Vines here grow on overhead trellises to catch the sun. (Elsewhere in Spain they are earthbound.) The wine they make, *albariño*, is reminiscent of hock.

I was on the way to Padrón, famous for a tiny pepper. *Pimientos de Padrón* are so small that 20 form a portion. Deep-fried and served with coarse salt, they are a lottery as in every plateful two or three will be hot ones! They are an admired *tapa* across Spain.

In honey-coloured Pontevedra the camellias in the main square were flowering for Christmas. With its old streets and good pilgrim museum, the port is at the head of a river. It was the perfect place to stop for lunch and sample shellfish.

Plain-boiled, there are plenty to choose from. Huge deep-water prawns (*langostinos*), pink-clawed scampi (*cigalas*), wonderful small shore crabs called *necoras*, and St James's own lobster with a flat head (*santaguiño*). There is also a curious (and very expensive) barnacle called *percebes*, which stands from the rock like a miniature bear's claw: black with white fingernails. We snap, break, squeeze, peer and poke into the shells, heads and legs, trying to extract every last succulent white piece from piles of shellfish, from the best fishing waters in the world.

It is for scallops that Galicia and Santiago de Compostela will for ever be remembered, for these succulent shellfish became the food of pilgrims and are the potent symbol of the only apostle to have a known resting place – according to legend. We made the pilgrimage for St James's Day, to celebrate Spain's national day in its spiritual capital, in local company and in local style (see pages 48-50). After scallops came mussels for which we made a separate expedition to the treacherous west coast.

Half Spain's fish is caught off this ragged, rocky coast: Vigo is the main fishing port of Europe. Oysters are exported by the barrels: 'their flavour is spiritual,' I heard. Locally, fish goes into *caldeiradas*, different fish layered upon each other (often six types at a time), with onions or potatoes. Turbot are now farmed here (on the island of La Toja), as demand is so great for them. *Rodaballo gallego* is cooked with potatoes, a few peas and paprika, with a garnish of baked red pepper.

Galicia is divided from the rest of Spain by more than mountains. For a thousand years it was occupied by the Celts, never the Arabs, and they left a different culture, the shadow of an ancient paganism. The cuisine stems from them and is based on pork fat. You can see it in Santiago market: great yellow rolls of *unto*, marked with string. *Lacón*, the salt-cured pig's foreleg, is another speciality and the tripe is excellent.

Galicia is a place with its own language and legends. The Romans came – and brought the bagpipes. The worship of nature and natural things is an enduring strand that ran for centuries beside the Christian one. It survives now in herbal medicine from the village healer. Local cures are now given on the radio. Bread still has a ritual element. Great rye loaves, wrapped in leaves, are sold by the chunk and there are also breads with cornmeal. Vast tub-moulded rounds were on sale with *pasas* (raisins) in them for Christmas.

Galicia claims to have invented the double-crust pie: flat affairs with bread dough (see page 147) or wheat or cornmeal pastry. These are festive fare but also work pies: stuffed with *xouba* (a skinny sardine) or lamprey, pork loin or *zorza* (paprika mince, ready for sausages).

With rain and a rich black earth, north Galicia raises vegetables for the whole of the country. The potatoes are famous, eaten as *cachelada* with *chorizo* sausage. The turnip tops are a favourite vegetable. The leaves (*grelos*) and young flower buds (*navizas*) are eaten with prawns or ham and go into egg dishes. Galicians claim to have invented watercress as a salad, and now grow kiwi fruit. Galician beef is better than most, and there are cows, and milk puddings, like those of Asturias. Cider is made here, and quince paste, called *marmelo*, gives us the English word marmalade.

Another discovery was the chestnuts. In Galicia they were (perhaps still are) associated with poverty: the only crop possible from poor land. But the associations are wider and the chestnuts dishes splendid. I went investigating. In Santiago market one can see a sight that has almost died out in Europe: women carrying shopping on their heads. Their baskets are from chestnuts, too, broad thin wood strips, interwoven, with a square bottom and round opening.

I was in Galicia for the Christmas market at Villalba. It squeezes into the space under the turret of the old Condes de Villalba. For this town is famous for capons, which used to be king of the Christmas table. Sunday is market day and there were lemons and fresh walnuts, garlic bulbs and great heads of domed *repollo* cabbage. The local smoked St Simon cheese, like a shiny brown pear, and a soft white breast-shaped one, some golden, some net-covered, and appropriately called *tetilla* (titty), were being unloaded from a van.

In the smaller squares the sellers were all local: eggs on sale from shopping baskets, or two or three rabbits gently pulsating in cardboard boxes. The hens were magnificent: red-crested, russet and ginger. I watched a man feel their breasts with a gesture that looked sexual. Capons, I discover, are the size of a 5 kg/11 lb turkey.

Aguardiente (eau-de-vie) is the local distillate, a drink to keep out winter weather. A headache-maker called *orujo* is poured from unlabelled bottles in the bars, and is made (like French *marc*) from pips and grape skins. They say it takes three men to drink it – one with the glass and two to hold him up.

Galicia, for me, is a land of stones and magic, and of the *meigo* (male witch), in his triple cape and hood-of-straw, chanting to San Telmo. This is the ritual of *queimada* – no mere punch. Into the three-legged pot goes 2 litre/3½ pt of clear *aguardiente*, strips of lemon and 1½ glasses of red wine for colour and 250 g/8 oz of cubed sugar. He sets fire to a ladle of liquid with islands of sugar, lowering it to ignite the rest of the liquid. Blue flames leap up! They are used for divination: foretelling someone's death or marriage.

THE PILGRIMS' WAY AND SCALLOPS

Santiago de Compostela – even the name has the reverberation of great bells tolling. It holds the shrine where St James the Apostle is reputed to lie. In the Middle Ages it was the most visited place in Europe. His saint's day, 25 July, is now Spain's national day, and we made the pilgrimage through France to celebrate it.

The pilgrims once walked across Spain to get here, wearing a scallop shell, the badge of St James. Scallops are associated with St James, Santiago, throughout Europe – *Coquille St Jacques* or *pélérin* in France, *Jacobsmuschel* in German. In the past, I reflected, pilgrims were the only civilian travellers. Modern pilgrims may still hang a shell around the neck, and I saw a few pilgrims with the traditional staff and gourd attached, as a drinking bottle.

We travelled the *camino francés*, south of the mountains. Each night was spent in old pilgrim resting places, like San Marcos in León. Outside, its Renaissance frontage is more suited to an opera house – or its present role as a grand hotel. Inside it is a monastery, with scallop shells round the inner courtyard.

Several days driving westward, and always ending towards the setting sun, a gleaming goal that became identified with Santiago. From the east, the view of the city cannot have changed greatly: a valley full of vines below the city wall. The cathedral, with three domed towers, dominates the town. At the west end, the great Obradoiro facade of the cathedral faces a large square. Its saints and scrolls in the honey-coloured stone look like sculptured marzipan, rising upwards. Finally, between the towers, St James looks down on the tourists from under that famous wide-brimmed hat.

The troop of pilgrims mounts the steps and through the double Door of Glory, where St James's feet are polished by caressing hands. The organ pipes splay out across the nave like trumpets. Ahead, down the darkened church, lies the sanctuary of beaten gold and silver, so ablaze with chandeliers and television lights it seems that approaching figures must leave a shadow.

Santiago is a medieval town en fête, the crowd moving on foot through its narrow arcades and passages, and in great good humour. It is a good Catholic tradition that the day before a feast day is also a feast. For an important saint, so is the day before that. Jugglers, sword swallowers, earring makers, pipers entertain the crowd, as do pavement artists. The entertainment cannot have changed much since medieval times. A competition is announced with a procession of drums and squealing bagpipes. It is for the best village dance team and brings girls in pretty shawls and bands of men in two-thumbed hats.

First God then food, celebrating in a city crammed for festive eating. Octopus is popular in Galicia (less so elsewhere). On feast days it presides on all the bars, like a pink wig on a stand; the legs, covered with rings, curl away in all directions. A pile of wooden plates stand by it, for *polpo a feria*, octopus with paprika and oil.

People, cigarette smoke and great trays of mussels cram the restaurant. Baked scallops are a 'must' to try: *vieras de Santiago*, crisp-topped with crumbs and rich with brandy and tomato. Then *lacón con grelos*, a vast mound of ham hocks with favourite green turnip tops; a dish to bring tears to the eyes of exiles. And to end, almond *tarta de Santiago* (see page 213).

We slipped into mass by a back door on the Eve of St James, to a service for the soldiers. At the centre of cathedral, where the nave crosses the transept, was an open space with a trailing rope. A large brass urn was attended by six hefty clerics. It was as big as any of them.

The organ began to play and the crowd roared out the marching tune we know as 'My eyes have seen glory, The glory of the Lord'. Impelled by 10,000 eyes, the great thing began to rise into the air. It was Santiago's famed incense burner, the great *botafumeiro*. A vast ballistic, on precarious ropes, it went swinging across the transept, from the north to south, higher on each swing, towards open doors where the crowd pressed in to see it. Belching flame from its caged mouth, it was willed upwards by a sea of faces, then plunged again, trailing clouds of perfume. Once, nearly 500 years ago, it fell: in front of Catherine of Aragon on her bridal voyage to Henry VIII and England – a bad omen fulfilled.

MUSSELS AND GREEN WINE

We set out for the End of the World: Cape Finisterre on the north-west tip of Spain, jutting into the stormy Atlantic. We never reached it, for on the way we found a mussel heaven at Muros. The best mussels, in a country that is the world's greatest producer. They grow in the *rías baixas*, deep bays like Norwegian fiords, that bisect this ragged coast. A Mecca for mussels!

I was not expecting to see a Chinese fleet there. At least, that is what it looked like. Round the corner of the bay and there on the water was a mass of floating houses, platforms round them. Were they sampans, were they junks? My idea of Chinese boats is hazy. And what were they doing in a quiet Spanish bay, with the evening sun behind them?

The answer was: growing mussels. They were wooden platforms with ropes beneath them, on which the shellfish cling and prosper. Scallops and oysters, as well as mussels, grow better off the seabed. The French call them '*bouchots*'.

We stopped for the day and ordered mussels by the plateful. They lay like fat chunks of some exotic fruit, bright orange in their jet-black shells. They were enormous, sweet and tender (though big ones can often be tough). The lip of one shell is the knife to prize free the next one. So good plain, with lemon!

Green wine made the perfect partner. The vines were brought here by German monks long ago, the same grape as Portuguese *vinho verdes*. But the *albariño*, a peasant over the border, is an aristocrat here. Very crisp with a delicate perfume, it is straw-yellow in colour: green refers to its youth. Made in the traditional way, and absolutely without additives, this is probably the most modern wine industry in Europe, with gleaming steel vats and water-cooled pipes the French would envy. Some wines have a faint fizz. And one is made at a palace-on-the-shore, Fefiñanes, which we visited later.

CHESTNUTS FOR THE DEAD

The smell of chestnuts on the brazier, rich but slightly acrid, signals autumn has come in Spain. Most towns squares have a chestnut seller. In Pontevedra, on the coast, the hand-carts were modelled on old railway engines. The chimneys puffed smoke and trays of hot nuts filled the stoking compartments.

In the countryside, chestnuts are associated with mourning. Chestnuts and new wine together symbolize death and life. In the old days, All Souls, 2 November, was celebrated by a vigil in the graveyards with lighted candles. Lots of waiting, but hands kept warm by hot potatoes and chestnuts. Now it is just a graveyard visit.

In the poorer, southern part of the province chestnut trees cover the hill-sides. These are the 'goodbye' lands from which too many people have departed. As I drove, smoke columns from burning chestnut leaves hung motionless in the air.

On a dull day I picked up chestnuts, glossy, tuft-topped and like new trea-sure in their open, spiky caskets. The wind had blown them into dunes, full of twigs and the smaller ones rejected by yesterday's pickers. Last night's fall was fresh and green, and a small wind brought another crop bouncing down. My small bag filled quickly and I tried to leave. But I couldn't pass a fat nut – just one more, just another – and another half-hour passed.

Spanish chestnuts have the finest flavour in Europe: most floury, least oily. Roasted at the end of the afternoon, they were my best chestnuts ever, and the easiest to peel: 40 minutes in the oven at 150°C/300°F/Gas 2, with no pricking or bursting!

I had joined three jolly women (each of whom owned a pig). We talked about chestnuts: creamy soups with milk, lemon and pepper, and the dried-chestnut soups of summer. Before the potato came in the eighteenth century, chestnuts and turnips were the staple fare here. Now chestnuts are served with *chorizo* sausage and accompany partridges in sweet old wine. They make a good purée with fresh fennel.

The thing for capons (which used to be the king of the Christmas table), I was told, were rolls soaked in milk or wine, plus chestnuts and flour. For the stuffing, I thought – but found it was to fatten up the birds! For stuffing a capon (or a 5 kg/11 lb turkey) use 350 g/12 oz peeled cooked chestnuts, with the same amount of diced russet apple and soaked prunes. Rub the bird's breast with pork fat, then baste it with brandy.

The best of all chestnut desserts is made in Galicia: chocolate and butter beaten with chestnut purée. The ingredients are local, but was this sweet bliss invented here, or in Italy? There are also sugary Galician *marrons glacés*. Alexandre Dumas thought them the best in the world. I carried them home for Christmas.

THE GALICIAN RECIPES ARE:

Zamburiñas rebozadas, cuatro en una (Fried baby scallops, four to a shell), see page 102.

Vinagreta de mejillones (Mussel and potato salad with paprika dressing), see page 113.

Empanada de berberechos (Cockle or clam pie), see page 147.

Sardinas rellenas asadas (Baked sardines with oregano stuffing), see page 151.

Gallina a la gallega (Buttered Galician chicken with noodles), see page 167.

Castañas con berza (Chestnut, cabbage and sausage pie), see page 187.

Callos con garbanzos y costillas (Tripe with chick peas and pork ribs), see page 188.

Lomo de cerdo con castañas (Roast pork with chestnuts and cognac), see page 190.

Tarta de Santiago (St James's almond tart), see page 213.

Asturias and Cantabria

MISTY AND APPLE-GROWING, THIS IS THE NORTH
COAST AND 'GREEN SPAIN'. THE CANTABRIAN RANGE,
500 KILOMETRES OF MOUNTAINS, SEPARATES IT FROM
THE PLATEAU. NO WONDER THE REGION HAS A
SEPARATE HISTORY! KNOWN FOR BEANS, MILK AND
CIDER, THERE ARE DISHES HERE SIMILAR TO THOSE
OF NORMANDY.

THE FLAGS STILL fly in the casino city of Santander, where the Spanish
royal family made seabathing fashionable in the nineteenth century.
Spaced leisurely round two beaches, the city is a starting point for the
corridor along the north coast. Here, round curved sandy bays and in fishing
villages, Spanish families can holiday untroubled by trippers, at what must
be Europe's last undiscovered seaside.

Cantabrian cooking has some of the Basque virtues. Hake is fished
from the Bay of Biscay, and savoury sardines, 'richer than those of Levante',
I was told, are served simply in tomato sauce or, in August, roasted and
eaten outdoors with the fingers. Excellent small squid, called *raba*, are
floured (rather than battered) and served as many as 100 tiny ones to a
portion.

For this coast is blest with the roaring, scouring Atlantic. It makes the
locals confident that the *calderetas* (mixed fish stews) made in all the little
ports are superior to French bouillabaisse 'because Atlantic fish are superior
to Mediterranean'. There are mixtures of fish and meat, too, from a peasant
economy, just as there are in Catalonia.

The Arabs never came here and for more than 1000 years it was a Celtic
kingdom. The difference shows in the kitchen. The parallels with Normandy
are obvious: almost identical recipes for spiny lobster and for tripe, the same
fondness for black pudding. Both make and drink cider, and cook with it.
Both prefer lard (pork fat) to oil, and are less-than-lavish with garlic. Both
like milk and butter, while the local *frixuelo* crêpe is like the Breton one.

Made with milk for a dessert, this crêpe can also be made of fish stock to enclose mussels (or with blood after pig slaughter).

Milk and apples are the two ingredients most obvious to passers-by. Milk is for drinking and for making pudding (see page 207) with rice, which found its niche in the north, in the eighteenth century, as a dessert ingredient. *Quesada* is the local cheesecake in the Vega de Pas, below Santander, a grassy and gently rolling valley known for soft (and blue) cheeses. A buttery sponge called *sobaos*, popular for breakfast, is also made here, and sold all over Spain.

Below the Picos de Europa, in the lap of the mountains, is a green, wooded land with 100 million apples on the bough in summer. They mostly go for cider. The bars here are *chigres,* cider houses – and there is a ritual to cider pouring. One hand high above the shoulder holds the bottle. The other, as low as you can reach, has the glass – the two as far apart as possible, to get air into the cider. A wide-mouthed glass increases the chance of catching it – not much, for amateurs. You must drink your cider very fast, while it has a thin head and is fizzy – and throw the dregs on floor, if you can't down it immediately. Perhaps this is why it is 'happy making'.

Sober, and driving west again, along the bucketing shore road, I was made aware how much locals also look to the sea to make their fortunes. All the big houses were built by the *indianos*, successful exiles who made fortunes in Mexico or Venezuela, and then came home to spend them. There are hydrangeas, the glossy *Magnolia grandiflora* with white wax flowers, and the occasional palm tree. They were planted as a reminder of the 'Indies' (anywhere abroad), where the exiles had made their money.

On the coast the slag heaps from the coal mines of Oviedo interrupt the green fields. You can't avoid the factories in this area of serious industrialization. (Others are the Basque country and Catalonia.) Spewing bilious smoke, these factories are often stylish and modern, gleaming with red- or blue-coloured overlays.

Beyond Oviedo, *horreos* instantly mark the landscape. They are different from the Galician ones: larger, square and made of wood with galleries, balancing on stone toadstool feet. They make a rodent-proof store for potatoes, while white beans and corn cobs are dried on their wide balconies.

Asturias is famed for Spain's best salmon rivers, so I drove to Cornellana (due west of Oviedo), the salmon capital. Up a long valley, with rippling water, winding through deciduous trees and nut bushes, it reminded me of Wales. And I was told the same story that I have heard in Scotland and Norway, of servants stipulating that they are not to eat salmon more than twice a week! Nowadays demand is so great that they have *piscifactorías*. Local recipes were simple: salmon steaks soaked in milk, then grilled, or a big middle piece roasted whole with oil: the skin comes off in one piece.

The Cantabrian mountain range is so long and high that it includes some of the wildest land in the country. There are three sorts of deer in the Bierzo, at the west end, while the high peaks of the Picos de Europa at the eastern end are over 2500 metres/8000 feet and form one of Europe's largest wildernesses, still wandered by ibex and bears. We once drove up from Potes looking for bears, to Fuente Dé, where the cable car whisks you almost a kilometre into the sky – and were snowed on in July.

Little wonder that stews are popular locally. The *puchero montañes* is a warming combination of mutton, ham, hen, beans and sausages. And it is for beans that Asturias is best known. Beans keep out the rain, they say, and they are ballast for the labouring man in Spain's main mining region. *Pote asturiano* (see page 129), comes from the remote Muniellos, in the Bierzo in the west. Local versions add rice, turnips or carrots too, or a slice of the local *botiello* sausage.

Spanish beans do have a European reputation – though I had yet to learn that they could outperform the French *cassoulet* (itself of Spanish derivation). Reluctant Gascons and Tuscans might not give Spain the accolade I (at the end of the day) felt their beans deserved. There was the evidence of the plate! But Spanish cheese is altogether another matter. With such superb natural advantages as mountain pastures, and the choice of cows', sheep's or goats' milk, why should they make such a poor showing internationally? These were questions to look into.

BEAN QUEEN

She was a bean snob, I decided, Angelina with her elegant upswept blonde hair and her oh-so-slim hips in black and white houndstooth trousers. Then I discovered they are all bean snobs, all Spaniards. They choose the beans for a dish the same way a Mexican might choose the correct chilli, or a Frenchman select the wine. And Spaniards are willing to pay big prices for these vegetables. *Fabes de la granja*, the favoured 'beans from the farm', cost more than milk-fed lamb at Easter! They come from the sierras of northern Spain, and are reminiscent of avocados in texture and colour once cooked.

Fabada is the famous dish of Asturias, made with great flat beans that melt in the mouth and the dry, wrinkled *morcilla* (black pudding). Smoked locally, this blood sausage miraculously swells and returns to life in the stew. 'Heavy on the stomach,' said Angelina, 'with all those *chorizos*. Impossible to eat at night!'

Hare and partridge go into other good Asturian bean dishes, while *fabada con almejas*, with clams and saffron, was a real discovery – like the second beautiful sister in a family. They were my introduction to beans with seafood.

The beans must be *fabes de la granja*, said Angelina, 'soaked overnight. To see if they are ready, blow and the skin comes off. When they are done they should be *suave* (smooth), like a person's skin.' She cooks them in the soaking water. When I raised the problems of gas associated with eating beans, it was not one she had met. 'Cook beans slowly,' she said; 'four hours is right. And always cover with water, one or two fingers. Don't stir – even with a wooden spoon. It might break them up.' But reheating wasn't a problem. She thought them sweeter done ahead.

And so I learned to be a bean snob too. I have met about 40 sorts, now, and am still counting. *Fabes* in Asturias, *feizos* in Galicia, *mongetes* in Catalonia, red beans in the Basque country (where they are three times the price of other beans) and *michirones* in Valencia. The latter are broad beans, very sweet when tiny and eaten fresh – and the worst fart-makers when dried. Broad beans were once the staple diet of Europe, and this is at least one good reason why haricot beans were so popular when they were introduced after the discovery of America.

Every region adopted and developed its own kidney bean. And there lies the problem. The names are all local. On my kitchen table *fabes de la granja* look little different from *judiones* from El Barco de Ávila or *garrafones* from Valencia: all vast, flat and buttery in texture. *Garrafón* actually means a carboy. And 'quite different from *fabes*,' I was told. The *alubias* of León and the *judías* of El Barco de Ávila may be identical if they are both *redonda*, smallish, rounded and white – or they may not. Both are legally protected names. And always the locals will tell you, there, just in that corner of the world, grows the perfect bean for that local dish. There are often ten to choose from.

Size distinguishes some of them: my smallest white beans were called *arrocinis* (rice beans). And colour helps: some are cinnamon-coloured, others beige, or red, or black. I bought *fabes de la Virgen*, greenish-grey – a mint tinge – with an 'eye' like a pea. They were wonderful: plump and ripe when cooked, like buttocks straining against the stitching of jeans. I will never eat beans from a can again.

MILK, CHEESE AND CASINO COWS

Drizzle has its own name in Asturias there is so much of it. No wonder the countryside is green! In small villages like Porrua the wooden overshoe is still worn against the mud: the *madreña*, a pointed clog with bars under it.

The best milk in Spain comes from Asturias. It used to come from the sweet-faced *casino* cow but, like the native *lacha* sheep, they are being phased out. Here cows can graze in the glorious hay meadows, rich with blue speedwell, purple-pink vetches and bee orchids. Later the hay is cut for winter and pulled away by oxen in carts with medieval wooden wheels.

Up in these high pastures live some of the most primitive communities in Europe. The cattle-minders celebrate midsummer with a dance that goes back to the early Bronze Age: a view backwards across time.

There are almost as many cheese as there are meadows, including the blue Picos, Gamonedo and the strong *afuega'l pitu*. Cabrales, Spain's superb blue cheese, is made here from cow's milk (or with other milks added). It is often compared to Roquefort, for the blue veins develop in caves, but it is creamier and more acidic. Locally it is wrapped in plane leaves (though not for export). Both Cabrales and Picón Bejes-Treviso are *Denominación de Origen* cheeses: two of the 13 in Spain which are tightly regulated.

Spain has, on last count, 280 listed cheeses, only a few dozen behind France. More are made locally and they show great variation in style. Goats' milk cheeses, which predominate in the south, are generally light and crumbly; they have a distinct clean flavour, much less pungent than their French opposite numbers. The best-known goats' cheeses are the terracotta-coloured Ibores from Extremadura and Catalonia's Garrotza, which has a grey, cave-induced coating. From Ávila in the west, comes Cabra de Tietar; semi-cured it turns buttery in texture.

The central plateau is famous for its well-matured, dense, ewes' milk cheese, grainy and strongly flavoured (see pages 30–31). Manchego, of course, is the most widely distributed, but also well regarded are the D.O. regulated Zamorano and Idiazábal (from *lacha* sheep) in the Basque country. Iberico, widely exported, is similar, but combines all three milks.

Here in the north, cheeses are generally made from cow's milk and are exceptionally creamy, for they are eaten on the young side. Fresh cheese (*requesones*) are also popular.

The problem with Spanish cheeses is that they are mainly artisan cheeses (with Manchego the main exception), and so are expensive. Even in their own country they cost more than imported cheeses. In the past, too, I was told, the best cheeses were kept in Spain, and the worst sent abroad.

There is no tradition of cooking with cheese in Spain. They are served as *tapas*, while the creamier ones become desserts. Spain's fierce climate has made the choices for the cheese maker. If they are not to be bland, then they must mature until strong and hard. This gives them their role as a fitting partner for the strong charcuterie. As a consequence, outside the favoured few – Manchego *curado*, Mahón, Galician *tetilla* ... – they find little favour with foreigners. My advice is to look for the big names on holiday, them eat then as they do, at the beginning of the meal. You may be agreeably surprised.

The north is the dairy of Spain, supplying supermarkets round the country. Down on the farms vast SAM milk tankers are backed into tiny farm-yards. And round a corner you may well come upon a Danone yoghurt factory.

The rich milk makes traditional local desserts like *leche frita*: not fried milk, but hugely popular squares of melting, smooth custard fried with a crunchy coating. Crêpes called *frixuelos* or *filloas* are fried and folded to make ears, or are served like the Gallegan carnival *filloas a la crema*, enclosing custard and flamed in liqueur. *Nata con nueces* is rich whipped cream with walnut halves and honey poured over. And there is thick cream aplenty in *bebedizo*, the after-dinner coffee with *coñac*.

THE ASTURIAN AND CANTABRIAN RECIPES ARE:

Croquetas de huevos (Egg croquettes), see page 98.

Chirlas o almejas con arroz verde (Clam and green-rice soup), see page 128.

Pote asturiano (Asturian bean, sausage and cabbage soup), see page 129.

Fabes con carabineros (Beans with giant prawns), see page 158.

Caldereta asturiana (Mixed shellfish and fish stew), see page 159.

Perdices con verduras (Partridges in wine with cabbage), see page 176.

Arroz con leche requemado (Rice pudding with caramel topping),
see page 207.

Casadielles (Walnut puff pastries), see page 208.

Tarta de manzanas (Apple batter cake), see page 214.

The Basque Country

THERE IS A RESTAURANT IN THE BASQUE COUNTRY,
THEY CLAIM, FOR EVERY 1000 INHABITANTS. A SMALL
PROVINCE IN THE GREEN NORTH, SNUGGLED
AGAINST THE PYRENEES ON THE ROAD TO FRANCE,
THE BASQUES ARE SELF-STYLED GOURMETS, AND HAVE
LONG BEEN ACKNOWLEDGED AS SPAIN'S BEST COOKS.

A TANGLE OF MOTORWAYS on the French border leaps over a countryside of fields dotted with little houses. Like the south of Britain, there are no empty spaces: country – but full of people.

The coast, too, is crowded. Small fishing ports, where steel shrouds clap against the masts, mix with long-established resorts. Bilbao is a major port and industrial centre, an Hispanic Glasgow, full of energy, spewing dirt but making money. In contrast, San Sebastián makes an elegant capital, with the perfect bay location. Fine buildings and the spaciousness of a nineteenth-century resort recall more elegant times. There are dishes in keeping, like chops *a la Berritz*, three grilled together. The outside ones are thrown away and only the centre one is eaten.

As a nation – the beret-wearing Basques have their own language, near-independence from Madrid, and the title of País (Vasco) – they have always been outward looking. Most of Spain is cut off from France by butter and cream. Spaniards don't use them. Not true here in the Basque country, where they still covet 'their' provinces over the French border and share many cookery traditions. For example, *piperada*, the soft, moist, red French-style omelette with peppers, is unlike any other Spanish egg dish. Alone in Spain the Basques make good chocolate, notable Vitoria's truffles.

They also share French enthusiasm for new-style cooking, creating *la nueva cocina vasca*, in the late '70s and early '80s. 'Our chefs caught the bug from big stars like Bocuse, the Troisgros brothers and Outhier in France.' Chefs like Juán Arzak and Pedro Subijana in San Sebastián had Basque connections over the border, who helped point the way.

The strong point of *la nueva cocina* is that it emphasized local ingredients:

white squid dishes sauced with their own black ink, for example. It is only line-caught squid (fished on this shore) that still have any ink. Squid automatically squirt ink when in danger, so those fished in nets turn up in markets elsewhere without it.

The new cuisine has had the happy effect of giving everyone confidence in their local cooking, and encouraging development of existing traditions, rather than chasing after foreign fashion. It has also done great deal to civilize the excesses of oil or lard in peasant dishes right across Spain.

The Basque country is blest by near-perfect ingredients: the only good beef in Spain, well-hung for enormous *chuletones* (wing rib chops); the first mushrooms in April, eaten with scrambled eggs as *revuelta de zizak*; good chickens; and beautiful vegetables, such as soft artichoke hearts and beans of many colours.

The first to adopt maize and cornmeal from America, the current fashion is for the spicy *pimientos de piquillo* (see page 43), grown round Lodosa, cooked, for example, with rabbit. Game birds wing over from the Pyrenees, and many dishes are shared with Rioja. But they make their own red sausage, a skinny one called *chistorra*, and even lamb sausages.

Red beans are the favourite, though Tolosa is famous for a black bean stew. 'The beans of Tolosa were red, not black, when I was young,' stated one old lady. There are also special dishes to celebrate fresh haricots, with and without the pod, like quails with beans, *pochas con codornices*.

'The Basques know quality when they see it,' said Palomita Tomé, long-time cook and passionate about it. 'There is excellent cooking in the little villages. People bring a few things to sell. Everything is in season. They eat *chipirones* (small squid) in the north *Virgen a Virgen* (26 June to 15 August, the Assumption). By November they aren't *chipirones*: they're too large. You can get *chilenos* (squid from Chile), but they have lost their ink. Not good. In Madrid people buy them, and don't recognize that they are imported. In Bilbao people realize the difference and don't eat them.

'Basques pilfer the sierras for things to cook – game, mushrooms. But there has been a change, over 30 years, in the quality of the produce. More additives. Nowadays things are cooked more rapidly but have less flavour. One reason is food is not so immediately seasonal. In prime season things are better. There is also a need to cook ahead. Many dishes need to sleep (*dormir*). Without the rest, I won't guarantee them – big beans, squid, *bonito* – especially dishes cooked with olive oil.'

The brisk Atlantic, which washes into the Bay of Biscay (anglicized from *vizcaína*), produces wonderful shellfish, like the *txangurro*, the spider crab. It is strong, so 'some mix it with hake, parsley, garlic and brandy, then stuffed back into its own shell. But the authentic *txangurro* has no fish.'

Hake, the Spanish fish par excellence, is fished in the Bay of Biscay. *Cogote*, hake head, is typical. You may also find potatoes cooked in the same green sauce like hake. They enjoy classic recipes: like sole with mushrooms, young garlic and white wine. There are four basic Basque sauces, each with their harmonies and colours. Red is *vizcaina* (see page 146), white is *pil-pil*, black comes from squid ink (see above) and green is most famous with hake. The local white *txacoli* wine, appley and dry, is ideal for cooking.

But, traditionally, the Basques are deep-sea fishermen and sailors. A Basque, Juan Sebastián Elcano, was the first to skipper a ship round the world (Magellan never made it home). And their shipboard stews are famous. *Marmitako* with the white tuna (*bonito*) and peppers, and steaks from its *hijado*, stomach – '*¡Jesús: es exquisito!*' They catch cod in the North Sea and salt it, for their most famous dish, *bacalao a la vizcaína*, salt cod with pork fat, dried peppers and onions plus, in modern times, fresh peppers and tomatoes.

A *macho* society – it *is* a Spanish word – Basques are famous for bar-hopping and *cofradías*, which help keep their cooking traditions alive. Food is their passion, the invention and promotion of delicacies: *bocartes* (small sardines) in sauces and *angulas* (elvers). In the 1930s they invented *kokotxas*, a triangle from the hake's throat eaten fried or in white *pil-pil* (see page 154). It is the identical cut to the American 'cod's tongue', which has a longer history. Clubs – with their sexiest overtones and luxuries – were certainly one area to investigate further.

The Basques are a nation of bar-hoppers, so *tapas*-crawling was clearly another query – even though the custom stems from Andalusia. My third choice for more study was salt cod, for its continuing attraction is a mystery to many people outside the Mediterranean.

The most famous Basque cheese is the smoky Idiazábal, with its firm paste texture and caramel-coloured rind. From high-pastured *lacha* sheep it is D.O. (regulated) and regularly exported. Many desserts are based on milk: *canutillos* (cream horns), *natillas* (custards) and *leche frita* (see page 58). The pastry tart, *gateau basque*, has a custard filling here (though the French version features cherries).

Still a village culture, the three Basque districts of Vizcaya, Alava and Guipuzcoa are prone to criticize and compete against each other. But a feature common to them all is the hamlet walnut tree, with nuts to make creamy *intxaursalsa*, the dessert for Christmas Eve.

MEN'S CLUBS AND THE STORY OF THE WOODEN FORK

Cofradías are the famous (or infamous) all-male Basque food clubs. San Sebastián alone has some 30 of them. Men have to have somewhere to get away to. And what do they do, when they are alone with other men? In the Basque country they cook! Women come twice a year, on the city's major festivals; they also wash up.

The clubs also run sports and charities. But their business is to talk about, and sample, food. Self-appointed gourmets, they take their responsibilities seriously. Every member has the right to cook, and afterwards puts money in a box, to pay for what he has taken.

The clubs create food fashions, opening their November season when the *angulas* arrive. Ninety-odd years ago only modest fisherman round the Bay of Biscay ate these tiny elvers. In nearby France they were sold as pig food.

A mere finger long, and as slim as spaghetti, elvers have made a mysterious journey. Freshwater eels breed in the salt Sea of Sargasso and their young travel back along the Gulf Stream, scenting the rivers from whence their parents came. They are caught in rivers like the Nervion, on the way to the port of Bilbao, San Juan de la Arena in the Asturias, the delta of the river Nalón (and even at Cadiz, on the lower Guadalquivir). Galicians and Valencians gobble them too.

Highly perishable, they are dipped in a tobacco solution to kill them – 'whichever brand you smoke'. Nicotine, apparently, saves them from insipidity. They are then washed 10 times to lose their slime. In the most famous recipe, *angulas a la bilbaina,* oil is heated in an earthenware casserole, with garlic and hot *guindilla* chilli. In go the elvers and are turned a bare minute – 'the oil should not be too hot'. They are eaten with a wooden fork.

Sadly, pollution has put paid to most Spanish elver rivers. The softest, whitest *angulas*, I was told, now come from France and Northern Ireland.

SALT COD: A LENTEN FAST TURNED FEAST

Bacalao started as a Lent necessity, but has become a passion through the year. The coming of the freezer has changed nothing. Spaniards continue to demand and treasure it, for salt cod excites the same sexual nerve as caviar or Stilton.

From the market in San Sebastián, the Mercado de la Bretxa, I went to a bar. And there was yet another new book devoted entirely to *bacalao*. 'My sister-in-law has a recipe in it,' said the owner. '*Bacalao* with the fruits of autumn' – a sauce with crushed pine nuts and almonds. I called round to shake her hand.

The Basques acquired the taste four centuries ago – it was newish when Don Quixote ate it. For cod is not a Mediterranean fish. It first came to Europe in a big way in 1481 when, so the latest theory goes, Bristol fishermen discovered the Newfoundland Banks – and kept quiet about them! As the big fleets of Britain and northern France moved west to America, the Basque whalers took over the North Sea – and turned to cod. Now Spanish cod boats are away for 6–7 months at a time. In the *casa de bacalao* – and most towns have one – salt cod from Iceland and the Faroes is prized above that of Newfoundland. Icelandic salt cod is white and fleshy, while that of the Faroes is yellow and much stronger. Four types of fish are salted, including ling.

The Spanish demand for salt cod is much more sophisticated than the Italian. The dirty, white kite-shaped fish, stacked in the corner like a pile of old newspaper, is still to be found in the south. But the north has a greater choice. So-called white *bacalao blanco* is moist to the finger (though safely salted), easier and more pleasant to cook, as the middle cuts look like fish. Soaked, its weight increases only marginally. *Bacalao inglés* is less salty still and yellower, resembling smoked haddock. It is soaked and eaten raw. It was this that opened my eyes to its virtues. In a salad (see page 110) raw salt cod has a texture and intensity more exciting than smoked salmon.

Different cuts command different prices, and are used for different dishes. Cured flat, the centre is sold as loin. Squares to crumbs, from best to worst, all are labelled with the names of classic dishes.

The know-how is in the soaking: to get the palatability of a fresh fish, but retain the magic taste of a cured one. Here is the approved method. Cut the fish into squares about 7 cm/3 in and cover with water – at least twice its volume. After 11 hours, turn over the fish by hand, and cover with fresh water. 11 hours further on, put it in a pot at the back of the stove and let it soak in hand-hot water for 2 hours. Always soak it for 24 hours, changing the water three times – the last couple of hours in warmish water. Keep this water for cooking – a spoonful or so is often needed.'

Rock-hard and powdery, cut from the stiff fish, *bacalao* will need 36 hours under water. I recommend a bowl in a sink under just-running water, for the smell of soaking cod can haunt a house in hot weather. Lion dung was author Gerald Brenan's comparison! It will double its weight, but (unless it is a middle cut) you will lose the extra in discarded skin and bones.

There is a different method for fish which is to eaten raw – largely because it will be shredded. Toast the stiff fish, which breaks it up. It can then be flaked, so soaking is much quicker.

Among the proud Basque dishes are *bacalao a la vizcaína* made scarlet with dried *choriceros* and – nowadays – fresh peppers, and the mountain *ajoarriero* (see page 146). *Porrusalda*, a soup with potatoes and leeks, is also popular.

Pil-pil is one of the Basques' most famous dishes – and almost the only bad dish I have ever eaten in Spain. By an apprentice hand, it can be a caricature of Spanish cooking: grey fish shapes and garlic swimming deep beneath a sea of oil!

Correctly made, *pil-pil* is the lightest of white sauces – though it needs Basque talent to make it well. For it uses the gelatine in the skin of the tail (sometimes throat pieces of hake; see page 154) to thicken the sauce. The fish is fried in oil and then the whole casserole is revolved or shaken to extract the gelatine and blend it into the oil making a hot emulsion. Fish stock or wine are then worked in, to complete it.

The taste for salt cod is shared right across the country. Cuenca, on the Castilian plain, makes *atascaburras*, a beaten cream with potato and oil, eaten on Christmas Eve with walnuts in it. The Valencian *giraboix* is a stew with potatoes, green beans and chilli, served with garlicky *allioli*. And Seville invented *soldaditos* (soldiers), batter-coated and the original fish finger!

TAPAS CRAWLING

Bars and discos together in Spain equal the number of drinking places in the whole of the rest of the EC put together! Here in the old quarter of San Sebastián, where every third building is connected to food or drinking, you can see why.

San Sebastián is home to the *tapas* crowd. A supremely urban hobby, *ir de pinchos* means a tour of the bars, to see what titbits are on offer. *Poteo* (I tip the jug) puts rather more emphasis on the drinking. But *tapas* and alcohol go together. You can't do it on coffee. The food is there for moderate drinkers *'para tenterte en pie'*, to keep you on your feet. *Tapas* is a communal activity – and definately peripatetic. Each bar is visited for its speciality: Negresco for its shellfish, La Espiga for its fried food. They are sampled, discussed, and then we move on. Here in the north *tapas* also carries the idea of meeting new people. And in *chicas de alterne*, there is an added hint of female temptation.

Elaborate counter displays, like jewellery in trays, offer immediate temptations: piles of pink prawns, gleaming salads with mayonnaise, fish pudding, *tortillas* the size of birthday cakes, and veal stew. Food is the means to lure in passers-by. In Spain people eat when they drink – and drink when they eat. Drinking is moderate. The wide-mouthed glasses contain a few fingers of wine; a *zurito* is a small glass of the local lager.

A *tapa* should be an individual portion, on a small saucer, one per drink. And each new drink should bring a different one: dishes are not repeated. They should be tiny, for they come before the meal, and each one should have a new flavour or texture. A good chef offers a gastronomic adventure, a succession of tempting morsels for the gourmet, not a meal. As such, *tapas* are Spain's most interesting contribution to the food world.

San Sebastián is a sea city on an enclosed bay with a fine *concha* of white sand, backed by tamarisk trees. Fish must be first choice here, like pots of *txangurro*, baked spider crab (called *centolla* elsewhere). Europe's best anchovies are fished on this coast, marinated raw and served white as *boquerones en vinagreta*. Prawns are deep-fried in batter as *gambas en gabardinas*. I love the name, with its reminder of Napoleon's army invading from the north in their caped macintoshes. Both dishes are copied across the country.

Enter the bar door, and it is the hams you notice first. They hang in ranks over every bar in Spain, each with a tiny inverted paper umbrella beneath, to catch the drips. I look at them with a southern eye, because in Andalusia charcuterie is pre-eminent. But all Spaniards like a good name that guarantee quality, sausages and hams *con apellido*, 'with a surname'.

Tapas are indisputably an Andalusian creation, the gift of an age less hectic, less obsessed with productivity, than our own. They offer a lazy way of unwinding in the heat of the day, or in the evening after exertion, and as such are one of Spain's most endearing rituals. In essence it is a way of spinning out a drink or two without getting drunk – a sop with accompanying alcohol.

The word *tapas* means a 'cover', and the custom is nineteenth century, at first a piece of bread, balanced over a glass to keep out the flies in hot weather. The bread was soon topped sausage or cheese and, so the story goes, they were first served to horsemen as they rode into an inn. The glasses must have been slim ones, perhaps the tulip-shaped *copita* of sherry. Nowadays they are as likely to be *cañas*, tall tubes of chilly Seville Cruzcampo, served from the pump.

Tapas are a pastime, not a meal – though a *ración* (larger plate) will serve the hungry tourist. In Andalusia, sitting on chairs in the street at night, under rows of naked light bulbs, small snacks come, like crisps with beer: *chocos*, which are yellow lupin seeds, sunflower seeds, toasted chick peas, soaked *chufas* (see page 86) and *encurditos* (pickles), sold ready-skewered in variety in many Spanish markets.

Tapas bars in the south, and particularly Seville, have also an intimate connection with bullfighting; one reason, perhaps, why they are largely standing bars – it permits demonstration! Loaded cocktail sticks become *banderillas* here, after the sticks, with their flying banners, used to pierce the bull's shoulder before it is killed.

Bars are also male haunts, at least in origin, in a country where drinking is done away from home. The hot food reflects this: dishes with gravy, like mother made, with overtones of the nursery. The southern favourite, *riñones en jerez*, kidneys in sherry, is widely copied, and there are stews with bread and meatballs in tomato.

Of course different parts of the country also have their own specialities. In the Basque country in winter you may find *angulas*, baby eels or elvers, of a gossamer thinness, tossed with hot chilli. Bechamel-based croquettes are called *bolas* in the north, and may contain spinach, shrimps or cheese. Barcelona's best is *patatas bravas*, fried potatoes in chilli-tomato sauce so hot 'it is manly to eat them' – even in the latest designer bar by Javier Mariscal, where people go primarily to be seen with the in-crowd. Madrid favours *tigres* (see page 101) and strips of tripe on cocktail sticks. And in country places beyond the capital there are *montaditos* (toppings on bread) and *pepitos*, rolls sandwiched with good things like fried veal.

Good ideas are copied everywhere. Galician *pimientos de Padrón* (see page 46) are found all over the country. *Ensaladilla*, Russian salad, too, is a national number, achieving popularity during the Civil War because fresh vegetables and mayonnaise were easy ingredients to buy. A very few *tapas* are the invention of a single person, such as *flamenquines* (pork, ham and cheese roll-up, deep-fried), elaborated from a simpler item.

Some medieval things survive because people continue to ask for them: like squares of blood (set solid with vinegar) 'to give men strength at night'. But crisply fried anchovy backbones – in Empordà – turned out to be modern. The main change of the last ten years is the increasing number of bars offering gourmet items: *botargo* (grey mullet caviar) and the ham of the fish world, *mojama*, Arab in origin and the salted, dried back of the blue-fin tuna. Classics like fried whole *chipirones* (baby squid) have been joined by sea urchin coral, baby octopus in oil and a big variety of fish eggs.

THE BASQUE RECIPES ARE:

Pinchos (Titbits on cocktail sticks), see page 97.

Zurruputuna (Salt cod soup with garlic and peppers), see page 124.

Endivias al Roquefort (Chicory with Roquefort cream), see page 137.

Revuelta de delicias (Spinach and sea treasures with scrambled egg), see page 142.

Budín de merluza (Pink souffléd fish pudding), see page 144.

Bacalao al ajoarriero (Mule-driver's salt cod with garlic), see page 146.

Merluza a la koxkera (Hake or cod with clams), see page 154.

Gastañka (Ray or skate with chilli oil), see page 161.

Arroz a la vasca (Rice with everything from a chicken), see page 166.

Solomillo con salsa de berros (Steak with watercress sauce), see page 195.

Helado Neluska (Chocolate and toasted almond ice cream), see page 209.

Reinetas en salsa de limón (Baked apples with lemon sauce), see page 210.

Aragon and Navarre

ARAGON AND NAVARRE HAVE THEIR HEADS IN HIGH
MOUNTAINS, BUT FEET IN THE WARM RIVER VALLEY.
HUGE ARAGON, ONCE A PROUD KINGDOM, STRADDLES
THE EBRO VALLEY THAT RUNS PARALLEL TO THE
PYRENEES. TINY NAVARRE, TO THE NORTH, BORDERS
RIOJA, AND MAKES FASHIONABLE FRUITY WINES.

T HE GREAT, SNAKING, wooded pass of Roncevalles, full of rocks, looming
trees and potential ambushes, forces its way through the Pyrenees into
Navarre. The west route into Spain, there are signposts in France,
almost 900 km away, to Santiago de Compostela. It is a place full of ghosts:
Roland's lost army, massacred 1200 years ago, and pilgrims to the shrine of
St James, who walked here in medieval times.

Two million pilgrims a year travelled to Santiago 500 years ago. They
shaped the road system to run west, not towards Madrid, as it tries to now.
The hillsides here are full of monasteries, usually in inaccessible places.
Pilgrim dishes remain too, like *bacalao al ajoarriero*, a white dish of salt cod,
eggs and garlic, which has tomato added in modern versions (see page 146).

Old ways endure still, but for how long? *Migas*, fried breadcrumbs crisp and
hot from the pan, are served with chocolate sauce or grapes – and in Aragon
with pork *torreznos* (see page 31). 'Very fatty and so *good*!' I was told. Behind
it are older dishes. *Migas* were once just flour, stirred and stirred in the frying
pan. They do this still, with golden cornmeal, to make *gachas* in Zaragoza.
Regañaos is a primitive pizza, a flat bread with *pimiento* in it, topped with
sardines. And *sopa cana* is related to the original blancmange (found across
Europe, with almond milk and minced chicken). Nowadays it is sugared bread
and hot milk, enriched with chicken fat. It is still popular as dessert.

Aragon has crops, too, which no one else cultivates, such as borage with
its bright blue flowers with black points and hairy stalks. 'It takes a morning
to wash it,' housewives sigh. It is served with potatoes and oil, especially on
fast days, while the leaves make sweet fritters.

Cooking here is simple: grilled chops are popular. *Costillas a la baturra*,
they are called, 'cooked by a country bumpkin'. But rustic cooking also

embraces spit-roast lamb and goat, served in hot hunks with melting golden garlicky *allioli*. These mountains rear some of the best lamb in Spain. *Ternasco* is lamb roast young and small with garlic lending its savour to new potatoes, while tender lamb strips in lemon make *cochifrito* (see page 196).

The region is called the *zona de chilindrones*. Quite why these stews should be named after a card game, no one knows. But I learned how to play it: a simple patience, for two or four people. The stews are flavoured with peppers, once with dried *choricero* (see page 43), but now with the fresh vegetable.

The Pyrenees form a truly formidable barrier, both high and wide. Entering the first range from Navarre, we stopped at the eleventh-century monastery of Leyre. I ate my first cardoons that night at supper. They are the largest of vegetables, huge ribbed stalks related to artichokes. In the field they look like enormous bushes with black bags tied round them, for they are blanched (like celery), to whiten the stalks. This is how the kitchen cooked them.

Cut the stalks in lengths: they need a lot of washing. Cook them in boiling water with the pulp of ½ lemon, to keep them white, for about 40 minutes. Pass them through flour, then eggs beaten with salt, and fry them in plenty of oil. Make a little white sauce by frying onion in the cooking oil, then add flour, some cooking water and a little milk. It's a dish many Spaniards eat on Christmas Eve, with a little ham added and perhaps a handful of walnuts as well.

Mountain foods include freshwater crayfish, flavoured with the same peppers, and *conejo con caracoles*, rabbit with snails (which eat wild rosemary and so form a walking bouquet garni). Equally famous are the fine brown trout. *A la navarra*, they are cooked in red wine with thyme, and are perfection fried in the pan with raw ham (one version is on page 155). The cathedral city of Teruel, across the Ebro, makes one of the finest raw *serranos* in Spain. A favourite ham dish is *magras con tomate*, ham slices in fresh tomato sauce.

We drove once more to the rim of the Pyrenees, air icy with the tang of old snow, up to the Vall d'Arán. Forty years ago it was cut off from Spain for six months of every year, until the tunnel was built. Now a ski area, every *borda* (barn restaurant) has gourmet ambitions, and offers home-cooked stews on Villeroy and Boch plates.

Game birds are netted flying through the mountain passes. *Perdices al chocolate*, partridges in chocolate sauce, came from Aragon, and is now popular across Spain. Turtle doves are cooked on the grill, basted with lard, vinegar and red wine, and quail are roasted in fig leaves. Quail are at their fattest when hunting starts on 15 September, and their return is joyously celebrated in a stew of fresh kidney beans, *pochas con codornices*. 'They must be the fresh ones, not dried ones – even *fabes de la granja*.'

History dominates Navarre as much as geography. The Arabs came, leaving behind brick houses in the Mudejar style, and dishes like *pollo en pepitoria*, fried chicken with a delicate sauce of saffron, garlic and pounded nuts. In early spring the lower plains of Navarre have kilometre on kilometre of flowering almonds from Arab times. (They are cultivated, not relegated to the hills, as they are to the south, in Andalusia.) In the cake shop in Tudela's colourfully painted square, I counted 12 different almond cakes, including a *turrón de Tudela*. There are almond sweetmeats, too, like *guirlache* (see page 212).

Perhaps the citizens had infidels in mind when the horrors of hell were carved on the cathedral Judgement door in Tudela. Little is left of the Jewish quarter; there are better preserved ones at Hervás and Gerona. In the twelfth century Benjamín de Tudela was a noted rabbi here. In agriculture and commerce – and, of course, the *cocido* (see page 37) – what a lot Spain owes to both its *descreídos!*

One is constantly reminded that Aragon was once a powerful kingdom, ruling the south of France and land as far away as Sardinia, Naples and Sicily. And Sos del Rey Católico – a dust-coloured hill with a very plain palace – is the birthplace of King Ferdinand, for ever remembered for uniting Spain by marrying Isabella of Castile – the Catholic Monarchs.

The great Ebro valley is a vast vegetable garden stretching towards the sea. It is famed for its asparagus, as fat and white as rich men's fingers, canned for the whole of Spain. *Merluza a la ribera navarra* (from the riverbank), with green peas and asparagus tips, is so popular that many restaurants serve it for *merluza a la koxkera* (see page 154).

Some French influence is visible in Navarre: dishes with Bayonne ham and many vegetables. *Pote con coles* is a solid cabbage soup, rather like *garbure* in neighbouring French Béarn. And Navarre red wines can be reminiscent of beaujolais nouveau. At Roncal a fine hard D.O. (protected) cheese, with rice-sized holes, is made. Much of it goes to France. Junket, *cuajada*, is sold everywhere in earthenware pots and eaten with honey.

But it is the fruit that I best remember. Zaragoza to Teruel, endless orchards, with plums, cherries and apples. The *melecotones* (peaches) of Zaragoza must be the world's largest. They were memorable baked in red wine, tops just clear and crusted in baked sugar. The chocolate-coated candied fruit are also delicious! Fruit is also made into *retacías* (ratafias), with spirits. Sloes from the mountain slopes go into *pacharán*. It is a mild, anis-flavoured brandy, drunk on the rocks. Zoco, the principal brand, is coloured red for export. It is Spain's most popular liqueur.

Navarre makes fines *rosados* (rosé) wines and Aragon makes purplish reds in Cariñena and somewhat lighter ones in Somontana. In Olite, on their saint's day, we had plenty of opportunity to sample local wines in their proper setting.

OLITE FESTIVAL: KINGS AND CASTLES

Olite castle, once home to the kings of Navarre, would look familiar, even to those who have never visited Spain. For these are the towers and little turrets copied by Walt Disney for every fairy castle. They are so well restored that they have a Lego-land feel about them, but their profile lends enchantment to the square.

It was late September and the town was en fête for its saint's day. The first impressions was that everyone was wearing white, with a red neckerchief or red scarf attached at the waist. There were scarlet berets too – normal gear for Basque policemen. Even a baby in a pram had espadrilles laced with red ribbon.

Great stout gates cordoned the exits from the main square. The bulls had clearly been through earlier. But now it was all bands and dancing, a tune, followed by a recurring chorus. ¡Ya! ya! ya! Now! now! now! we shouted each time it came round, left then right hand punching in the air.

Not one but three bands were on duty, drums banging and blowing mightily. Here came the chorus again! Spectators rose from their perches and we revolved once more upon the spot.

The *gigantes* and *cabezudos* arrived, three tall kings and queens, their stilts covered with faded cottons robes. The *cabezudos* had vast heads of papier maché. It distorted their proportions to Disneyland dwarfs. One had a blown-up pig's bladder on a stick, which he blobbed round ankles, making people jump. I knew it was a medieval trick, but had never seen it.

The band passed round a *porrón* (glass drinking kettle) between numbers. A thin spout of wine arched towards the mouth: a wettener, no more. There seemed little drunkenness, just immense good spirits. The crowd drank beer and ate *tapas* of bread with *lomo embuchado* (cured pork loin) or *chorizo de Pamplona,* an orange-fleshed salami, spattered with lighter flecks. It is the best of the *tapa* sausages.

Two bands set off round the town, each with a troupe of dancers. Now I noticed costumes. Teenage trios wearing the same – black or Batman capes. What hours the young can dance! As they passed beneath the walls, they called to the people smiling in the balconies above. Throw it! Throw it! And glasses of water, sometimes buckets, were emptied down on the dancers to cool them. Occasionally it was a bottle of wine. Then, to general cheering, a boy positioned himself beneath, arms wide, mouth open to catch the spout, and down the gullet.

THE RECIPES FROM
ARAGON AND NAVARRE ARE:

Cogollos de Tudela (Lettuce hearts with anchovy), see page 107.

Lentejas de Ordesa (Lentils with leeks and mushrooms), see page 134.

Truchas con serrano y hierbabuena (Trout with raw ham and mint),
see page 155.

Pichones con pasas y piñones (Pigeons with raisins and pine nuts),
see page 177.

Conejo con patatas (Rabbit stewed with potatoes), see page 179.

Cochifrito (Fried lamb with lemon juice), see page 196.

Chilindrón de cordero (Lamb stewed with peppers), see page 199.

Guirlache (Almond and aniseed candy), see page 212.

Catalonia

ON THE EAST COAST, WHERE THE PYRENEES AND
THE MEDITERRANEAN MEET, CATALONIA EMBRACES
THE COSTA BRAVA, A HINTERLAND OF MOUNTAINS
AND VINEYARDS, AND A STAR, IN BARCELONA.
IN MANY WAYS A NORTHERN CITY — EFFICIENT AND
INTERESTED IN MAKING MONEY — BARCELONA
HAS AN EBULLIENT, SOUTHERN STYLE.

SALVADOR DALÍ PUT bread loaves all over the outside of his house at Figueres. And why not? Made of yellow plaster, they are dotted regularly against a deep strawberry: the Catalan round loaf, twiddled at three corners, then slashed between them. He has vast brown eggs around the cornices, too. Don't go in summer. The Spanish adore his eccentricities and queue to enter.

Barcelona is the only city I know that has blue pavements: a pattern of snails and pumpkin leaves, designed by Gaudí along the Passeig de Gràcia, the major fashion street. Gaudí's buildings round the city are all disturbing. On La Pedrera the stone balloons look like the fantasies of a pastry cook; elsewhere it drips like a sauce. The towers of the Sagrada Familia are shaped like hock bottles, topped with bursting rockets. The inlaid ceramics in the Parque Güell have the colours of an *amanida* (arranged salad). Food is important in Barcelona. It is the universal hobby, in a city with 10,000 eateries.

All Catalan meals start with *pa amb tomàquet* – ripe tomato and good olive oil pressed on to very lightly toasted bread. Simple but excellent, topped with *serrano* ham. Local ways with vegetables include many decorative salads. Called an *amanida*, salad takes its name (like our word) from salt and means seasoned. The *amanida catalana* often includes sausage and cured fish together.

The meat is good, and barbecued well. The best is *al sarmiento*, meaning grilled over a fire of vine prunings (true of all Spain's wine provinces). This fire of intense heat means fast cooking, unlike most charcoal, which cooks quite slowly. Mixed grill is a *graellada*, splendid when it's fish and shellfish together, and this is often served Catalan style with *allioli* (oil, egg and garlic sauce). Indeed, *allioli* (see page 149) accompanies many things here.

Snails and cuttlefish are much appreciated, the latter often with peas. But the coast is famed for fish stews and *sopa de musclos*, mussel soup with tomato and anis *aguardiente* (eau-de-vie). The local *bullabesa* is much like the French one – and is arguably its forerunner. *Suquet* is the favourite fish stew: a wonderful mixture of fish and shellfish with tomato and potato (the latter can be mashed in on the plate). *Sarsuela* (local spelling) is an even more ambitious medley of fish with saffron and anis-scented brandy. Colours and shapes proliferate: the name, roughly, means 'operetta'. There is also the divine *romesco de peix* (see page 160), to my mind the most sophisticated, because of its subtle sauce.

L'Escala, on the Costa Brava, is famous for its large salted anchovies – as is the whole coast, as far as French Collioure. Almost every *amanida* seems to include them, while anchovy toasts may be served with the subtle, smoky, cooked *escalivada* salad (see page 108). In contrast, many *tapas* bars sell fresh *boquerones*, simply filleted and macerated for a couple of days in vinegar and lemon juice. The result makes them white – and very different.

Salt cod goes into salads such as *esqueixada*, made with strips of red pepper and tomatoes. *Xato* (pronounced 'château') is a dish I rate highly. Basically an escarole salad, it combines bitter leaves with translucent flakes of raw salt cod, just challengingly salty, and two more cured fish – canned tuna and canned anchovy fillets – in a light dressing of *romesco* sauce.

The Ebro reaches the Mediterranean in Catalonia, a great delta growing rice. Calasparra, Spain's best rice, grows here. There are local rice dishes like *el rossejat*, rice first fried until coloured, then cooked in fish stock. This is served with *allioli* stirred into it, like the Murcian *arroz en caldero* (see page 148). In L'Empordà, *arròs negre* (black rice) was invented, a striking dish coloured with the ink of cuttlefish.

Barcelona also has its own *paella. La parellada* was created for Julí Parrellada at the beginning of the twentieth century (his house is now the Barcelona Atheneum). Without bones, shells or any other interruptions, its popularity has spread – you can eat it with your eyes shut – which has given it the name *paella ciega* (blind paella) in Majorca.

Barcelona was once the capital of the kingdom of the House of Aragon that ruled southern France, and as far away as southern Italy and Sicily. There are dishes and foods with Spanish names across Languedoc still. Catalonia leans towards France, though the weight of Spain is towards Africa. There is often a French way of looking at things – the ç with a cedilla (pronounced s), for instance, as well as white sauces, and *jamón de pato* (cured duck breasts).

Catalonia has sauces, too, to challenge the Basque ones. *Samfaina* is made with tomatoes, peppers, courgettes and aubergine on a fried onion base.

Salmoretta (see page 148) is similar but fishy. And there's *allioli* with garlic, and *romesco* (based on nuts and chillies).

In Catalonia the *picada* reaches perfection. It is a final condiment, puréed in a mortar, and the idea is familiar throughout Spain, for it is of Moorish origin. Here there is almost a standardized version, with a nice balance of garlic, bread, nuts and parsley (to which fish livers are added if it is to be served with fish). It serves the double purpose of thickening a visible amount of liquid and seasoning at the end of cooking.

Vic is known for sausages – *salchichón* of the salami type (but with larger fat flecks), and the surrounding hills for a smell of piggeries. But Catalonia's chief sausage is the fresh white *botifarra*, famous with beans as *mongetes amb botifarra*, and eaten with *rovellones* (wild mushrooms) in autumn. There is also a black one – and even a sweet *butifarrón dulç* with sugar and lemon. From the mountains come dishes such as rabbit with herbs and hare with chestnuts. *Escudella i carn d'olla* is in the same tradition as the Madrid *cocido* (see page 37). It provides a soup first, then the *carn d'olla* is the meat from the pot, veal, *morcilla* (blood pudding) and a huge dumpling of meat which is garlic-flavoured. A century ago it was eaten daily, except in Lent and Semana Santa. This is the season for *panadones*, pies of spinach, raisins and pine nuts.

'*¿Tienes pasta?*' 'Have you any cash?' As in our slang, dough is synonymous with money. Pasta has 500 years of history here. Rice dishes come in pasta versions. *Fideos rossejat*, for instance, short spaghetti lengths fried, then cooked in fish stock, and served with *allioli*. *Fideos* are also eaten with sausages. More recently, Italian immigrants brought cannelloni. These are now stuffed with pork and veal, or with luxuries like foie gras or seafood.

The parallels between Barcelona and Italy are clear. Italian chefs in the nineteenth century made Barcelona one of the best restaurant cities in Europe. Spain in the 1990s has that buzz of creativity and going-somewhere that made Italy such an exciting place in the 1970s.

The general ebullience and desire to break the mould, evident in the art world, turns up in food too: birds with fruit, for instance – goslings with pears for Christmas and duck with figs. There are dazzlingly brave combinations – though not the eccentricity of the Italian Marinetti. Hot apple rings with anchovy, for instance, or peaches stuffed with ham and then baked in a sauce with chocolate. Catalans are not the inventors of surf and turf: it dates from the Romans. But *mar y muntanya* is a live tradition: pork with mussels, chicken and scampi (see page 170) or chicken with lobster in an elaborate sauce with puréed nuts and bitter chocolate.

A fun food occasion here was the spring onion festival. I'm told the field workers used to barbecue the green onions with their tops, freshly picked, on old mattress springs. The grill was big enough for a party! Now an annual festival has grown up round the new vegetable. Definitely a day out for me!

Allioli is a much more important local food. One might guess – from the noise they make in Nice – that the glorious garlic sauce *aïoli* was a French invention. No such thing! Investigating these two were my best expeditions in Catalonia, though Barcelona's world-famous Ramblas market could not be missed, and a glorious day mushroom picking in the Pyrenees was worth recording.

Vast orchards in Lérida produce fruits for dessert. Cream cheese is eaten with honey (*mato con miel*) and *menjar blanco* is an almond milk pudding that once contained chicken. In *crema catalana* there is the best (and possibly the original) crème brulée. Redolent of cinnamon and lemon, the net of grilled sugar is now copied in top French restaurants. Festive fritters include *bunyols* and the All Saints' *panallets*, little cakes based on sweet potato and pine nuts.

Catalonia makes some of the best white wine in Spain, on French models, and often with French grapes in Penedès and Allela. There are good cabernet sauvignons from Jean León and Raimat and cherry-red *rosados* from Apurdán. And to celebrate it all, glasses of sparkling *cava*, for Sant Sadurní de Anoia is the world's biggest producer of wines by the champagne method. Tarragona makes fine *vi rancios*, dark, strong and rounded like an old dry sherry. The Costa Brava is also famous for *cremat*, a drink of flamed rum (together with brandy – or moonshine made from sugar locally) poured into hot coffee.

SPRING COMES WITH GRILLED ONIONS

The idea seemed eccentric. Celebrate spring by eating new onions? Find something better! That was before I ate a *calçot*!

The return of warm weather is the time for *la calçotada* on the east coast. The sun has some heat again, and everyone thinks of going to the country. Driving across the province of Tarragona, these feasts seem to be universal. Farms advertise the onions for sale, and restaurants have hordings outside, about making bookings. There were also *calçots* in every market: chunky spring onions, milder and sweeter than those we know, fatter than a finger and a good hand's length, well trimmed for domestic consumption.

Valls and Cambrils are known for their onion feasts, but Valls celebrates with barbecued onions *and* a human pyramid, with seven tiers of bodies. The TV cameras recorded them at the Barcelona Olympics. I can't say which I find more frightening, to be the cherry on the top (with all those people to clamber past safely) or to be the stolid legs, thighs and bottoms that bear up 30-odd people.

The feast is quite different. Grilled in the open, the onions arrive in bundles, inside a curved pantile (which keeps them warm). No trimmed leaves: the herbiage is like something in a wheelbarrow. I watch my neighbours distastefully grasp the leaves above the blackened objects, trying to avoid the ashes, and strip off the outside layer. Then they dip them in *romesco* sauce (see page 160) and, facing heavenwards, held them high, dribbling onion into a waiting mouth, It is a messy business and bibs are provided.

Then an acceleration, like the backwash from a liner: they start to eat faster. Cramming in the onions: grubbing for the next one. Counting how many are left in the communal pile, and what each person's share is. Skipping on the peeling, hurrying on the chewing. How fast can you eat to get a new one? Where is the sauce, and is there a full one down the table? Then, thankfully, replenishment comes from the grill again. Good humour resurrected, competition subsiding and general contentment!

LA BOQUERÍA: BARCELONA'S MARKET

Food is entertainment in Barcelona. It is not by chance that the market of La Boquería faces on to Las Rambles, the principal pedestrian walkway. It is a show with several acts. There is a wide arch, with a border of orange and yellow glass rondels on blue. Metal crosses hang on either side, like orders of merit.

Inside a huge pile of strawberries scents the market. They are in season for Easter and San José – 19 March and Father's Day. I watched a woman arranging piles within some cabbages leaves.

I had come from the north and winter, so the spring produce was most appealing. Tongues of lamb's lettuce, still bearing water drops, and new peas. These were ready-podded peas, forming conical piles in a plastic bag corner. There were tiny black potatoes from la Isla. Were they Spanish? 'No, from France.' Fat white heads of asparagus were labelled Navarra and were bigger than Churchill's cigar. There was also green wild asparagus, with chanterelles and green cauliflowers. Beautiful pears were individually displayed in yellow papers.

Local produce included a hot, slim chilli called *bitxo* (used for *romesco* sauce) and Spanish sugar cane, in a length for sawing, *pasas de Málaga* (huge muscatel raisins), kumquats and custard apples. There were imports, too: tamarind pods, physalis lanterns and enchanting baby pineapples. Even the eggs looked tempting!

The market women wear white embroidered pinafores with shoulder frills – very decorative. The oldest (at 82) is Lola de la Langostas – Lobster Lola. In Spain the same care goes into fish that the French give to butchery. I watched a woman working delicately with a huge cleaver with a round front corner. She took out the top fin from a hake, cutting a delicate V on either side in two movements. Then she sliced it into cutlets. The results was elegant: the neatness of something in a packet, but without the question mark as to its origin.

The market has the buzz of a good restaurant, the hustle of anticipated eating. Luxuries include *chanquetes* – invisible if not heaped – and *espardeñes*, an orangish, jellied sea slug. Some cuttlefish are mottled, like pebbles at the bottom of a rock pool; others are ready-skinned, round, white and gleaming. The pink skin on the squid show how fresh they are; it will go grey later. Under the spotlights the sardines make a brilliant glitter. The hall looms darker above them. The octopus are brown, as though rusty. Mixtures of small fish are sold for soup: long pink things, with baby groupers and scampi, one on its back with leg flapping. Fine marble sinks display salt cod ready-soaked for cooking.

Market wisdom distates which are the best stalls. These are packed with knots of women. The olive stall offers dozens to choose from. Green *obregones*, almost as plump as walnuts and tiny aromatic *arbequines* from Lérida, some of them reddish and not much bigger than raisins. Small green *manzanillas* and *aliñados* are olives for work days, the latter marinated and crushed. There are black Aragón *extras*, shiny with oil and large *perlas negras*. The stall also sells capers.

I watched two nuns choosing sausages. The *chorizo extra* has the bumps and lumps of a gut expanding, but the Catalan *fuet* is long, skinny and has mould on the outside. A fresh *longaniza* was curled round and round in a brown earthenware bowl with cream markings. The Catalan sausage is the pink *botifarra blanca* that goes white on cooking – a mammoth banger. Sausage for slicing included a *chorizo* from Rioja, with marbled meat, and a orange-red *chorizo de Pamplona*, with paprika in it. A *morcón ibérico* (bits of the black pig) is like a grenade, segmented by its string.

I want to gather up everything. It would need a wheelbarrow!

TARRAGONA AND ALLIOLI

Pontius Pilate was born in Tarragona, Caesar Augustus commanded from a tower that stills stands here, and St Paul came to convert the city. Principal actors in one drama. *Allioli* was also present, first recorded here by Pliny. The name comes from the Latin: *allium* is garlic, while *oleum* is oil. The correct Catalan spelling has two *l*s, pronounced as one. In other provinces the sauce is called *ajoaceite*.

Don't eat it before a wedding, when you will be kissing a lot of people. This is really the only advice you need about *allioli*. It is easy to make, simple, delicious, and *very* healthy if you make the classic one – whisking crushed garlic with olive oil, both of them known to lower cholesterol.

In its pure form *allioli* is white and shiny 'like a lemon sorbet'. It is best made with Spanish oil, with its high acidity, which holds the emulsion stable. *Allioli amb ous* includes egg yolks, as do Provençal aïoli and Languedoc's aïllade.

Warning! You can't purée garlic with bought mayonnaise – it splits. One easy way to make sure there are no lurking pieces of garlic is to chop the cloves, then crush to a paste with a pinch of salt, on a board, using the flat of a knife. Garlic never seems to dissolve enough in a blender, though a herb mill (like a coffee grinder) is excellent. Crushing garlic is the first step in the typical Catalan *picada*. This is a very common way of making a sauce in Spain – other things are added for a condiment that finishes off the sauce.

Tarragona has not one, but two famous sauces. To sample them both, a perfect menu here might be *calçots* served with *romesco* sauce (see page 160), followed by grilled fish and *allioli*. The alternative is *arrossejat* (rice cooked in fish broth) with *allioli* followed by *romesco de peix*.

Along the coast here grow pines, hazelnuts, almonds and olives. *Romesco* sauce embraces all of them. It was born in the Barrio del Serrallo of Tarragona, and is equally wonderful served with fish, roast chicken or rabbit. The basis is the dry *romesco* pepper, *bitxo* which lends heat, plus a *ñora*, which lends piquancy and sweetness to the ground nuts. The sauce also includes bread and garlic which indicate an ancient origin.

MUSHROOM PICKING IN THE HIGH PYRENEES

We climbed in search of lammergeyers – a bearded vulture and Europe's largest bird of prey. There were rumoured to be two breeding pairs in this part of the Pyrenees. 'You will know it, if you see it, by the *alas inmensas*' – a wing span of 2.5 metres/8 feet.

A day, in late September, without seeing another car, snaking upwards, then again, to a high cliff where, on one side, all the Pyrenees stretched out in the sunshine. We set up a watching point. Griffon vultures wheeled in flights overhead, lazily inspecting me as lunch, for I wore a carrion-coloured shirt.

At the back of the cliff sloped a pine wood. I have never seen so many mushrooms: russulas, red, green, black, white, so many it was like a Disney cartoon. And which were safe? I needed guidance. Then I suddenly realized the woods were full of people. Serious men, not quiche-eaters, pick mushrooms in Spain. My new companions were only interested in one mushroom.

A stunning golden-yellow underneath, and so big they had become cup-shaped, the *rovelló* was reminiscent of a communion chalice. A penknife through the stalk produced a single drop of blood, like some medieval miracle. This was *Lactarius deliciosus*, the bleeding milk cap. It is Spain's best-loved mushroom, and the picking season is a social event. They are known as *níscalos* in the Guardarrama, outside Madrid, *miscalos* in Extremadura, and *esne-gori* in the Basque country, but supremely they are a Catalan mushroom. As we descended to the valley, the roadside was full of mushroom-sellers with their baskets. We ate them in Martinet, high in Lérida, done simply, with garlic and parsley. What a wonderful country, where celebrating each new food is season seems to turn into a party!

THE CATALAN RECIPES ARE:

Escalivada amb anxoves (Barbecued vegetable salad with anchovies), see page 108.

Crema fría de melón con virutas de Jabugo (Iced melon soup with raw ham shreds), see page 121.

Lechugas a la catalana (Braised stuffed lettuce), see page 133.

Allioli (Garlic, oil and egg sauce), see page 149.

Romesco de peix (Shellfish stew with hazelnut and chilli sauce), see page 160.

Pechugas de pollo Villeroy (Chicken breasts in cream and crumb coating), see page 169.

Pollastre amb escamarlans o gambas (Chicken with scampi or prawns), see page 170.

Levante

'WHERE THE EAST WIND BLOWS.' LEVANTE TAKES IN
MOST OF THE EAST COAST, INCLUDING VALENCIA,
ALICANTE, MURCIA AND A GOOD MANY OF THE
SUNSHINE BEACHES. VALENCIA IS SYNONYMOUS
WITH ORANGES BUT IT IS FOR PAELLA, SPAIN'S
MOST FAMOUS DISH, THAT THE REGION WILL
FOR EVER BE REMEMBERED.

A SHOWER OF RICE (naturally) greets the happy wedded couple in Valencia. They emerged from the church into the quiet Plaza de la Paz behind the cathedral, and a cloud of pigeons descended on the bride, white feathers and lace veiling all fluttering together. Rice is the most visible record of Arab occupation – they were driven out by El Cid in 1094 – though the yellow, copper-green and blue handpainted Manises pottery is another. Rice grows in the Ebro delta and beside the Guadalquivir too. But here, round Lake Albufera, is the *zona de los arroces* and the home of *paella valenciana*. To pay homage, I drove round the famous *paella* villages, and was lucky to be the guest for a wedding *paella* on Valencia beach. But these are worth their separate stories.

Paella's history is a short one, for Spain's most celebrated dish is less than 200 years old. It was invented by men, combining fish and meat in rice for the first time. It is also an outdoor dish – and a lunchtime one – made on a dying fire. Every village here has its *tío*, uncle-expert, who will hold forth on how to make it. I soon found mine. Lake Albufera is famous for eels and they have uncles, too, an *allipebrotero* to give his counsel on the proper pepper sauce to cook them in.

The uplands that back the coast have also given the region some filling dishes. I met them in the form of *michirones* (broad bean stew) in Valencia, but it also has other *hervidos* (stews), and north of Castellón in the Maestrazgo heavy stews are based on potatoes, cereals and wheat. This region is also known for good meat – and makes *cecina* (beef hams). And, as always, there are stewed salt cod dishes, like *giraboix*, with green beans and cabbage.

On the coast orange trees everywhere earn it the name of Costa de Azahar, of fragrant, heady blossom. The problem is to dodge the industry that also comes with a major port. I found a route through the rice fields, up the river Júcar through groves where the fruit hung like lamps on the trees. 'When are they picked?' I asked, used to the idea of flowers in the autumn and fruit at Easter. 'In all seasons.' This is agribusiness, not nature. The preferred orange here is the navel, and not the valencia, though that is the world's most-eaten orange. There are lemons too, chiefly the juicy Verna. Here they grow 80 per cent of Spain's crop.

Driving south, the bluest of blue seas and continual sand stayed at my left elbow, and beaches where the sun turns all bodies (whatever their shape) into gold. I stopped at Gandía, famous as the home of the Borjias (Borgias). They are remembered locally for their saint, not their pope. Here *fideuá* was invented, a wonderful noodle (*fideos*) version of *paella*, with seafood in it. There are also sea dates, the brown mussels for the best of mussel soups.

Reaching Alicante, it would be easy to mistake it for North Africa, bare mountains in the background. Every roofline is broken by tufted palms and the light has an exceptional clarity. There are a million date trees here, Europe's only major grove and the most northerly. You can see them from the road from Elche to Orihuelo, though there is no way to count them. The dates were round, plump and yellow. I bought them on the frond.

Murcia is the third kingdom of the coast, proud of its Arab past. Moors ruled here until 1609 and the land is the richer for it, one vast, irrigated vegetable garden. Peppers (introduced from America) are the thing they are now proud of. But Arab dishes are still eaten, like *zarangollo*, a slow-cooked hash of onions and courgettes. The local pie, *pastel murciano*, has much in common with the Moroccan *b'stilla*. The filling is veal, ham and *chorizo*, inside a shortcrust shell. But the top of *filo* pastry rises, flower-like, in concentric circles. 'Do you make it at home?' 'Oh no, we buy it.'

Every market has new surprises. In Valencia it was snails: more follows later. In Murcia it is the superb capers. Their pickled leaf tips are used in several salads. Capers are canned here for the whole of Spain, though they grow in the Balearics. Another acid taste (and Arab invention) is *escabeche* (see page 114), meat or poultry lightly pickled in vinegar now adopted in Spain to fish.

This is a coast of *marismas*, pools and salt marshes, mirroring the sky. It has been famous for salt since Carthaginian times. The Mar Menor is a small sea, pollution-free, divided from the Med by the sports colony of La Manga.

The fish and shellfish here are astounding, for they absorb salt and iodine from the water, and gain incomparable flavour. The famous dish is *mújol a la sal* (see page 157), grey mullet baked in a salt jacket and cracked open at the table. There are also *salda gorda*, fat prawns from salt water. I ate *dorado*, gilt-head bream, cooked quite simply – and perhaps the best fish of my life.

Salt from San Pedro del Pinatar, behind the Mar Menor, is used to make *arencas*, salted and pressed sardines, and the thinly sliced, mahogany *mojama*, cured blue-fin tuna, a delicacy since Arab times. There is *huevos de mújol*, grey mullet roe, too, the 'caviar' of the Mediterranean.

From Alicante to Valencia, the coast is famous for muscat grapes, their tawny plumpness fed by the sun. Kumquats grow here, as well as fat green-gages called *yemas* (yolks) and a wealth of other fruit I had never seen: like white plums called *chinchols*, and a flat, white peach called a *paraguaya*.

Desserts are sweet too, from Arab days. Valencia is famous for its Christmas almond and honey *turrón*, which has been made commercially for four centuries. There is *tocino de cielo* (see page 206), heavenly in name and nature, and a *pan de Alá* (same idea, different faith) of pressed figs with almonds. The summer festival season brings *dulces de sartén* (morsels from the frying pan), little cakes of sweet potato, and *bunyols* (see page 204).

REAL PAELLA

The men were going to cook *paella*. Would I join the party? It was to celebrate a marriage. But the hosts (except one) were unemployed – the owner of the bar, and the men who spent their day there. We were in working-class Malvarossa, the last back street of Valencia, on the beach edge. No one swims here because of pollution from the port. But the sand drifts into the bar door, open 18 hours a day.

Breakfast comes with a tot of something, and the cooks were pacing themselves when I arrived. Manolo was the bar owner and chief chef, middle-aged and vast. 'You will recognize him by his glass eye,' I was told. He was fortifying himself with *ponche* (herbal brandy) from a silver bottle. Second (and silent) cook was José, with a neat crescent of ginger beard and respectable jeans like a carpenter's. For 10 people they had bought: 3 kg/6½ lb squid, 3 kg/6½ lb small clams, 2 kg/4½ lb *rojas* (large red prawns) and 3 kg/6½ lb scampi, plus the necessary extras, like chickens, rice and saffron.

The *paella* pan on the stove was the cheapest sort, with green handles and a dimpled bottom. It seemed as big as a bicycle wheel and gas burners in concentric rings, attached to an orange butane bottle, were needed to heat it. In it were chicken pieces in a ring, scampi and prawns, squares of white translucent squid: all arranged with the precision of a stained-glass window. The smell of oil was awful, the kitchen a windowless hole, like so many in Spain. I fled, but I went back to taste the fish broth and saffron as it went in.

Non-cooks started drifting towards the table, dragging chairs, at the arrival of *sangría*. In an unglazed jug, this was not the namby-pamby lemonade stuff made for tourists, but the real thing: wine, citrus juice and a heavy slug of Soberano brandy. It signalled the closing of the bar, metal shutters crashing downwards. Non-guests were encouraged towards the door.

There were three dishes of *mariscos* to start. The first was cooked by José-the-honest, non-drinking long-term bar companion, for whose marriage the feast was given. It was clams *a la marinera* in a sauce of garlic, plenty of paprika and a Moriles wine that was much like *fino* sherry.

This was followed by prawns *a la plancha*, unctuous, rich and the colour of steak grilled rare. There was a suggestion of black where they came off the griddle, and of blood as they spluttered open. The big heads were an embarrasment on the table, which was quickly littered. Then came boiled scampi, beautiful with their long pink claws – three well-balanced dishes, I noticed wryly.

Opposite me sat José-with-the-crash. His shirt was plentifully spattered. Did he own another, I wondered? Newly out of a detoxification unit, his face was half-bashed, though whether from a recent accident or a birthmark that had caught the sun and peeled, I dared not ask.

José-with-the-beard brought out the *paella*, wrapped up in sheets of *El Mercantil Valencio*, and placed it on more newspaper, to wait 10 minute for the grains to separate. He remarked (the second time he spoke) that of ten at table, five were called José (counting me, for Pepita is a diminutive of Josephine). Our fifth was José-minus-the-legs. So very little was left, one wondered what he sat on. He had recently been to London to attend a conference on the handicapped and been introduced to Princess Margaret. But the simultaneous translation had broken down, and he had slept throughout.

Andréas with bright eyes and exuberant curly beard atop two bird-like legs was the last man. His wife was a junkie and his child had gone away to grandma. This had made him a philospher.

It was news to me that three sorts of beans are needed for *paella*. *Garrafones* are big and flat like butter beans, *talvillas* (young haricot in a pod) and flat green *ferrauras*. 'Unknown outside Spain,' I was assured by the philosopher (though they looked like tender runner beans). He moved on to brick-laying and ended up with Handel, without my quite following how he got there.

The newspaper came off! Of course it is the seafood that catch the eye, but the rice is a real star. Plates were loaded for the 'two girls' (the bride and I), while a dirty two-year-old appeared from under the table and was given rice (but no seafood). But she got the crisp bit underneath in the middle, the *soccarat*, which is what I fancied.

More drinks. A conconction by José-with-the-beard of kiwi syrup and gin, whisked with egg white and diluted by *cava* (local champagne) – and then another with Moscatel and something. Of the 10 assembled to eat the great *paella*, five took a plateful, five barely put their forks in the pan. But for everyone it was a day to remember.

Was it the greatest *paella* in the world? I couldn't fault it. It was cooked with the classic ingredients, in exactly the right place, by people who had done it a thousand times before. It was also done with love for a special occasion – enjoyed for a day and slept off. The shutters were down for the whole of Monday.

LAKE ALBUFERA: DUCKS, RICE AND EELS

The rice harvest was late in September, because the weather was good. Normally the month brings rain to Valencia (again in spring) – and floods. *La gota fría*, it is called: the cold drops. It's the floods that make rice viable in this flat coastal strip in the bay of the east coast. Spain is the major rice producer in Europe.

I drove out beside Lake Albufera, one of Spain's largest natural freshwater lakes. The names of the villages I passed were familiar to me: the *paella* roll call of honour. First Catarroja (now industrialized), then El Salar and El Palmar, later El Perellonet, El Perelló, Silla, Sollana, Sueca.

From the tree shade of the shore a soft grey sheet of water spread out to the mountains. The Arab 'mirror of the sun' and space to breathe after Valencia city! To the south, banks of reeds shelter migrating birds – duck with orange was an early dish here. The lake is also famous for its eels (now diminished by pollution). Rice grows in the black mud and, when I eventually reached the western edge, the ripe rice stretched out, golden like the proverbial cornfields.

Paella was invented in this countryside, a peasant rice dish, and a Lenten one. Eels, snails and green beans with rice were its origin, put together outdoors by men cooking. El Palmyr is one of the few lakeside villages approachable by car, for punts and ancient motor boats are the local transport. Little bridges with square, dark cobbles cross a series of green canals between islands of swaying bamboo. The traditional cottages are thatched with rice straw, *barracos* steep-roofed against the rain. There are not many left.

On to El Perelló, on the coast, where I fell into conversation with Señor Manoli on the beach, and was delighted to find his wife was the *maestra paellera* (best cook) of the coast the previous year. I admired her trophy and was amused to discover she was born in León in the north. 'Paella valenciana is the most famous dish, but it is not really home food. It's for Sundays out. In these villages we make *paella* with chicken and rabbit, but no fish.' The chicken feet were essential for good stock.

Though the things that go into rice catch the attention of foreigners, locals care more about the rice. It is this that wins the prize. 'Rice is the principal actor,' I was told. 'There are good dishes with rice served with nothing in it. *Paella* is a 'dry' dish. When it is done the grains must be separate. That is why it is important to wash the rice first.' I had already met *soccarat* (the crust underneath), but I found its name was that of the next village on the coast.

And life before *paella*? 'Rice has been here since Arab times. It used to be cooked in casseroles in the oven. And that meant the baker's oven, since homes had none in this heat.' In Catalan it is called *arròs passejat* – walked rice. One of the famous ones is the rice dished out to the Jijona factory workers. *Empedrat*, it is called – 'cobbled' – just rice and beans, but the latter look like paving stones.

Elche is famous for a *paella* like a pie – rice with a crust, *arròs amb costra* in the local dialect. Beaten eggs are poured over the half-cooked rice with the mixture of chicken and ham, *chorizo* or *morcilla*. This protects it in the oven.

Soupy rice dishes – 'wet' rice – come from a different tradition. These often contain bits of pork, like *arròs amb fesols i naps*. With dried beans, I find, and the yellow swede (not turnips). Not what you expect in the heat!

We got on to saffron and fish soups, the oldest rice dishes on this coast. But the yellow colour of much rice comes from *ñoras*, the pepper called *romesco* in Catalonia (see page 160). They are important when the rice is *arroz abanda* – eaten alone as a first course. The famous dish is from Castellón de la Plana, and made with rascasse, which is then eaten with *allioli*. Murcian *arroz en caldero* (see page 148) is related to it.

'The rice is cooked in the rich broth that was used for the fish. *No* water.' I was rebuked. 'Valencian water is only for soup. To cook rice it must be good *caldo* (broth).' However he relented, and told me the story of a Valencian family bottling town water (well-known for its bad taste) to take to Madrid, to add that authentic local 'something' to *paella*.

CREEPY CRAWLERS: SNAILS IN VALENCIA

Women who sell apples don't have to pursue them, with a grab and a whoop, to prevent them walking off the table. But the snail-seller I met in Valencia moved quickly to recover one that had made it further on the road to liberty. Snails don't have a good press in non-Latin countries, but this one was quite endearing. The movements of its head were like those of a cat pricking its ears.

There were great baskets of snails on sale: dark-shelled *paellitas*, *vaquetas de oliva* with grey and black whorls, and similar *cristianos* and *sonetos*. The biggest were great, gross black ones called *moros*, and the tiniest cream *avellanets*. 'Those are best in a tomato sauce with *pimiento* and a few bits of raw ham (or *chorizo*). Bags of chillies were sold alongside them.

I asked about the recipes. 'The two larger types of snail are much less good to eat. Roast them on the grill. But in the interior of Valencia you can buy the *vaqueta*. There's a snail! They are very expensive, £4–5 for a dozen – if you can find them. For *paella* and rice dishes.' For a good rice dish she was emphatic it must be *vaquetas* or *zonetas* (mountain snails), not the *negros* (blacks) or *moros* that she was selling. Indeed, I was assured later, one of the nicest *paellas* was snails with runner beans (*ferrauras*) and butter beans (*garrafones*) – eaten outside in the shade of a broad-topped fig tree or under a hanging vine.

This was September. Was it specially good for snails? No, spring was the time for snail festivals – even a freshwater snail feast, as the river dried out at Os de Balaguer in Lérida!

But the famous festival – *la cargolada* – marks the return of warm weather. The snails are cooked outdoors on a grill, 200–300 a time. At the last moment a torch is made from a piece of lard, wrapped in greasy paper, and the fat is dribbled along them, so a tiny drop enters each snail shell. They are eaten from the communal dish. Everyone has their own bread slice, for a plate, and piles it high with golden *allioli*. And the empty shells are collected, to count at the end like cherry stones. 'More bread and *allioli*? 'Yes, and a good *porrón* (drinking kettle) of red wine.'

TURRÓN, NUTS AND OTHER SWEETS

Xixona – Jijona: obviously Arab. A brown village on the edge of the Sierra de la Carrasqueta, in rocky hills the colour and texture of toasted almonds – almost as though the main ingredient of *turrón* was mined here, not manufactured. For Jijona is celebrated for a type of nougat which has been made in the town for four centuries. The whole of Spain eats it at Christmas and, increasingly, throughout the year.

The finest Marcona almonds are at least half the weight of all *turrón*. Riding the village bus from Alicante, through the village of Muchamiel (lotsahoney), I reflected there must be lotsascrub in the mountain and lotsabees around too, for honey is the other main constituent of this nougat.

The *turrón* made here is soft and sticky; the meringue-covered nuts go into the grinder, then are beaten until creamy, to make a coffee-coloured, almond-scented paste. The other version is studded with whole toasted nuts – like the white El Almendro from Alicante, and the Lérida *tarta imperial* (the best in Spain). There is also a dark caramelized version, *guirlache* (see page 212), in Aragon.

The Spanish sweet tooth and taste for nuts is also indulged with the drink called *horchata*. Alboraya, just outside Valencia, is the world capital of *chufas*. 'An Arab from Saudi owns the lot,' I was told. 'His supply is sent weekly on a plane.'

The *chufa* is an underground tuber, an irregular little brown pebble to look at, textured like a peanut shell. It is produced by a type of sedge – toughest hummocks of grass (not unlike rice), growing in the fine black sand. It is harvested in summer by burning off the foliage.

The taste is between almond and coconut, and it is made into a long refreshing drink, and sometimes an ice cream. It is sold in cafés in Valencia. To make *horchata* the *chufas* are steeped in water, strained and ground: 1 kg/2 lb nuts, 800 g/1¾ lb sugar flavoured with a little lemon zest, and water makes 5 litre/8 pt. A good profit, as the nuts are only £1 a kilo. But good cafés make it daily and throw it away if not consumed.

I find *horchaterías* are a Jewish-Arab tradition. In Madrid the same men may also make *persianas* (venetian blinds) or *zapatas* (rope-soled shoes). Poor trades; they switch to making *horchata* in summer and *turrón* at Christmas.

THE LEVANTINE RECIPES ARE:

Ajotomate (Tomato salad with tomato dressing), see page 107.

Esgarràt (Red pepper and cured fish salad), see page 110.

Bajoques farcides (Cold stuffed peppers with rice and tuna), see page 132.

Arroz en caldero (Rice with peppers and allioli followed by fish), see page 148.

Mújol a la sal (Whole fish baked in salt), see page 157.

Pollo all y pebre (Peppered chicken), see page 168.

Caracoles Lola (Snails with piquant sauce), see page 172.

Arròs amb forn (Oven rice with pork and tomato), see page 184.

Paparajotes (Fritters with lemon or bay leaves), see page 203.

Bunyols de vent (Hot orange puffs a wind could lift), see page 204.

Tocino de cielo (Sweet temptation), see page 206.

Granizado (Iced lemonade), see page 216.

Carajillo (Brandied coffee), see page 216.

The Balearic Islands

SPAIN'S BIGGEST MEDITERRANEAN ISLANDS ARE
MAJORCA AND MINORCA (LITERALLY THE MAJOR
AND MINOR ISLANDS) AND IBIZA. THE LATTER WAS
THE ONE PART OF SPAIN NEVER OCCUPIED BY THE
FASCISTS. ONE REASON, PERHAPS, WHY IT BECAME
THE MEDITERRANEAN'S FIRST HIPPY COLONY
IN THE 1960S.

ONCE GOT LOCKED in Palma cathedral. The cathedral is vast and late
Gothic: slender soaring pillars (with chandeliers round them) and light,
with coloured glass and a wide rose window. A moment of panic as I
struggled with the outside lock in the pitch-blackness of a double-porch.
Never mind! I had my *ensaimada* with me in a paper. Such comfort, as I bit
into that glorious breakfast pastry, many layered, its flaky softness coiled
under a dusting of icing sugar. Workmen arranged my exit.

Eight in the morning is the time to see Palma de Mallorca, when the city
is untroubled by the tourists that will engulf it later. And March is the time
to be there, to experience the elegance that once gave it its bon-ton image.
The bay is very beautiful – and a major sailing port in summer, which still
brings the King to the Marivent Palace. March to April is the opera season,
and in a shop on the arcaded Avenida Jaime III I saw a windowful of male
opera gear, white silk scarves matched to different shirts and styles of dinner
jackets. The Hotel Formentor, in the north of the peninsula, is part of this
same elegant tradition, built in 1929 as the first of the twentieth-century
luxury resort hotels. In summer some such retreat is needed: tourist beds on
the islands outnumber those in Greece!

I hadn't expected the island to be so beautiful. First the bay of Palma,
dominated by the cathedral hulk and buttresses, then the interior of the
island, where agricultural life goes on as usual. I passed a field of almond blossom (so late it was obviously in a frost pocket). The Sierra de Tramonte
forms a ridge down the west of the island and rises to 1500 metres/4500 feet
in places. Though pink in the morning light, it is grey and without vegetation.

The rough stony *garrigue* grows a profusion of herbs, which are the basis of domestic and commercial green herb liqueurs. In the valley are gnarled olive trees, some over 1000 years old. Ancient and grey, often split down the middle, they are as old as those on the Mount of Olives. I watched a woman picking up *muertas* – ripe black olives left to shrivel and drop. Beyond the ridge is the west coast road, with incomparable views of blue sea and the villas of the discerning.

Majorca is known for solid soups and vegetable dishes. *Sopa mallorquina* is almost solid with bread, more like a juicy pudding, though I ate a very good one with three sorts of greens – *bledes* (chard), cabbage and spinach, plus stock (and bits) from pork and rabbit. Perhaps the pleasantest of these dishes is *tumbet*, with layered, lightly fried aubergine and potato in tomato sauce (see party version, page 136).

Minorca's popular soup is *oliagua* (see page 127), one of the few dishes not to start with a fried *sofrito* of onion and tomato. For these vegetables, with potato, are the basic fare. *Trempó* is the local salad – mixed tomato, peppers and onions, sometimes with fruit or wild groundsel. Many recipes include bread, a good way to use up a stale loaf (though Majorca has a dark saltless bread that lasts). There are also flat breads called *cocas*. Sugary ones are eaten for festivals and they are made in many flavours, though I find them less good than pizzas.

Pork is basic, as is the use of lard for cooking. There was local uproar at the time I was there because of an EC threat to outlaw the family *mantance* (pig-killing). Much pork goes to make the raw, red sausage, *sobrasada*, so soft that it is bread-spreadable. In the western market town of Soller, eggs are fried and served on slices of *sobrasada*, then covered with a milky sauce with puréed peas in it. Sausage also enriches *escaldums* (see page 171) and *perdices del capellán* (chaplain's partridges), which are veal escalopes rolled up with ham and sausage.

Fish is often eaten simply, like sardines barbecued on the beach over old rosemary bushes from the stony *garrigue*. Sauces are traditional, like Ibiza's *burrida de ratjada*, ray with a sauce of pulverized almonds. The fish stews, *calderas*, have great variety and freshness. Most start with a *sofrito* of onion and tomato and lightly fried fish is added. Wherever possible peas seem to be included, and they are very common with cuttlefish.

Summer is celebrated with spiny lobster in all the islands. The most glamorous dish is *caldereta de langosta*, with a tomato sauce containing peppers and bread, spiked with the local herb *aguardiente*. I was amused to find it was assumed this was *salsa americana*. I met other good lobster dishes, one called a *greixera* – the name of a flattish brown casserole, and therefore of many local dishes. The lobster was baked and peeled, then layered with about one-third of its bulk of cooked spinach mixed with eggs and milk, flavoured with cinnamon and lemon juice and topped with breadcrumbs.

At Alcudía, a port with sugar-brown city walls built in the fourteenth century, I joined the party of a local *cofradía*. Sucking pig in Majorca is roast plain or stuffed with its own spiced liver, apples and cherries. But this was the festive *mero con lechona a la mallorquina*. From beneath the roast piglet's splayed legs came the tail of a grouper. Pork and fish together! Beneath it were layered vegetables and a sauce that contained raisins, pine nuts and paprika.

I saw precarious two-wheel carts practising for the trotting races in Manacor. But it was cultured pearls, made here by Majoríca, that really caught my eye. Their sheen is borrowed from the belly scales of certain fish. Black pearls are the ones I covet, to wear to the Baile de Piñata (Carnival Ball) on the first Sunday of Lent. The famous *bolero*, I learned, comes from an eighteenth-century ballroom dance in Palma.

After the cathedral, the most famous building on Majorca is the Cartuja de Valldemossa. The Charterhouse owes its fame largely to George Sand, who came here in 1838 with the consumptive Chopin. She found it draughty, and wore trousers. The locals hated her (and she took her revenge by disparaging them in *Un Hiver à Majorque*). I inquired about what she might have eaten: pickled hocks are the local speciality. The favourite of a later famous author, Robert Graves (who wrote *Goodbye To All That* here), was rabbit with onions cooked down to a confit.

Waves of invaders have occupied these islands. Bronze Age people left *taulas* (T-stones) scattered across the interior of Minorca. Greeks planted the flat-topped Aleppo pine (source of pine nuts) in all the islands, and left a sweet cheesecake called *flao*. The Arabs named all the villages starting in Bini (son of) in Minorca and bequeathed a sweet tooth. There are still shops called *sucrerías* (sugar sellers) and the Arabs are credited with the pastry *ensaimada*.

Flat Minorca, to the British eye, still has many English traces: Windsor chairs and English tallboys in private houses – and willow-pattern dinner services still on wedding present lists. The British had a long and benign occupation. Gin (drunk seriously strong) and gravy (*grevi*) are well-known here. Ex-English words have become local argot – *boinder* is a bow-window, *potato* instead of *patata*. There are turkeys and soda biscuits called *crespells*, plain or layered with jam. I was also given lemon meringue pie, which my hostess said was an old Minorcan recipe. Governor Richard Kane introduced dairy Friesians to replace goats, planted *enclover* to feed them, and so formed the local cheese. The excellent square, orange Mahón is semi-hard, is D.O. (protected) and is now sold abroad.

Indisputably the most famous product of these isles is mayonnaise, getting its name from the Minorcan capital, Mahón. The French claimed it and the Spanish named it. As a classic sauce for the whole Mediterranean basin, its origin needed investigations in the place of origin.

MAHÓN AND MAYONNAISE

Horatio was here, Nelson, and the British fleet for nearly the whole of the eighteenth century. The Mahón harbour in the Balearic Islands is one of the best in the world, an inlet a couple of kilometres long (I walked it) and 200 metres or so wide, with a cliff to the west offering shelter. On that day there was a stiff breeze blowing, of a kind that makes sailors want to be at sea. It was easy to imagine the harbour full of ships of the line and British frigates.

The English must have been so happy! Decent, white and clean, there is something here reminiscent of Devon. Sash windows (inconceivable in the Mediterranean) and well-painted solid shutters are prevalent in Mahón. And in El Castell at the harbour entrance (Georgetown in the British era) I saw six-panelled Georgian doors that would not have been out of place in Greenwich or Woodstock. Halfway down the harbour, on the eastern shore, is San Antonio, a red villa with a lookout tower, where Nelson reputedly lived with Lady Hamilton. It is certainly in the perfect semaphore position.

The harbour was lost briefly to the French – and thereby hangs the story. There is an engraving in the museum of the party when the British got it back again, full of wine, dancing and babies. There must be a lot of Minorcans with English great-grandparentage.

In 1756 the French took Mahón – and the legend of mayonnaise was born. Did a Frenchman invent it, or did the English miss it entirely? An English engineer, John Armstrong, wrote a good account of the island's food in 1752 without remarking on it. The French took it back to France in triumph.

A widespread local legend associated it with Maréchal Richelieu. It is said his chef served it to enliven the local greenstuff during the siege of San Felipe castle. But Elizabeth David lends support to a local origin in *French Provincial Cookery*: 'It seems likely by the 1750s the sauce was already known in Spain and Provence.' The probability is that it is *allioli* without the garlic. The local dialect name is *maionesa* (from Maò) and Spaniards often favour a spelling, *mahonesa* (from Mahón), that emphasizes the local origin.

Mayonnaise is a southern sauce, and sensitive to cold. Spanish oil, with its high acidity, is ideal for it, and probably why it was born here. The oil blends at once and never separates. An acidity of 0.8 per cent, I was advised, is perfect for mayonnaise: in Spain acidity is marked on oil labels in big numerals. It is a sauce in which virgin oil is not successful. This goes in, if at all, after the emulsion is formed, to add to the flavour.

Start by diluting salt with vinegar (or lemon juice – even top chefs can't agree on the perfect recipe). Vinegar is better, though, for it will kill off any salmonella bug lingering round the yolks.

Then drip in the oil slowly. Sod's law applies to this (like meringue): the recipe is simple and works for everyone – but not when you are in a hurry! One egg will go on absorbing huge quantities of oil without the emulsion breaking; the sauce just gets thinner. Real mayonnaise should be thick, even cuttable! It then can be diluted to pour, or take other flavours. Once made, good Spanish mayonnaise also doesn't separate: witness mayonnaise in warm soup.

Ybarra is the local make, and a steady export. But my attempts to find purely local recipes that use it were rather frustrating. Invariably the answer was 'todo' – with everything. I was reminded, though, that Ernest Hemingway liked it mixed with a little tomato sauce and a spoonful of paprika over a tail of monkfish.

THE BALEARIC RECIPES ARE:

Cocarrois de Mallorca (Chard or spinach pasties with raisins and pine nuts), see page 103.

Mahonesa (Mayonnaise), see page 112.

Oliagua amb escarrats (Tomato and garlic soup with asparagus), see page 127.

Motllo d'alberginies de Mallorca (Aubergine timbale from Majorca), see page 136.

Calamares rellenos a la menorquina (Squid stuffed with pine nuts, mint and raisins), see page 143.

Escaldums d'indiot o de pollastre (Turkey or chicken fricassée), see page 171.

Ponx d'ous (Rum and milk punch), see page 215.

Ponche de sanguíneas (Iced white rum with blood oranges), see page 215.

The Recipes

CHAPTER ONE

Tapas

Aceitunas aliñadas

Marinated olives

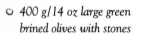

- 400 g/14 oz large green brined olives with stones
- 2 fresh oregano or thyme sprigs
- ½ lemon, cut into 4 long wedges
- 10 black peppercorns
- 1 dried chilli
- 200 ml/7 fl oz virgin olive oil

I can hardly bear to eat supermarket brined olives these days, so crude do they taste after Spanish marinated ones. But they can be turned into proper nibbles to go with drinks. Use the olive oil, as the jar diminishes, for making superior salad dressings.

Rinse the olives well in a colander under running water, drain well and blot with kitchen paper. Put a handful into a clean 600 ml/1 pt jar and add the herb sprigs, lemon wedges, peppercorns and chilli, arranging them attractively.

Make sure the bottom layer of olives is pushed well into the corner of the jar, then pack in the rest of the olives. Cover with virgin oil and put on the lid. Keep at least a week before eating. They will become spicier the longer they are kept.

For aceitunas a la importancia – olives decorated for a party – buy the big fat 'queens' or the purply heart-shaped Gordals. Rinse and dry them. Cross the top with a small thin strip of canned *pimiento* and another of canned anchovy fillet, split and halved. Jab in a cocktail stick to hold the decoration in place.

THE BASQUE COUNTRY

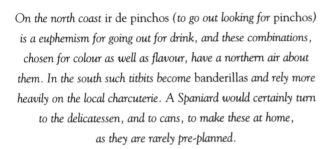

Pinchos

Titbits on cocktail sticks

On the north coast ir de pinchos (to go out looking for pinchos)
is a euphemism for going out for drink, and these combinations,
chosen for colour as well as flavour, have a northern air about
them. In the south such titbits become banderillas and rely more
heavily on the local charcuterie. A Spaniard would certainly turn
to the delicatessen, and to cans, to make these at home,
as they are rarely pre-planned.

Assemble any of the following on cocktails sticks:

1 Chunks of *chorizo* (or salami) with squares of fresh green pepper on either side of a cube of Manchego or Gouda. Half-gherkins go well, too.

2 Small slices of *serrano* or other raw ham, rolled up and pierced, with fat black grapes or half figs on either side.

3 Chunks of cold pork are good with wedges of apple in lemon juice, pineapple cubes or halved plums.

4 Rolled, canned anchovy fillets (Cantabrian if possible) – or anchovy-stuffed olives – alternating between cubes of Manchego or mature Gouda.

5 Green and red pepper squares with chunks of canned mackerel fillet, or tuna belly (look for *ventresca*). Home-pickled fish are also good (see recipes on pages 114 and 115).

6 Galician canned mussels in sauce, with a mild black olive or a cherry tomato.

7 Slices of roast red pepper (see page 110) or canned *pimiento*, looped over and speared with cubes of Idiazábal, St Simon or another smoked cheese.

8 Cubes of goat's cheese alternately with cubes of jellied quince paste. This is called *membrillo* in Spain, and is sold in Italian delicatessens as *cotogna*.

ASTURIAS AND CANTABRIA

Croquetas de huevos
Egg croquettes

Another immensly popular tapa, for Spaniards love things newly fried. These are very creamy in the middle, crisp on the outside – and so hot! At home, garnished with little watercress, they make an entremes *(starter) before roast meat or a ham salad.*

SERVES 5–6

- 500 ml/18 fl oz milk
- 1 bay leaf, crumbled
- 75 g/3 oz plain flour
- 90 g/3½ oz butter
- salt and ground white pepper
- freshly grated nutmeg
- 1 large hard-boiled egg (see note), finely chopped
- oil for greasing

FRYING

- 3–4 tbsp plain flour
- 1 large egg, beaten
- 8–10 tbsp stale breadcrumbs
- olive oil for deep frying

Warm the milk with the crumbled bay leaf. Make a white sauce (a *besamel*) in a saucepan: cook the flour in the butter for a couple of minutes, then, off the heat, strain in some of the warm milk, beating to a smooth paste. Add the remaining milk and simmer 2–3 minutes, stirring gently. Season to taste with salt, white pepper and nutmeg.

Stir in the egg (any addition must be very finely chopped). Pour on to an oiled platter, in a layer about a finger thick, and pat into a rectangle. Leave to go cold and hard.

Cut into fingers, then into about 30 pieces. Make bullet-shapes, rolling them lightly in flour. Coat with beaten egg, then crumbs; they should be well sealed. Deep fry in a basket, in oil at highest heat, in batches of about 8, for 3–4 minutes. Drain on kitchen paper and serve immediately.

Note: 50 g/2 oz cooked peeled prawns or raw ham can replace the egg, or cooked chicken with 1 tsp chopped fresh tarragon.

NEW CASTILE AND LA MANCHA

Tortilla de patatas con azafrán
Potato cake with eggs and saffron

Tortillas *stand proudly on every bar in Spain: dense moist cakes so very different from an omelette. Saffron makes this version of the national favourite more sophisticated – and a vibrant yellow.*

SERVES 8 AS A TAPA, 2 AS A SUPPER DISH

- 3 potatoes (*rather larger than the eggs*), diced
- 100 ml/3½ fl oz olive oil
- 1 onion, chopped
- 20 strands saffron
- 3 tbsp hot stock
- 6 large eggs
- salt and freshly ground black pepper

The best frying pan for this is about 22 cm/9 in across, with vertical sides. Heat a generous quantitity of oil until very hot. Add the potatoes and onion and stir to coat. Reduce the heat and cook until soft without letting them colour. Meanwhile crumble the saffron in your fingers, then soak in the stock for 5 minutes.

Move the potatoes and onion with a slotted spoon to a bowl with kitchen paper at the bottom. Drain the oil from the pan, leaving about 2 tbsp of oil. Beat the eggs with the saffron liquid and seasoning. Remove the paper and pour the eggs over the potatoes, so they are well coated.

Pour into the hot oil, spreading the potatoes evenly. Cook for a minute at high heat, then turn down to a low one. Use a spatula to pull the egg off the sides of the pan, shaking it to and fro occasionally, to make sure the bottom isn't catching.

When the top has ceased to be liquid, cover with a serving plate and reverse the pan. Return the *tortilla* and cook for a further minute. Serve hot, or cold, but in portions and speared with cocktail sticks.

Torta de gambas
Prawn-glazed loaf

~

SERVES 8 AS A TAPA,
4–6 AS A SALAD
LUNCH

*A modern tapa with pizzaz and colour for when the cava
(champagne-style wine) comes out, and corks start popping.
With tall cañas of iced beer, it also makes an elegant snack lunch.*

- ○ *500g/1lb big boiled prawns, peeled*
- ○ *1 small round white bread loaf, about 18–20 cm/ 7–8 in across, 1 day old*
- ○ *100 ml/3½ fl oz fish stock or white wine*
- ○ *1 scant tsp powdered gelatine (or fish aspic)*
- ○ *1 drop of cochineal (optional)*
- ○ *parsley sprigs, to garnish*

STUFFING

- ○ *250 ml/8 fl oz mayonnaise*
- ○ *100 g/4 oz smoked salmon*
- ○ *2 tbsp lemon juice*
- ○ *2 ripe avocados*
- ○ *pinch of garlic salt*
- ○ *pinch of cayenne pepper*
- ○ *freshly ground black pepper*

Make the glaze for the prawns (or use fish aspic): heat the stock or wine, sprinkle with the gelatine and leave 3–4 minutes, then dissolve over hot water. Add a drop of cochineal to a spoonful of cold water and add half to the jelly. Leave to cool until starting to set.

Slice the bread loaf horizontally into three layers, removing the domed top if there is one. Turn the loaf over, to give it a flat crust top.

Spread the bottom bread layer with two-thirds of the mayonnaise. Cut the salmon into strips (*tiritas*) as long as the radius of the loaf and arrange over the top, pointing into the middle (easier to cut). Sprinkle with 1 tbsp lemon juice. Cover with the next layer of bread and press down well. Purée the avocados in the blender and season with 1 tbsp lemon juice, garlic salt, cayenne and black pepper to taste. Spread over the bread with the back of the spoon.

Cover with the bread lid (once the bottom). Spread lightly with mayonnaise and arrange the prawns in a wheel on top. Dribble with the just-setting glaze and decorate the centre with parsley sprigs. Leave to set for 6–24 hours. Slice like a cake.

Note: The stuffing can be varied. Tomatoes with basil are good, with anchovies and black olives instead of the smoked salmon. The layers must moisten the bread, so if necessary sprinkle the bread with a little vinaigrette.

MADRID

Tigres

Stuffed crumbed mussels

~

Madrid's most popular tapa is not normally served at home, except as a first course. The traditional way to make these is to fill them, then egg and crumb the top and deep-fry them once they are well chilled. But at home grilling is a lot easier. The addition of chopped pepper and tomato comes from a friend.

First check that each mussel is alive: their shells should be closed, or close when tapped – throw out any that remain open.

Heat the wine with the garlic in a large saucepan. Add half the mussels, clap on the lid and cook over high heat for a couple of minutes until the mussels are all open. Discard any that have not opened. Remove with a slotted spoon and add the rest. Remove the bodies from the shells, saving half of the biggest shells and the cooking liquid.

Melt half the butter, stir in the flour and cook for 1 minute. Work in the hot milk, stirring until smooth and thick. Strain the liquid from the mussels, through muslin inside a sieve. Stir in enough to make a smooth, thick sauce (in the summer months you might not need it all, as mussels hold more liquid then). Add the diced peppers and tomato paste and season, adding nutmeg and cayenne.

Chop the mussel bodies into 2–3 pieces and stir into the sauce (at this point, everything should coagulate). Use a spoon to fill the mussel shells, laying them out on a cake rack. Fry the crumbs in the remaining butter plus the oil and sprinkle over the tops. Refrigerate until needed on baking trays.

Put under a hot grill for 2–3 minutes before serving them on saucers or small plates. Pass serviettes to pick them up, and remember dishes for the empty shells!

SERVES 8 AS A TAPA, 6 AS A STARTER

- *1.5 kg/3 lb large mussels, cleaned*
- *4 tbsp dry white wine*
- *1 garlic clove, finely chopped*
- *175 g/6 oz butter*
- *6 tbsp plain flour*
- *500 ml/18 fl oz milk, hot*
- *2 tbsp finely diced red pepper*
- *2 tbsp finely diced green pepper*
- *1 tsp tomato paste*
- *salt and freshly ground black pepper*
- *freshly grated nutmeg*
- *pinch of cayenne pepper*
- *about 8 tbsp stale white breadcrumbs*
- *1 tbsp olive oil*

GALICIA

Zamburiñas rebozadas, cuatro en una

Fried baby scallops, four to a shell

~

SERVES 4

- 16–24 small scallops, depending on size (350 g/ 12 oz shelled weight)
- 3–4 tbsp plain flour
- salt and freshly ground black pepper
- 1 large egg, beaten
- 3–4 slices of stale bread, crusts removed, crumbed
- about 4 tbsp olive oil
- lemon wedges, to serve

The most wonderful scallops of my life were eaten plain fried with garlic and parsley. So large were they that they resembled poached eggs in reverse – an orange roe circling right round the white meat. In the rich waters of the north-west, scallops grow swiftly to extraordinary size. But the ria de Arousa in Galicia is famous for these tiny ones – and nowadays the tiny ones are all most of us can buy. They are served in a top shell, for everyone to help themselves.

Clean the scallops, removing any frill attached to the base, and rinse them. Blot with kitchen paper. Roll in seasoned flour then in beaten egg. Coat with crumbs.

Fry briefly in plenty of hot oil – about 1 minute each side – and serve in the top shells of large scallops (or 4 small dishes), accompanied by wedges of lemon and cocktail sticks.

THE BALEARIC ISLANDS

Cocarrois de Mallorca

Chard (or spinach) pasties with raisins and pine nuts

~

A little closed pizza, with the edges making a wavy 'crown' (hence rois) on top, this is a Cornish pasty gone Spanish.

In a large bowl beat together the egg, lard and oil with a wooden spoon until creamy. Add the orange juice and sugar, then little by little beat in the flour until smooth. (The old method works well in a food processor.) Pull the dough together and chill while you prepare the filling.

Heat the oven to 180°C/350°F/Gas 4. Wash and drain the leaves. Wilt the spinach in the water clinging to the leaves in a covered pan, turning the top to bottom. Cook chard leaves in boiling water for 10 minutes. Drain as well as possible, pressing to extract excess water, then chop.

Toast the pine nuts in a heavy frying pan over a low heat, tossing for 3–4 minutes until coloured and smelling richly. Drain the raisins (and seed, if they are Spanish muscatels). Chop coarsely with the pine nuts, then mix with the spinach and add a little salt, pepper, paprika and the oil. Mix well.

Roll out the dough on a lightly floured surface and cut circles round a saucer (15 cm/6 in across) – or make 12 balls, then roll out each one. Put the filling in a bullet shape in the centre of each one. Dampen round the edge with a finger and draw up the side to meet along the top. Squeeze together, then use finger and thumb to crinkle it to and fro. Push in the ends slightly, so there is no empty pastry. Move to a lightly oiled baking sheet and bake for 30 minutes. Eat warm or cold.

SERVES 6

PASTRY

- 1 large egg
- 50 g/2 oz lard or butter
- 50 ml/2 fl oz sunflower oil
- juice of 1 large orange
- 1 tbsp caster sugar
- 350g/12 oz plain flour

FILLING

- 750 g/1¾ lb spinach or leaves from 1 kg/2 lb chard (425 g/15 oz prepared leaves)
- 25 g/1 oz pine nuts
- 50 g/2 oz raisins, simmered in water to cover for 10 minutes
- salt and freshly ground black pepper
- ½ tbsp paprika
- 1 tsp oil

CHAPTER TWO

Salads

ANDALUSIA

Ensalada de alcauciles y pimientos rojos

Artichoke and red pepper salad

~

SERVES 4

- 8 soft spring globe artichokes
- 1 large red pepper, seeded
- 6 tbsp best olive oil
- 2 garlic cloves, finely chopped
- 2 large red tomatoes, skinned and seeded
- salt and freshly ground black pepper
- 2 tbsp vinegar
- 12 black olives

Alcauciles *is the local Andaluz word for artichokes, called* alcachofas *in the rest of Spain. Introduced here by the Arabs, they were part of the cuisine by the thirteenth century – long before they became fashionable in Italy. If you grow tarragon (a Seville herb), add a little to the dressing.*

Prepare the artichokes, cutting off the stalk and tops of the buds, then paring round to remove most of the outside leaves. Cook in salted water for 20 minutes.

Meanwhile cut the pepper into thin strips. Heat 2 tbsp oil in a frying pan and fry the pepper, adding the garlic towards the end. Slice the tomato flesh, add to the pan and cook for 5 minutes, then season with salt and pepper.

Drain the artichokes. If they are very soft the whole can be eaten. If not, push out the hairy choke with a teaspoon and thumb and strip any harsh leaf stubs from round the sides. Quarter them, add to the pan and turn in the oil.

Make a vinaigrette by beating the vinegar with 4 tbsp oil and seasoning. Turn the hot vegetables into a salad bowl, dress them, add the olives and leave to cool before serving.

LEVANTE

Ajotomate

Tomato salad with tomato dressing

~

One of the oldest salads on the East coast, it uses tomatoes at different stages of ripeness. The acidity in the fruit keeps the dressing in a fluffy suspension like a mayonnaise. The name simply means 'garlic tomatoes'.

SERVES 4

- 4 firm salad tomatoes
- 1 very ripe beefsteak tomato, or about 300 g/11 oz ripe tomatoes, skinned and seeded
- 4 garlic cloves, finely chopped
- ½ tsp salt
- 200 ml/7 fl oz good olive oil
- 1 tbsp sherry vinegar
- freshly ground pepper
- ½ tsp cumin seeds, finely ground (or paprika)

Cut the salad tomatoes in rounds and put in a salad bowl. Purée the garlic with the salt – in a mortar or on a board with the flat of a knife. Purée the ripe tomato flesh with the garlic (in a blender), adding oil and vinegar to make a smooth emulsion. Taste and check the seasonings. Pour over the sliced tomatoes, dress with a little cumin (or paprika) and stand for 30 minutes before serving.

ARAGON AND NAVARRE

Cogollos de Tudela

Lettuce hearts with anchovy

~

Good as a side salad and also as a starter.

Buy pointed, hearted lettuces, such as Little Gem – one per person. Wash as necessary and put in a bag in the fridge to chill. At serving time, cut each lettuce into 4 wedges, dribble with vinaigrette and arrange a split canned anchovy fillet in a cross on each one.

CATALONIA

Escalivada amb anxoves

Barbecued vegetable salad with anchovies

SERVES 4

○ *4 small aubergines, about 250 g/8 oz each*

○ *4 red peppers*

○ *4 onions, 75–100 g/3–4 oz each*

○ *1 big bulb of fennel, sliced thickly*

○ *about 4 tbsp virgin olive oil*

○ *salt and freshly ground black pepper*

○ *50 g/2 oz canned anchovy fillets, drained*

Firm vegetables are barbecued to soften them – and literally blackened: the Spanish name is from a verb meaning 'cook in the ashes'. They are then peeled and eaten cold. The recipe is one of the big success stories of the 1990s, and you will find versions in restaurants from San Francisco to Sydney, with London thrown in. The rather crisper fennel slices are a successful modern addition to the dish.

Best barbecued outside, nevertheless this is still good cooked in the oven. Heat it to 200°C/400°F/Gas 6. Bake the aubergines, peppers and onions together on a baking sheet for about 1 hour, turning them over once. Then cool and remove the outside skins.

Grill the fennel slices, brushing them with oil and turning them. Arrange the fennel pieces on 4 plates, putting them to left and right. Slice the other vegetables; aubergines reduce to a quarter of their former volume. Arrange the strips together in the centre of the plates and dribble with virgin oil and season-ing. Arrange a few anchovy fillets over the top (or on some lightly toasted bread) and serve.

NEW CASTILE AND LA MANCHA

Pisto Semana Santa

Peppers, tomatoes and onions with tuna

～

Pisto *is well known as the Spanish (and probably an earlier)*
version of the French ratatouille, which has barely 70 recorded
years. In Castile pisto, *served plain, used to precede Manchego*
cheese. Elsewhere it often goes with ham. This version, for fasting
during Holy Week, contains pickled fish instead. Good hot, it is
better still cold. Parsley is a luxury in a Manchegan summer,
but enhances the cold dish.

SERVES 4

- 3 large green peppers, seeded and chopped
- 5 big ripe tomatoes, skinned and seeded (or 800 g/ 1 lb 10 oz canned tomatoes, with juice)
- 2 Spanish onions, thinly sliced
- 3–4 tbsp olive oil
- 3 garlic cloves, finely chopped
- 3 big courgettes, thinly sliced
- salt and freshly ground black pepper
- 4 tbsp chopped parsley
- 200 g/7 oz canned tuna
- 2 hard-boiled eggs
- 2–3 tbsp virgin olive oil (to serve cold)

Soften the onions in the oil in a flameproof casserole, over
medium heat so they caramelize. Add the garlic near the end.
Add the chopped pepper, then the tomatoes and courgettes, as
they are ready. Season with salt and pepper and cook gently for
20 minutes until the flavours blend.

Stir in the parsley and flaked tuna and check the seasonings.
Garnish with the chopped eggs. Sprinkle a little virgin oil over
the cold dish (or use more in cooking if planning it this way).

Note: Like all peasant dishes, *pisto* is infinitely adaptable to the
season. In early summer it may contain green beans, and in
autumn pumpkin goes in.

LEVANTE

Esgarràt

Red pepper and cured fish salad

SERVES 4

○ 250 g/8 oz bacalao inglés *(flexible centre fillet pieces of salt cod), or a dry tail piece of salt cod*

○ 4 tbsp extra virgin olive oil

○ 6 large red peppers

○ 2 garlic cloves, finely chopped

My favourite red pepper recipe is also one of the best ways to eat salt cod. This the ideal way to try bacalao if you have never tried salt cod, and suspect it is all too much effort. The more expensive mojama *(cured tuna) is sometimes substituted, while canned tuna can also be used.*

Well ahead, simply soak the *bacalao inglés* for 3–4 hours and drain it, patting it dry. If you can't get this, then soak an equal weight of stiff salt cod for 24 hours, changing the water 3–4 times, then remove the skin and bones and flake the flesh. Mix the oil and garlic and marinate the fish flakes for 24 hours.

Put the peppers on a hot griddle (*la plancha*), or under a grill, and turn them regularly until charred on all sides. Leave until cool enough to handle, then strip off the skin (on a plate to catch the juices) and remove the seeds. Cut into long strips and mix these, and their juices, with the fish and dressing.

Note: *Bacalao inglés* is for eating raw – it is less dry, and so quicker and easier than the salt cod sold in Italian delicatessens. The flavour is nearer to salt herring, which is another possible substitute.

ANDALUSIA

Remojón
Salt cod and orange salad

~

A popular Lenten salad, this recipe comes from Antequera, an ancient town in the north of Andalusia. It's the classic recipe, using fish which is toasted before soaking – stronger-tasting and firmer, with a finely judged, exotic flavour. I am told this was once made with Seville oranges in season, but I found these too bitter for modern taste. Hard-boiled eggs are sometimes included.

SERVES 4

- 250 g/8 oz thin outside piece or tail end of salt cod (or 200 g/7 oz canned tuna as a short cut)
- 8 oranges
- 75 g/3 oz marinated black olives, stoned
- 6 spring onions, chopped
- ½ small garlic clove, finely chopped
- tiny pinch of salt
- 1 tsp sweet paprika
- 1 tsp vinegar (if not using Seville oranges)
- 5 tbsp good olive oil

Toast the salt cod in the oven at 200°C/400°F/Gas 6 for 20 minutes. Break up the fish roughly and put it in a dish. Cover with water and leave to soak for 4 hours (the name of the dish just means 'soaked'). Taste the fish – it should be edible, but exquisitely salty.

Drain the fish, discard the skin and bones and shred the flesh finely with two forks so that it looks like pieces of wool.

Slice the oranges into rounds (on a plate to catch the juices), quarter them and put in a serving bowl. Add the fish shreds, olives and chopped white and green of the onion and mix gently. Make a paste with the garlic and salt, crushing it with the flat of a knife. In a bowl, mix with the juices on the plate, the paprika and vinegar and beat in the olive oil. Dress the salad 30 minutes ahead of eating.

THE BALEARIC ISLANDS

Mahonesa
Mayonnaise

**MAKES ABOUT
300 ML / ½ PT**

- ○ juice of ½ lemon or 1 tbsp white wine vinegar
- ○ salt
- ○ yolks of 2 large eggs, at room temperature (plus 1 egg white, if making in a blender)
- ○ 300 ml/½ pt Spanish olive oil, preferably one with 0.8% acidity, at room temperature, or 3 parts plain oil (even sunflower or corn oil) plus 1 part good virgin olive oil

OPTIONS

- ○ 1 garlic clove, chopped (then crushed with the salt)
- ○ 2 tbsp finely chopped parsley

Here is the classic recipe from Mahón – and the way I find it is often made now. Temperature is important for a successful emulsion. Warm the oil gently if it seems chilly. Below are the two best local serving suggestions.

Put the lemon juice or vinegar and a pinch of salt in a bowl (or blender) – the acid element is important as the sauce won't emulsify without it. (A smidgen of crushed garlic can go in here, if it matches your recipe.) Add the egg yolks (use 1 whole egg plus 1 yolk in a blender) and whisk (or work) to a cream. (Parsley goes in here, in a blender.)

Add the oil (start with the plain one), drop by drop if working with a whisk, until the mixture emulsifies. Add more oil, in larger quantities as the mayonnaise thickens, until it is all absorbed. Virgin oil can be used once the sauce has emulsified. Taste and correct the seasonings.

This mayonnaise is quite thick and can be thinned with 1–2 tbsp boiling water if it is to be kept.

For Mahón potato salad: Mix chopped parsley and a little more vinegar into the mayonnaise and coat rounds of cold potato. Decorate with anchovy fillets and lemon slices.

For Mahón mussel salad: Steam open the mussels and remove the shells, then serve in a pile, covered with mayonnaise and parsley. Garnish with a radiating ring of mussel shells, bedding them a little under the salad. These can be used to scoop up the mixture.

GALICIA

Vinagreta de mejillones
Mussel and potato salad with paprika dressing

~

Simple – and simply delicious! Both mussels and potatoes are at their best in Galicia. Spanish olive oil makes a very light dressing, as it stays in the suspension once whisked. This red version, with sweet paprika, is called ajada. *It is a popular dressing in Galicia for all sorts of things, including turnip greens.*

Cook the potatoes in their skins in boiling salted water until just done. Drain and leave a few minutes, then peel and slice or not, according to size. Mix with the shelled mussels.

If you haven't a mortar (or can't be bothered to wash it), mash the garlic on the board with the flat of a table knife, working the salt in to form a paste. In the mortar or a bowl stir the wine vinegar into the garlic and then beat in the oil to make a light cream. Add the paprika, dissolved in the water, plus pepper to taste. Pour over the potatoes and mussels.

Note: Freeze mussel stock. The juice of one shellfish is particularly good as stock for a different one.

SERVES 4

- 2 kg/4½ lb mussels, opened (see page 101)
- 500 g/1 lb cachelos or best salad potatoes (Jersey Royals, Pink Fir Apples, Charlottes)

PAPRIKA VINAIGRETTE

- 1 garlic clove, finely chopped
- ¼ tsp salt
- 3 tbsp wine vinegar
- 100 ml/3½ fl oz olive oil, preferably Spanish
- 1 tsp sweet paprika
- 2 tbsp cold water
- ground white pepper

ANDALUSIA

Salmonetes en escabeche
Red mullet salad

SERVES 4

- 4 red mullet, about 200 g/ 7 oz each, cleaned
- 2 tbsp olive oil
- 1 small onion, finely chopped
- 1 large garlic clove, finely chopped
- 175 ml/6 fl oz dry white wine
- 175 ml/6 fl oz wine vinegar
- 2 sprigs of fresh thyme or 1 bay leaf
- salt and freshly ground black pepper

An old Arab way of preserving fish in lightly spiced jelly for a summer lunch, I ate these charmingly named pink fish accompanied by avocado on a terrace shaded by old, rambling bignonias. The pink and green colours were perfect. Fennel, which grows wild in Andalusia, is another green salad choice.

Scale the fish by scraping from the tail towards the head. (Scales pop off easily, but look like dropped contact lenses.) Cut off the fins with kitchen scissors.

Heat the oil in a pan that will just hold all the fish and fry the onion gently until soft, adding the garlic at the end. Put in the fish, then the wine and vinegar. Add just enough water to cover them and tuck in the thyme or bay leaf and season. Bring to the boil, then cover and simmer for 10 minutes.

Move the fish carefully on a fish slice to a shallow dish. They can be served whole, or the fillets can be removed – easy when cooked and cold – and served without the bones. Strain the cooking juices over them and refrigerate until needed. Provided the juices completely cover the fish, the dish keeps 2–3 days.

A chilled *rosado* wine, like a Navarra Gran Feudo, perfectly matches the colour of the fish.

EXTREMADURA

Escarapuche

Cold trout in vinegar with chopped salad

When I was in Cáceres, tench were on sale everywhere, but this
recipe makes a lovely summer dish for small trout. The name
means pickled, though there is not enough acidity to keep them.
I was told small fish (young carp, barbel etc) could be grilled
uncleaned: not true of trout!

Salt and pepper the fish, then brush with oil. Barbecue or grill
them for 4–5 minutes on each side.

Remove the skin, fins, heads and bones, using a foil-
covered tray to catch the fish juices. If the fish were grilled on
foil, retain any oil and juices from this too. Put the fish and
their juices in a flat dish in which they just fit.

Put the chopped onion, tomato and coriander in a bowl
and add 2–4 tbsp oil, the vinegar, lemon juice and seasoning.
Spoon the dressing over the fish, spooning it back over them
several times. (The gelatine in the juices is a part of their
dressing.) Chill and serve cold.

SERVES 2

- 2 trout or tench, cleaned
- salt and freshly ground black pepper
- 3–4 tbsp olive oil
- 4 tbsp finely chopped Spanish onion
- 6 tbsp chopped tomato flesh
- 2 tbsp chopped fresh coriander leaves
- 2 tbsp red wine vinegar
- 2 tbsp lemon juice

CHAPTER THREE

Soups, Cold and Hot

ANDALUSIA

Zoque
Red gazpacho

SERVES 6

- ○ *1 garlic clove, finely chopped*
- ○ *½ tsp salt*
- ○ *5 slices of stale white bread, crusts removed*
- ○ *2 tbsp red wine vinegar or sherry vinegar*
- ○ *4 tbsp good olive oil*
- ○ *2 ripe red tomatoes, skinned and seeded*
- ○ *2 large red peppers, seeded and chopped*
- ○ *750 ml/1¼ pt iced water*

Everyone has heard of gazpacho, but few people know this reddest of red versions from Seville. It is much eaten in Spanish homes, because it appears in the Manual de Cocina (now on its 27th revision), presented to many brides. In the 1940s the power behind it, the formidable Pilar Primo de la Rivera tried to organize traditional Spanish cooking – in the same way her father and brother in the Falange tried to reorganize everything else. This cookery book was a much happier result.

Everyone now uses a blender, but this recipe has been shaped by pounding with a pestle in a mortar. Crushing is still the best way to turn garlic to a paste with salt. Alternatively, mash the chopped garlic into the salt with the flat side of a knife. Soak the bread in water, then squeeze it out and add morsels to the blender with the garlic, salt and vinegar. Purée until smooth.

Add the oil – a little at a time like mayonnaise. Add the tomato flesh and purée again. Add the chopped red pepper and reduce to a pulp. Chill well.

Stir in the icy water. Taste and season with more salt and vinegar if needed and serve very cold.

ANDALUSIA

Ajo blanco con uvas de Málaga

White almond and garlic soup with muscat grapes

Garlic and bread is one of the Mediterranean's oldest food combinations. This is the famous white gazpacho, and far older than the red version. It was originally made by pounding almonds with icy well water – very soothing in the summer heat.

The sultana taste of muscats is a big plus. It is one of those peasant dishes that is so successful it has stayed in the repertoire.

Basic variations may include dried bean flour, pine nuts, even potatoes. Ernest Hemingway claimed to have eaten a rice version.

Soak the bread in water, then squeeze it gently. Grind the almonds in a blender until smooth, adding a little of the bread to stop them turning oily. Add the garlic, salt and olive oil and blend to make a smooth cream.

Add the remaining bread in pieces with the vinegar and enough iced water to blend smoothly. Chill for at least 2 hours, then dilute with iced water. Float the halved grapes on top before serving.

SERVES 4

- ○ 8 slices of stale white bread, crusts removed
- ○ 100 g/4 oz freshly blanched almonds
- ○ 2 garlic cloves, finely chopped
- ○ pinch of salt
- ○ 3 tbsp olive oil
- ○ 2 tbsp sherry vinegar
- ○ 600 ml/1 pt iced water
- ○ 250 g/8 oz ripe muscat grapes, seeded

ANDALUSIA

Salmorejo cordobés
Chilled Cordoba tomato cream

SERVES 4

- 2 ripe red tomatoes, skinned and seeded
- 6 slices of stale white bread, crusts removed
- 2 garlic cloves, roughly chopped
- ½ tsp salt
- 6 tbsp good olive oil
- 3 tbsp vinegar
- 1 hard-boiled egg
- about 40 g/1½ oz serrano or other raw ham, such as prosciutto

Not really a soup (for it has no water), but an addictive, chilly cream, delicately flavoured with garlic and tomato. The tomatoes must have been added after the discovery of America, for the recipe goes back to Arab times. In its old form it was eaten in the great days when Cordoba was capital of Spain and the second city of Europe.

Soak the bread in water, then squeeze out lightly. Purée about a quarter in the blender with the garlic, salt and oil until smooth. Add the remaining bread in pieces with the vinegar. Add the tomato flesh and juice. Purée again until very smooth, then beat hard for 2 minutes, to lighten it. The cream should be thick, but not stiff. Season and chill overnight.

Ladle into small shallow bowls and garnish with shreds of hard-boiled egg and raw ham.

CATALONIA

Crema fría de melón con virutas de Jabugo

Iced melon soup with raw ham shreds

~

Two classic partners – melon and ham – rearranged to make an interesting chilled soup. The region of Balaguer is famous for its Piel de Sapo melons, now in our supermarkets, but if you can't find them honeydews can be used. Allow roughly 500 g/1 lb per person.

Halve the melon(s), discard the seeds and scoop the flesh and juices straight into a blender. Purée, then chill well. Ripe melon needs nothing more. Taste before serving (consider sugar, salt, pepper). Serve in bowls, over ice if you like, garnished with shreds of raw ham.

SERVES 4

- 1–2 ripe Piel de Sapo or honeydew melons, well chilled
- 50 g/2 oz raw Jabugo ham, or prosciutto, shredded

ANDALUSIA

Gazpachuelo

Warm potato soup with eggs and vinegar

SERVES 4–6

- *750 g/1½ lb new-season potatoes, diced*
- *750 ml/1¼ pt water*
- *½ tsp salt*
- *2 small eggs, separated*
- *about 4 tbsp vinegar*
- *250 ml/8 fl oz best olive oil*

In Spain this soup is associated with wakes, and so is also called sopa de duelo – mourners coming to sit with the bereaved need simple sustenance. It has vinegar in common with gazpacho but, said friends, 'we miss the garlic of gazpacho.' It's surprising that a soup with such simple ingredients should be so good and creamy.
'Nowadays,' I was told, 'the egg whites don't often go into the broth, because the mayonnaise is made in a blender and that needs whole eggs.' A good example of how traditional recipes are reworked!

Cook the potatoes in the salted water. When tender, remove the potatoes, saving the liquid. Beat the egg whites into the liquid; they will set like a Chinese egg-drop soup.

Let the stock cool a little while you make the mayonnaise (see page 112) with the yolks, 2 tbsp vinegar and the oil. Thin the mayonnaise to soup consistency by stirring in the stock and pour this over the warm potatoes in a serving bowl. Serve the soup warm, stirring in another 2 tbsp vinegar. Or pass a jug of vinegar so the acid content can be judged at table.

NEW CASTILE AND LA MANCHA

Sopa de la abuela castellana
Granny's garlic and bread soup

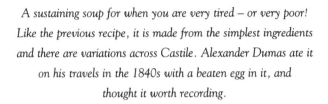

A sustaining soup for when you are very tired – or very poor!
Like the previous recipe, it is made from the simplest ingredients
and there are variations across Castile. Alexander Dumas ate it
on his travels in the 1840s with a beaten egg in it, and
thought it worth recording.

SERVES 4

- *4 garlic cloves, chopped*
- *6 tbsp olive oil*
- *4 slices of stale bread*
- *1 litre / 1¾ pt light stock or water*
- *100 g / 4 oz raw ham or gammon, finely diced*
- *salt*
- *1 tsp paprika*
- *½ tsp cumin seeds, very well crushed*

Put a casserole over the heat and add the oil and garlic. Remove the garlic the moment it looks cooked, and keep it. Then fry the bread on both sides until golden. Add the stock or water and the ham and bring to simmering. Return the garlic and season with salt and paprika. Simmer for 5 minutes, stirring to break up the bread.

Check for salt (it probably won't need it because of the ham) and sprinkle the cumin over the top just before serving. This adds special flavour.

THE BASQUE COUNTRY

Zurruputuna

Salt cod soup with garlic and peppers

SERVES 4

- 250 g/8 oz salt cod, soaked overnight with a change of water
- 3–5 tbsp olive oil
- 3 garlic cloves, finely chopped
- 2 slices of stale country bread
- 1 green pepper, seeded and chopped
- 3 dried choricero peppers, soaked for 2 hours, or 2 tsp paprika
- 1 dried guindilla chilli, seeded and chopped, or a pinch of cayenne pepper
- 3 tbsp sieved tomato (passata)
- about 1 litre/1¾ pt cod soaking water (see recipe)
- freshly ground black pepper

'The men got up at five, drank coffee and went to work. Then about eight, they came in for breakfast – a cup of milk and a couple of plates of zurruputuna – this was the workman's breakfast half a century ago.' One of many garlic soups, it has salt cod as a highlight, spiced with peppers. Eggs can be poached in it at the end.

Remove any bones and skin from the salt cod, keeping the last fish-soaking water. Heat 3 tbsp oil in a flameproof casserole, preferably earthenware, and fry the garlic. When it starts to colour, put in the salt cod pieces. Fry them until they have stopped looking gelatinous, then immediately remove them. Fry the bread (or toast it) and the green pepper in the casserole, adding more oil if necessary.

If using *choriceros*, scrape the pulp from the skin. Break up the toast and shred the fish on a plate. Return the cod flakes to the casserole with the *choricero* pepper and chopped *guindilla* chilli, or the paprika and pinch of cayenne, plus the sieved tomato and toast. Taste the cod water (to make sure it is not too salty – use more water, if so) and add enough to give a soup consistency. Stir and cook for a few minutes to break up the bread, then check the seasoning.

EXTREMADURA

Sopa de tomate con higos
Tomato soup with fresh figs

~

*A peasant soup using two fruits – so simple it must
be made slowly and correctly.*

Fry the onion in the olive oil very slowly until soft, then add
the garlic. Add the tomatoes (these must be skinned and
seeded first if you intend to blend them). Cook, with the bay
leaf and orange zest, very gently down to a sauce – 30 minutes
or so. (Ripe tomatoes don't need sugar, but supermarket ones
might.) Season with salt, pepper and paprika.

Sieve or blend. Return to the pan and reheat. Stir in the
virgin oil to give a creamy emulsion – don't boil from this
point.

Lightly toast the bread, put it in 4 soup plates and pour the
tomato cream over. Arrange the split figs on top of the bread,
or pass separately.

SERVES 4

- 1 generous kg/2½ lb ripe tomatoes, chopped
- 8–12 ripe black figs
- 1 Spanish onion, chopped
- 3 tbsp olive oil
- 2 fat garlic cloves, finely chopped
- 1 big bay leaf, crumbled
- 1 strip of orange zest (optional)
- 1 tsp sugar (if tomatoes aren't ripe)
- salt and freshly ground black pepper
- paprika
- 2 tbsp virgin oil
- 4 slices of stale country bread

NEW CASTILE AND LA MANCHA

Crema de Aranjuez
Aranjuez cream of asparagus soup

SERVES 4

- ○ 500 g/1 lb asparagus
- ○ 50 g/2 oz butter
- ○ 1 leek, white and pale green parts sliced
- ○ 1 carrot, sliced
- ○ 4 tbsp rice
- ○ 1 litre/1¾ pt light stock or water
- ○ 2 tbsp finely chopped parsley
- ○ 200–250 ml/7–8 fl oz milk
- ○ 2 egg yolks (optional)
- ○ salt and ground white pepper
- ○ tiny pinch of cayenne pepper
- ○ 4 tbsp whipping cream

Aranjuez has Spain's Versailles – a purpose-built summer palace, where the fountains play on festival days. It is the one green place on the dusty plain, and so a place for summer outings. The so-called 'strawberry train' runs there from Madrid at weekends and on public holidays. The royal connection gives this soup an elegance not often associated with Spanish food.

Reserve the asparagus tips, and peel and slice the stalks. Melt the butter in a pan and add them with the leek and carrot. Sweat them for 20 minutes, covered, then add the rice. Cook the tips separately in the stock for about 8 minutes, then set them aside.

When the rice has absorbed the pan juices, add the stock and simmer for 30–40 minutes. Press through a sieve with the parsley (or blend together). Bring back to simmering and thin with milk to a creamy consistency, heating the asparagus tips in the soup. Stir in the egg yolks, if wished, for extra richness. (They are traditional but not, I think, needed.) Season, including a discreet amount of cayenne, and serve hot with a dribble of cream.

Note: This also makes an excellent chilled summer soup, diluted a little with good jellied chicken or meat stock. Purée the tips with the soup and garnish with a delicate herb and a chopped hard-boiled egg.

THE BALEARIC ISLANDS

Oliagua amb escarrats

Tomato and garlic soup with asparagus

~

The name means 'oil soup' and it features the vegetable in season: cabbage, tomato or just parsley with garlic. I was given it with fine wild asparagus. With cultivated asparagus a practical solution is to cook the hard asparagus ends first, then discard them and make the soup with the asparagus water.

Put the onion, garlic, green pepper and tomatoes in a flame-proof casserole and add a glass of cold water. Cook very gently, covered, until the onion has softened, without letting it colour – a good 30 minutes.

Add the oil and stir in. Add the vegetable water, bring to the boil and season with salt, black pepper and cayenne. Press much of the solids through a sieve or blend (which is easier). This is really best done ahead and allowed to mellow.

Bring to simmering (when a slight skin forms on the surface), then add the asparagus, cut in manageable lengths. Simmer for about 15 minutes (wild asparagus can take longer).

Dry out the bread slices in a low oven or toast them. Put 3 or 4 in each soup plate and ladle the soup over them.

SERVES 4

- 250 g/8 oz thin wild asparagus or 500 g/1 lb green asparagus
- 1 onion, finely chopped
- 8 garlic cloves, finely chopped
- ½ green pepper, finely chopped
- 700 g/1½ lb ripe tomatoes, skinned and thickly sliced
- 4 tbsp olive oil
- 750 ml/1¼ pt vegetable water
- salt and freshly ground black pepper
- pinch of cayenne pepper
- 12–16 thin slices of French bread or good quality country bread

ASTURIAS AND CANTABRIA

Chirlas o almejas con arroz verde
Clam and green-rice soup

~

SERVES 4

- 1 kg/2 lb clams, rinsed (300 g/10 oz shelled clams)
- 1 onion, chopped
- 2–3 tbsp olive oil
- 1 green pepper, seeded and chopped
- 3 garlic cloves, finely chopped
- 6 tbsp chopped parsley
- 200 g/7 oz paella or risotto rice
- salt and freshly ground black pepper
- 1.5 litre/2½ pt fish stock (or water), incorporating mussel stock if possible
- 75 ml/3 fl oz dry white wine or strong cider

'Can you use long-grain rice for a dish like this?' I asked, explaining it was easier for me to get. 'If you must. But American rice tastes only of flour. Our Mediterranean rice has more flavour.' With long-grain rice this is more of a soup, so, emboldened, I tested this with Italian brown rice, and the result was nearer to a Spanish *sopa*, which are often quite puddingy in texture. Rice is eaten in many Spanish homes more than once a week and 'wet' rice dishes like this one are as popular as the more famous 'dry' paella.

Fry the onion in the oil in a large casserole, then add the green pepper, garlic and parsley. Turn the rice in the oil and season with pepper. Add the fish stock (or water) and cook for 20 minutes.

Meanwhile, heat the wine or cider in a large saucepan and add the clams. Cover tightly and cook, shaking the pan to bring up clams to the bottom, until all the clams are open. Add to the rice (discarding a few empty shells), check the salt and serve.

Note: If the stock is not up to much, put the bruised parsley stalks in too. Remove to serve.

ASTURIAS AND CANTABRIA

Pote asturiano

Asturian bean, sausage and cabbage soup

~

A traditional bean and pork dish from the mountains of the north.
This one contains fresh cabbage, fresh meat and unsmoked
morcilla (black pudding), which make it lighter than alternative
versions that use cured meat and smoked sausage. The traditional
one, called xuan, *is made from the pig's stomach.*

Put the beans to cook in a large flameproof casserole, packing
in the ham bone, pork rib, cubed pork belly and whole sausages
and adding fresh water to cover. Skim as they come to the boil
and cook for 1 hour, until the beans are almost tender.

Cut up the cabbage head finely and bring it to the boil in
a saucepan of salted water, then drain it. Remove the meat
bones, returning the meat shreds to the casserole. Take out the
sausages, slice and then return them.

Crumble the saffron with your fingers into the casserole,
with paprika, plenty of black pepper and salt (to taste). Add
the cabbage and potatoes; the liquid should cover them
comfortably. Simmer until the potatoes are tender, and check
the seasonings again. Serve in big soup bowls.

Note: If you cannot buy a ham hock, use 2–3 pork spare ribs,
plus a piece of boiling gammon.

SERVES 6

○ *275 g/9 oz fabes de la*
granja or big white kidney
beans, such as cannellini,
soaked overnight

○ *200 g/7 oz ham hock,*
soaked for 1 hour

○ *1 pork belly rib with meat*
on, about 150 g/5 oz

○ *125–150 g/4–5 oz fresh*
streaky pork belly, cubed

○ *3 fresh morcillas or 350 g/*
12 oz black pudding

○ *2–3 chorizos, paprika*
sausage or fresh garlic
sausage

○ *700 g/1½ lb dark green*
cabbage

○ *20 strands saffron*

○ *1 tsp paprika (2 tsp, if not*
using chorizos)

○ *salt and freshly ground black*
pepper

○ *500 g/1 lb potatoes*

CHAPTER FOUR

Vegetables

LEVANTE

Bajoques farcides
Cold stuffed peppers with rice and tuna

~

SERVES 4–8

- 4 small green peppers (or 8 slim pointed ones)
- olive oil for deep frying
- 1 small onion, chopped
- 2 tbsp olive oil
- 2 garlic cloves, finely chopped
- 150 g / 5 oz paella or risotto rice
- 2 tbsp fino sherry or dry vermouth
- 2 tbsp sieved tomato (passata) or tomato sauce
- 20 strands saffron, crumbled and soaked in a little of the stock for 5 minutes
- 1 bouquet garni
- 40 ml / 14 fl oz chicken stock or fish stock
- 200 g / 7 oz can tuna, drained
- mayonnaise, to serve

An unusual version of a very well-known recipe, it goes well before grilled meat, or makes a simple, filling lunch. In Spain it is made with slim pointed green peppers, but I have adapted it to morrones, the common, fist-shaped ones. I was advised to use Calasparra rice, the best in Spain.

Deep fry the peppers whole, putting them in at top heat for 10 minutes, until they have lost their plump football appearance (pointed ones need about half the time). Remove with a slotted spoon and drain on kitchen paper.

Make the filling: in a wide shallow pan fry the onion in 2 tbsp of oil until soft. Add the garlic, then the rice and stir. Add the sherry, tomato sauce, saffron and its liquid, and the bouquet garni. Add a third of the stock and let it simmer until absorbed, then add the rest in 2 batches. Simmer the rice for a total of about 20 minutes, until all the stock is absorbed. Leave it to sit for a couple of minutes, then add the well-forked tuna.

Slit the peppers from end to end and remove the stalk and seeds. Stuff with the rice mixture and reshape the peppers. When cold they will halve neatly. Arrange in a circle, green side up, and pile the mayonnaise in the middle.

CATALONIA

Lechugas a la catalana
Braised stuffed lettuce

~

One of the few hot lettuce dishes, this makes an excellent supper dish for 2, when served on slices of fried ham.

Heat 2 tbsp oil in a small flameproof casserole into which the letttuces will fit neatly and fry the onion and carrots, adding the chopped tomato flesh and parsley when the onion softens. Season and set aside.

Put the lettuces in a colander, pour boiling water over them in turn, then drain well. Chop the leek white, garlic and anchovies very finely (the food processor works well). Work in the butter, egg yolks and a little nutmeg. Salt lightly.

Squeeze the lettuces gently in kitchen paper to blot, then split them lengthways. Put the stuffing between the leaves, starting with the outside leaves and working towards the middle. Reshape them again and lay on the bed of vegetables, tucking in the bouquet garni and moistening with the wine. Cook very gently for about 1 hour, checking occasionally whether stock is needed (it depends on pan size). Check the sauce seasonings before serving.

SERVES 4

- 2 small Cos or Webb's lettuces
- 2–3 tbsp olive oil
- 1 big onion, finely chopped
- 2 carrots, finely chopped
- 2 very ripe tomatoes, skinned, seeded and chopped
- 2 tbsp chopped parsley
- 1 bouquet garni
- 100ml / 3½ fl oz dry white wine
- 100 ml / 3½ fl oz poultry stock (optional)

STUFFING

- white of 2 small leeks
- 4–6 garlic cloves
- 50 g / 2 oz canned anchovy fillets, drained
- 25 g / 1 oz softened butter
- 2 egg yolks
- freshly ground nutmeg
- salt and freshly ground black pepper

ARAGON AND NAVARRE

Lentejas de Ordesa

Lentils with leeks and mushrooms

~

SERVES 6

- ○ 500 g / 1 lb green lentils, soaked for at least 6 hours
- ○ 1 piece of ham bone (see note)
- ○ 2 tbsp olive oil
- ○ 1 onion, chopped
- ○ 2 leeks, white and edible green, sliced
- ○ 250 g / 8 oz mushrooms, preferably wild, cleaned and sliced
- ○ 2 big ripe tomatoes, skinned, seeded and chopped
- ○ 2 sprigs of fresh thyme
- ○ 1 sprig of fresh rosemary
- ○ 1 morcilla or 200 g / 7 oz black pudding
- ○ salt and freshly ground black pepper
- ○ 2–3 tbsp muscatel wine or anis liqueur (or Pernod)
- ○ pinch of sugar (optional)

The sweet alcohol makes a pleasant final addition to this pulse dish. When I use Pernod (which is not sweet) for the anis, I add a pinch of sugar.

Put the drained lentils in a pan with the ham bone (or bacon, if you choose this option) and add water just to cover. Skim if necessary and simmer for 1 hour.

Meanwhile heat the oil in a large frying pan and soften the onion, adding the chopped leeks and mushrooms towards the end. When these wilt, add the chopped tomatoes and herbs and cook until soft. When the lentils are done, remove the bone (if using – or shred the bacon) and add to the frying pan with the sliced *morcilla* or black pudding if using. Cook for 10 more minutes. Before serving season to taste, adding the wine, or liqueur, with a pinch of sugar if it is not sweet.

Note: Ham bones, sawn into rings, are available in most Spanish markets. A piece can be popped into a stew like a stock cube. Outside Spain I use a piece of unsmoked boiling bacon (about 200 g / 7 oz) to replace both this and the *morcilla*.

OLD CASTILE AND RIOJA

Judías del Barco de Avila
White bean pot

~

*Subtle – and a change from beans in tomato sauce. It is also
an excellent dish combined with roast game birds – try a roast
mallard. Meat shreds and pan juices go into the beans:
the carved bird is served on top.*

Drain the beans, put them in a pot with the pork and add the
leek, ½ of the onion (stuck with 2 cloves) and the garlic, all
unsliced, plus the bouquet garni. Just cover with the water and
put over a low heat. When it starts to simmer, add 1 tbsp of oil.
Leave to simmer (with no bubbles), covered, until the beans
are tender – about 1 hour. Keep an eye on it, adding a little
water if needed.

Heat the remaining 2 tbsp of oil in a saucepan with the
remaining onion quarter, finely chopped, and the green pepper
over low heat. After a few minutes raise the heat to medium
and cook, stirring occasionally, until they start to colour. Then
add the sieved tomato and paprika and cook a minute longer.

Fish the leek, onion quarter and garlic cloves out of the
beans. Discard the bouquet garni and cloves and purée the
vegetables (peeling the garlic cloves first) with a little of the
bean stock. Return this, plus the green pepper sauce, to the
pot. Shred the pork and return it. Taste for seasoning: it may
not need salt, if the pork gives it. Add pepper and a little vinegar to add piquancy. Cook gently for another 10 minutes.

Note: A little fried, crumbled bacon (cooked with the vegetable
sauce) can replace the pork.

SERVES 4

- 400 g / 14 oz judías del Barco or *white haricot beans*, soaked for 12 hours
- 150 g / 5 oz salt pork belly, Italian pancetta or boiling bacon (see note)
- ½ leek
- ½ onion
- 2 cloves to stick in the onion
- 4 garlic cloves
- 1 fresh bouquet garni or a sprig of rosemary, 3 sprigs of thyme and 1 bay leaf
- 600 ml / 1 pt water
- 3 tbsp olive oil
- 1 big green pepper, seeded and finely chopped
- 4 tbsp sieved tomato (passata) or tomato sauce
- ½ tsp paprika
- salt and freshly ground black pepper
- ½ tsp vinegar

THE BALEARIC ISLANDS

Motllo d'alberginies de Mallorca
Aubergine timbale from Majorca

~

SERVES 6

- 1 kg / 2 lb aubergines
- salt and freshly ground black pepper
- 500 g / 1 lb green peppers
- 25 g / 1 oz lard or butter, softened
- 2–3 tbsp grated stale bread
- 2–3 tbsp plain flour
- about 125 ml / 4 fl oz olive oil
- 500 g / 1 lb potatoes, in rounds
- 1 big bunch of parsley, chopped
- 250 ml / 8 fl oz sieved tomato (passata) or extra tomato sauce, to serve

TOMATO SAUCE

- 1 Spanish onion, chopped
- 50 g / 2 oz streaky bacon, chopped
- 2 tbsp olive oil
- 4–5 garlic cloves, finely chopped
- 750 g / 1¾ lb ripe tomatoes, skinned, seeded and chopped
- 4 tbsp chopped parsley
- 1 bouquet garni

A handsome mould with aubergines round the edge of the dish and the whole thing turned out, this is a party version of the island's well-known tumbet. Normally it is made in simple layers, topped with crisp crumbs. We agreed it is best assembled in the morning, to bake later.

Cut the aubergines in rounds 5 mm / ¼ in thick and salt them. Leave for a good 30 minutes, while you make the tomato sauce. Fry the onion and the bacon in the oil until soft. Add the garlic, chopped tomato flesh, parsley and bouquet garni. Moisten with ½ glass of water and simmer for 20–25 minutes. The sauce should be thickish.

At the same time grill the peppers until charred on all sides. Leave to cool in a plastic bag, then peel the skins off on a plate, to catch the juice. Remove the stalks and seeds and chop the peppers. Heat the oven to 190°C / 375°F / Gas 5.

Smear a 2.5 litre / 4 pt soufflé dish, particularly the bottom, with half the fat or butter. Dust with breadcrumbs, tipping out any that don't stick.

Rinse and drain the aubergine slices, pressing gently with kitchen paper to dry them. Flour them and fry in a generous quantity of very hot oil (they can absorb it so treacherously). Blot and fry the potato slices until well browned on each side.

Arrange a ring of aubergine slices on the bottom of the soufflé dish, overlapping them, with one in the middle. Make one row overlapping round the sides, bending them at the bottom, so they have something to sit on. Sprinkle the bottom with 2 tbsp parsley, and add a quarter of the peppers and of the freshly made tomato sauce, then more parsley. Layer in half the potatoes. Season, add more parsley and then repeat the peppers, sauce and parsley.

Using the better slices, edge the rest of the dish with aubergine. Then layer all the awkward ends into the dish and sprinkle with parsley. Repeat the peppers, sauce and parsley, and then the potato layer, seasoning again. More parsley, then top with peppers and tomato sauce. Sprinkle the top with breadcrumbs and dot with the remaining lard or butter.

Bake in the oven for 45 minutes. Run a knife round and turn out on to a hot dish. The mould is rather firm, so some hot sieved tomato (or tomato sauce) is welcome. Pour a little round the mould (and the rest into a sauce boat). Cut in wedges, giving each serving 2–3 tbsp of sieved tomato. Also good cold with *allioli*.

THE BASQUE COUNTRY

Endivias al Roquefort
Chicory with Roquefort cream

~

Roquefort is extremely popular in Spain, probably because it has the same sophisticated saltiness as the beloved salt cod.

SERVES 4

○ *8 small white chicory heads*
○ *15 g / ½ oz butter*
○ *200 ml / 7 fl oz single cream*
○ *50 g / 2 oz Roquefort, in pieces*
○ *salt and ground white pepper*

Bring a pan of salted water to the boil, put in the chicory heads and simmer for 10–15 minutes until just tender. Drain in a colander, squeezing lightly.

Melt the butter in a small pan over the low heat, add the cream and bring slowly to simmering. Crumble in the cheese, stirring as it melts. Season to taste (it is quite salty). Pour over the chicory and serve.

Surtido de verduras rellenas
Stuffed vegetable selection

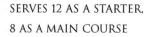

SERVES 12 AS A STARTER,
8 AS A MAIN COURSE

- 8 smallish tomatoes
- 8 small onions
- 4 oversize courgettes
- 8 small peppers
- 6 tiny aubergines
- 1 garlic clove
- 1–2 lemons, sliced in rounds
- 3 bay leaves

Meat balls

- 500 g / 1 lb minced veal
- 500 g / 1 lb minced pork
- 150 g / 5 oz raw ham or raw smoked gammon, finely diced
- 4 garlic cloves, finely chopped
- salt and freshly ground black pepper
- 6 tbsp finely chopped parsley
- 2 slices of stale bread, crusts removed, soaked in milk then squeezed dry
- 2 tsp ground cinnamon
- 1 tsp ground cloves
- 1 tsp freshly grated nutmeg
- 2 tsp paprika

Two grannies gave me almost identical recipes for this dish of concentric rings of stuffed vegetables. Their families are lucky, for it needs time to make (and cook) and some careful shopping. Buy a selection of vegetables that match (or can be cut to) a 50 g / 2 oz tomato – about 36 in all. Potatoes can be used as cups, though one version had a ring of tiny new potatoes between the stuffed vegetables. Use a 30-cm / 12-in diameter earthenware casserole.

Heat the oven to 200°C / 400°F / Gas 6. Rub a garlic clove round the inside of the casserole and rub with a little oil.

Prepare the vegetables by cutting off and keeping the tops and scooping out the insides to make cups. (Even onions respond to a firm revolving spoon.) Cut lengths of courgettes, and cut the peppers and aubergines short to fit the scale of the other vegetables. Arrange them all in rings in the casserole. Keep the scooped-out onion, tomato and aubergine for the sauce; discard the courgette seeds.

Combine all the ingredients for the meat balls, first reducing the garlic to a purée with 1 tsp salt in a mortar. Traditionally the parsley and the bread are puréed there too, before being worked into the meats. Make walnut-sized balls and use to stuff all the vegetables, then put back the vegetable tops as hats. Anything that has no hat can have a lemon slice. Use the remaining meat balls to make another ring inside the outermost vegetables, to fill the spaces. Push the bay leaves in round the edge.

Make the scooped-out onion insides up to 200 g / 7 oz, chop well and fry slowly in oil in a saucepan until soft. Add the garlic and the other chopped vegetable insides and cook until soft, then add the parsley and rub through a sieve (or blend). Return to the pan, add the tomato concentrate and some of the wine and season well.

Reheat the sauce and pour round the vegetables adding more wine as needed. Bake the vegetables in the oven for 1 hour, then turn down the heat to 180°C / 350°F / Gas 4. The dish needs a good 2½ hours to cook: cover with foil if the tops are burning. It reheats well, so is best made ahead.

SAUCE

- *200 g / 7 oz onion, including inside of onions*
- *3–4 tbsp olive oil*
- *4 garlic cloves, finely chopped*
- *6 tbsp finely chopped parsley*
- *2 tbsp tomato concentrate*
- *200–300 ml / 7–10 fl oz dry white wine*

OLD CASTILE AND RIOJA

Revuelto de ajetes o puerros
Cold scrambled egg with leeks and mayonnaise

~

An unusual starter, or something to join the summer salad plate, these eggs combine the smooth texture of a baked custard with subtle onion-family flavouring. In Spain, where everybody owns paella pans in several sizes, it is cooked in a bain-marie, one pan inside the other. Quantities can be larger. Put 2–3 dried beans between the pans, so the top one is not sitting directly on the bottom one and on the heat source.

Heat the butter in a saucepan until frothing. Add the garlic, leeks or onions and soften for 2–3 minutes. Beat together the eggs, cream and seasoning (I strain this, wanting a perfect texture). Pour on to the garlic or leeks.

Move the pan, to stand it in a small roasting tin of simmering water. Scramble the eggs, stirring regularly with a wooden spoon and removing from the heat while still just liquid. Turn on to a dish and leave until cold, then slice. Serve with 1–2 tbsp mayonnaise each.

SERVES 2–3

- *4 large eggs*
- *25 g / 1 oz butter*
- *4 green garlic shoots, or 2 small leeks, or 2 bunches of spring onions, white and palest green, chopped*
- *2 tbsp whipping cream*
- *salt and freshly ground black pepper*
- *mayonnaise, to serve*

139

CHAPTER FIVE

Shellfish and Fish

THE BASQUE COUNTRY

Revuelta de delicias

Spinach and sea treasures with scrambled egg

SERVES 4

- 350 g/12 oz young spinach, stalks stripped and washed
- 100 g/4 oz butter
- salt and freshly ground black pepper
- 4 kokotxas (*hake throats, see page 61*) or 50–75 g/ 2–3 oz white-skin sole fillet (¼ of a 500 g/1 lb fish)
- 3 tbsp olive oil
- 100 g/4 oz button mushrooms, cleaned and sliced
- 100 g/4 oz cooked peeled prawns
- 8 large eggs
- 2 tbsp thick cream

A sophisticated version, from San Sebastián, of a starter that is very popular on the north coast. Further west it might contain turnip tops and prawns. Stirring keeps the revuelta *eggs soft, in contrast to a* tortilla, *which sets to a golden crust.*

Heat 25 g/1 oz butter in a saucepan and add the well-drained spinach. Cover and cook, turning top to bottom once, until wilted. Turn on to a board and chop coarsely. Season well.

Cut the *kokotxas* into pieces, or the sole fillet into strips. Heat 25 g/1 oz butter and 1 tbsp oil in a frying pan and cook the mushrooms, adding the fish pieces and prawns. Add to the spinach and mix gently.

Using two frying pans, heat 25 g/1 oz butter and 1 tbsp oil in each until frothing. Divide the *delicias* between the two pans. Beat the eggs and cream together, season well and pour in, moving the *delicias* so they do not stick. Turn up to medium-high heat and scramble the eggs lightly, stirring the outside to the middle with a wooden spoon. Divide each pan between two people and serve with crusty bread.

THE BALEARIC ISLANDS

Calamares rellenos a la menorquina

Squid stuffed with pine nuts, mint and raisins

~

I first ate this – more than thirty years ago – in a bamboo-roofed hut on a tiny half-moon bay in Minorca, cooked by a friend of a friend.

SERVES 4 AS A STARTER, 2 AS A MAIN COURSE

- 4–8 squid, about 500 g/1 lb
- ½ small Spanish onion
- 4 tbsp olive oil
- 1 slice of stale country bread
- 25 g/1 oz pine nuts, toasted in a dry frying pan
- 75 g/3 oz raisins, preferably muscatels from Malaga, simmered 10 minutes in boiling water
- 12 fresh mint leaves
- 2 tbsp chopped parsley
- 1 egg
- salt and freshly ground black pepper
- about 2 tsp plain flour

To clean squid, use the tentacles to pull out the body. Cut off and keep the tentacles, with the fin flaps from either side of the body. With salted hands rub off the skin; flexing will pop out the spinal structure. Rinse inside and out.

Make the stuffing by chopping the onion finely (briefly in a processor) with the tentacles and pointed fins. Heat the oil in a flameproof casserole in which the squid fit neatly. Over high heat fry the bread. From this point all the stuffing ingredients can be added to the processor, or chopped separately and then combined.

Add the bread and pine nuts. Pip the raisins (if using muscatels) and add with the mint, parsley and egg. Season well with pepper and a little salt.

Stuff the squid and stitch them through the top with a cocktail stick to hold the stuffing inside. Flour the squid very lightly and fry them briefly in the casserole, turning until coloured.

Make the sauce round the squid if there is room. Fry the onion there, then add the garlic and tomato. Let this wilt a little, then stir in the wine and bay leaf. Simmer gently, covered – 30 minutes for large squid, 20 for small ones. Check the seasonings and serve the squid sliced in rounds.

SAUCE

- ½ small Spanish onion, chopped
- 1 garlic clove, finely chopped
- 350g/12 oz ripe tomatoes, skinned, seeded and finely chopped
- 125 ml/4 fl oz dry white wine
- 1 bay leaf
- salt and freshly ground black pepper

THE BASQUE COUNTRY

Budín de merluza
Pink souffléd fish pudding

~

SERVES 6

- 750 g/1½ lb hake or cod fillet
- about 700 ml/1½ pt fish stock, water and white wine, or salted water
- ½ large onion, finely chopped
- 1 tbsp olive oil
- 2 garlic cloves, finely chopped
- 750 g/1½ lb ripe tomatoes, skinned, seeded and chopped
- 2 tbsp finely chopped parsley
- ½ tsp sugar
- salt and freshly ground black pepper
- 40 g/1½ oz butter, plus extra for greasing
- 1 slice of stale bread, soaked in 2 tbsp milk
- 4 large egg yolks
- 3 large egg whites

'Many kitchen drawers in the Basque country have a cutting with a recipe for fish pudding,' I was told, 'because there was a wave of pudding mania when the New Cuisine came in. Some fish, like cabracho (*spiny scorpion fish*), are nicer without their bones.' This light pudding is also called merluza asalmonada because of its pretty salmon pink colour.

Heat the oven to 180°C/350°F/Gas 4. Heat the fish stock or other liquid, then slip in the fish (making sure it is covered by the liquid). Cover, bring back to the boil and remove from the heat.

Meanwhile, fry the onion in the oil in a saucepan. When it colours, add the garlic, chopped tomatoes and parsley. Cook until the sauce thickens. Press the sauce through a sieve (or blend) and season with sugar, salt and pepper. Grease a 1.5 litre/2½ pt bread tin well with butter, line the bottom and long sides with greaseproof paper or foil, and grease again.

Remove the fish from the poaching liquid and shred it with 2 forks, discarding skin and bones. Heat the butter in a wide saucepan and gently warm the shredded fish, forking in the crumbled bread. Add the tomato sauce and heat through. Check the seasoning again and then beat in the egg yolks off the heat.

Whisk the egg whites with a pinch of salt in a large bowl to soft peaks, then lightly fold in the fish mixture. Turn into the prepared tin. Stand in a small roasting tin and pour boiling water round to come two-thirds up the sides of the bread tin. Cook in the pre-heated oven for 50 minutes.

Wait a couple of moments, then run a knife round the pudding and turn out on to a serving plate. Best served hot (with a cream and parsley or tomato sauce if you wish).

OLD CASTILE AND RIOJA

Pimientos rellenos de merluza

Red peppers stuffed with hake or cod

The *great stuffed red pepper dish? It balances the flavours of two
types of pepper, one whole, one dried, with a white fish filling.
The sauce tastes of cream and tomato, but has neither. Usually
made with bottled* piquillo *peppers, which are smaller and spicier
than ours, I have adjusted this recipe for our common red peppers.*

SERVES 4 AS A
STARTER, 2–3
AS A SUPPER DISH

- 8 smallish red peppers
- 400 g/14 oz tail fillets of hake, cod or other white fish, without bones (or canned crab)
- 3 tbsp water
- about 5 tbsp olive oil
- 1 onion, finely chopped
- 2 garlic cloves, finely chopped
- 4 tbsp chopped parsley
- salt and ground white pepper
- plain flour for dusting

**BECHAMEL AND
PEPPER SAUCE**

- 2 tbsp plain flour
- 25 g/1 oz butter
- 200 ml/7 fl oz milk, warm
- 4 dried choricero peppers, soaked for 2 hours, or 1 tbsp paprika
- 1–2 tsp lemon juice

Heat the oven to 200°C/400°F/Gas 6.

Grill the red peppers until charred on all sides, giving them
a quarter turn every 5 minutes. Leave to cool in a bag, then peel
off the skins on a plate, to catch the juices. Remove the stalk
and most of the seeds through the stalk hole with a teaspoon.

Arrange the fish, in fat fingers (skin down), in an oiled
baking dish in which they fit exactly. Sprinkle with the water
and 2 tbsp oil. Bake in the oven for 10 minutes.

Meanwhile fry the onion in 2 tbsp oil until soft, adding the
garlic towards the end. When the fish is ready, flake the flesh
into the onion and add the parsley and seasoning. Don't turn the
oven off – just lower the temperature to 150°C/300°F/Gas 2.

Make the sauce: cook the flour in the hot butter for a
couple of minutes, then stir in the warm milk and simmer for
a couple more minutes. Add 4–5 tbsp sauce to the fish mixture,
then divide this into 8 and stuff the peppers. Lay these in an
oiled baking dish (or individual casseroles), brush with oil and
sift flour lightly over them.

Add the reserved pepper juices to the remaining sauce,
together with the *choricero* flesh or paprika and bring back to
simmering. Taste and balance the sauce with a little lemon juice
and seasoning. Pour round the peppers. Reheat in the oven for
about 10 minutes – or 25–30 if prepared ahead and cold.

THE BASQUE COUNTRY

Bacalao al ajoarriero
Mule-drivers' salt cod with garlic

~

SERVES 4

- ○ 500 g/1 lb salt cod, in 4 slices, soaked overnight with 3 changes of water
- ○ 4 tbsp olive oil
- ○ 4 garlic cloves, in slivers
- ○ 2 large eggs, beaten together

TOMATO SAUCE

- ○ 1 large onion, chopped
- ○ 2 garlic cloves, chopped
- ○ 4 pimientos de piquillo *or* 1 red pepper, seeded and chopped
- ○ 3 dried choricero peppers, soaked for 2 hours, or 2 tsp paprika
- ○ 4 big ripe tomatoes, skinned, seeded and chopped
- ○ 75 ml/3 fl oz white wine or fino sherry
- ○ 1 bay leaf
- ○ 1 tbsp vinegar, if not using piquillo peppers
- ○ freshly ground black pepper

Invented by the medieval equivalent of truck drivers, muleteers criss-crossed the country, introducing this dish throughout Spain. Basically, it is cod with garlic and eggs scrambled in at the end. But, because it is travellers' food, it sometimes include wild things like snails or mushrooms. Potatoes often go in too.

Heat the oven to 200°C/400°F/Gas 6.

Heat 3 tbsp oil in a small pan with the garlic slivers. When they colour, discard them. Pour the oil over the cod pieces in a flameproof casserole (preferably earthenware) and put into the oven to cook for 15 minutes. Alternatively, fry the pieces in the garlic-flavoured oil. When the fish is cooked, remove it.

Make the sauce in the same casserole, adding another 1 tbsp oil. Fry the onion gently, adding the chopped garlic towards the end. When it begins to colour add the chopped peppers, the *choricero* pulp or paprika and the tomatoes. Add the wine and bay leaf and cook to a sauce. Taste for sharpness and add vinegar as needed to accentuate this.

Meanwhile, shred the fish, discarding bones and skin. Drain it on kitchen paper and dry it as much as possible. Incorporate the fish flakes into the sauce and heat through. Add pepper to taste. Add the eggs and scramble everything together for 30 seconds or so.

Empanada de berberechos

Cockle (or clam) pie

~

A festival flat pie that smells wonderfully of the sea when cut. I ate it one breathless December day, on Shellfish Day, sitting on the sea wall of tiny O Barqueiro, on Galicia's north coast.

SERVES 8

- 1 kg/2 lb cockles, rinsed (300 g/10 oz shelled cockles or clams)
- 2 large Spanish onions, well chopped
- 3–4 tbsp olive oil
- 20 strands saffron

CORNMEAL DOUGH

- 250 g/9 oz yellow cornmeal
- 15 g/½ oz fresh yeast
- 1 tsp caster sugar
- 200 ml/7 fl oz warm water
- 2 tbsp oil, plus more for greasing and brushing the pie
- 2 eggs, beaten
- 250 g/9 oz plain flour
- 1 tsp salt

Make the dough first. Put the cornmeal into a large bowl (or food processor). Blend the yeast with the sugar until liquid. Add the water, oil and eggs to the cornmeal and beat well, then beat in the yeast. Gradually add the flour, sifted with the salt, to give a smooth soft dough. If working by hand, knead for a minute or two, until fairly smooth and not sticky. Return to the clean bowl, cover with a towel and leave in a warm place for 20–30 minutes.

Heat the oven to 200°C/400°F/Gas 6 and make the filling. Cook the onions in plenty of oil until golden. Open the cockles by putting them, in batches, into a large pan with a little boiling water and covering tightly. Leave a minute or two, then take off the shells. Pound the saffron in a mortar or crumble with your fingers, and add a couple of spoonfuls of cockle water. Add the cockles and saffron to the onions.

Grease a baking tray (about 35 x 25 cm/14 x 10 in). Divide the dough equally and roll out one part rather bigger than the tray. Lay it on the tray leaving a border hanging over the edge.

Spread the filling over the dough, leaving a clear margin. Roll out the top sheet and lift over. Trim off the edges, just bigger than the tray and keep them. Fold the outside edge inward, rolling it neatly, and pressing with a fork to bind. Decorate the top with long thin strips of pastry – these often mark the cutting lines. Paint with oil and prick with a fork in the squares.

Bake for 20–25 minutes. Cool for a minute or so, then cut into squares. Eat with your fingers – preferably with a sea view!

LEVANTE

Arroz en caldero
Rice with peppers and allioli followed by fish

~

The popular lunch in Murcia is just the rice course, made in a little witches' cauldron, with a suave creamy mousse of allioli. *No fish! However, the double course is very splendid. The ñora pepper was once the base of both the rice and the fish sauce.*

SERVES 6

- 400 g/14 oz paella *or risotto rice*
- 1.5 kg/3 lb fish fillet, such as grey mullet, or several types, cut in serving pieces
- 1 bulb garlic, in unpeeled cloves, smashed
- 2 ñora or 2 cm/¾ in canned Mexican jalapeño peppers, chopped (or 2 tsp paprika)
- 6–8 tbsp good olive oil
- 1 ripe beefsteak tomato, skinned and seeded
- 20 strands saffron
- 1.5 litre/2½ pt fish stock, from the bones etc. of the fish
- salt and freshly ground black pepper
- allioli for fish (see next recipe), to serve

SALMORETTA SAUCE FOR THE FISH

- 1 ripe beefsteak tomato, skinned, seeded and chopped
- 3 tbsp olive oil
- 3 garlic cloves, finely chopped
- 2 tbsp chopped parsley
- 100 ml/3½ fl oz fish stock (from the recipe)
- juice of 1 lemon
- 1 tsp paprika

For the rice alone, create a very quick base: fry the garlic (and *ñoras* if using) in oil, then remove. Fry the chopped tomato, then add it to the pulverized garlic, peppers and saffron in a blender, plus 1 litre/1¾pt fish stock, salt and paprika (if using). Easy!

For two courses, start by preparing the fish, cutting it into steaks and seasoning. Heat the oil in a *paella* pan and fry the garlic and chopped *ñoras* until the garlic colours, then reserve. Stiffen the fish in plenty of oil, then remove.

Fry the chopped tomato (and sprinkle with paprika, if using), reducing it to a sauce. Peel and pound the garlic, with the *ñoras* or *jalepeño* and saffron in a mortar or small blender. Stir the paste into the tomato. Return the fish to the pan and add the fish stock and a little salt. Poach for 5–6 minutes, depending on shape. Remove to a serving dish and keep warm. Reserve the stock for the *allioli* and the *salmoretta* sauce.

Press the stock through a sieve (or blend). Return 1 litre/ 1¾ pt to the pan, taste and season. Add the well-rinsed rice. Cook for 18–20 minutes: the rice must still have some bite. Make the *allioli* and serve together as the first course.

For the *salmoretta* sauce, fry the chopped tomato in the oil in a small saucepan. Pound the garlic cloves in a mortar with the parsley (or blend) and add the fish stock and lemon juice, with paprika and salt. Beat well and serve in a sauce boat with the fish as the main course.

CATALONIA

Allioli

Garlic, oil and egg sauce

~

Perhaps the Mediterranean's greatest sauce, allioli is indisputably a Spanish invention – even though French aïoli is better known. Classically it partners fish, but it is also popular with rice mixtures in Catalonia.

SERVES 6

EGG YOLK ALLIOLI

- ○ 6 garlic cloves, finely chopped
- ○ ½ tsp salt
- ○ 1 large egg yolk
- ○ 2 tsp lemon juice
- ○ 250 ml/8 fl oz olive oil, preferably Spanish, including half virgin oil

ALLIOLI FOR FISH

- ○ 1 small bulb of garlic, finely chopped
- ○ salt and freshly ground black pepper
- ○ 1 small potato (50 g/2 oz), boiled in its skin
- ○ 125 ml/4 fl oz fish stock
- ○ 1 large egg yolk
- ○ 125 ml/4 fl oz olive oil, preferably Spanish

For egg yolk allioli: a mortar is still the best place to make this. Crush the garlic with the salt in a mortar (or with the flat side of a table knife on a board), mashing it to a smooth paste (if necessary move it to a bowl). Work in the yolk, then the lemon juice. The oil must be at room temperature. Add it, drop by drop, working it in with the pestle, 'always in the same direction' (or whisk it in), until an emulsion forms. Continue adding the oil until it is all incorporated, to make a thick sauce.

Because there is little acidity in the mixture, *allioli* splits more easily than mayonnaise. Not to worry! This is called *allioli negat* and is often stirred into fish stews and sauces.

For allioli for fish: Pound the garlic with a pinch of salt in a mortar to a paste, or blend. Peel the potato and work it in, alternating with the fish stock, then the egg yolk. Add the oil drop by drop, like mayonnaise if working by hand. Season with salt and pepper.

MADRID

Merluza de Mama

Hake with two mayonnaises and a soup course

~

SERVES 4, IN TWO
COURSES

- 1 kg/2 lb middle piece of hake
- salt and freshly ground black pepper

STOCK

- 100 g/4 oz small onions, halved
- 100 g/4 oz baby carrots, in sections
- 4 small new potatoes
- 1 strip of lemon zest
- a bay leaf
- about 400 ml/14 fl oz water

TWO MAYONNAISES

- 300 ml/½ pt thick home-made mayonnaise (see page 112)
- 0.1 g packet powdered saffron
- 1 tbsp boiling water
- pinch of paprika
- 1 sliver of garlic
- ¼ tsp salt
- 5 tbsp finely chopped parsley
- 1 tbsp capers
- 1 tbsp lemon juice

An elegant and easy cook-ahead dinner for a hot day. Hake is perfect as the fillets roll off the backbone like the breasts of a chicken. It is cooked in a pressure cooker – a popular time-saver in Spain – and left unopened all day. The stock is then used for soup. Quicker to do than explain!
Cod, poached in the normal way (or baked – see page 145), is also delicious with these mayonnaises. I like to serve one mayonnaise plain, one coloured, though there is a choice of green or saffron-flavoured.

Put the stock ingredients in the bottom of a pressure cooker. Put in the bottom plate with enough water to reach it. Salt and pepper the fish, put it in and close the pressure cooker. Bring up to high heat with the vent open. Close the vent, according to your model, turn down the heat and start timing for 9 minutes. When this is reached, remove from the heat and leave unopened, untouched, until cold.

Open the pressure cooker and skin the fish, removing it from the bone on to a serving plate.

Make the mayonnaise. For saffron mayonnaise dissolve the spice in the boiling water and stir into half the thick mayonnaise. Dust paprika over it.

For green mayonnaise, pound the garlic sliver with the salt, then reduce it with 4 tbsp parsley and the capers to a green paste (easy in a small blender). Stir into half the master recipe for mayonnaise with the lemon juice. To serve, sprinkle with a little finely chopped parsley.

To make the bisque soup, remove the lemon zest and bay leaf and sieve (or blend) the stock base with the hard-boiled egg yolk (if using). Return to the pan, add the wine or vermouth and reheat. Add the prawns and season to taste. Garnish with the parsley and finely chopped egg white (if using).

Note: This is adjusted to the British standard of 15 lb per sq. in. Continental models of pressure cooker (such as Tefal, Duromatic, Silvinox and Sitram) all cook at much lower pressure than this and require about double the time.

SOUP ADDITIONS

- *1 hard-boiled egg (optional)*
- *100 ml/3½ fl oz white wine or dry vermouth*
- *100 g/4 oz cooked peeled prawns*
- *2 tbsp chopped parsley*

GALICIA

Sardinaſ rellenaſ aſadaſ
Baked sardines with oregano stuffing

Sardines are at their best in August. A rich dish as it includes the juices from the head and the fish are uncleaned. Ideally it is accompanied by the deep-fried miniature pimientos de Padrón.

Heat the oven to 190°C/375°F/Gas 5.

Scale the sardines by rubbing tail-to-head and rinse them. Slit them open from the back, cutting down one side of the backbone. (The guts are nothing much in small fish.) Open the pocket with 2 fingers and salt and pepper them inside.

Mash the garlic with ½ tsp salt in a mortar (or a small blender), then purée with the shallots or onions, parsley and oregano. Add the breadcrumbs, lemon zest, 1 tsp lemon juice and the paprika and reduce everything to a paste. Taste and season.

Stuff the sardines and lay them in a lightly oiled earthenware dish. Mix 1 tbsp lemon juice with the oil and brush or dribble over them. Bake in the oven for 25 minutes. Serve immediately, with crusty bread.

SERVES 4–6

- *1 kg/2 lb very fresh sardines*
- *salt and freshly ground black pepper*
- *6 garlic cloves, finely chopped*
- *2–3 shallots or the whites of a bunch of spring onions, finely chopped*
- *6 tbsp chopped parsley*
- *1 tbsp fresh oregano leaves*
- *8 tbsp dry white breadcrumbs*
- *¼ tsp finely grated lemon zest*
- *4 tsp lemon juice*
- *1 tbsp paprika*
- *about 1 tsp olive oil*

Fritura malagueña
Malaga mixed fried fish

~

Malaga people have a reputation for being particular about food, and the city was the first on the south coast to build a luxury hotel in the nineteenth century. There is an elegance about this mixture, while the dish is exceptional when one fish is pickled.

SERVES 4

- 4 small red mullet, about 175 g/6 oz each, fresh or pickled (see Escabeche, page 114)
- 8–12 small squid, about 7cm/3 in long
- oil for deep frying
- 2 small fillets of white fish, hake, sole, etc., about 400 g/14 oz together
- lemon wedges, to serve

BATTER

- 125 g/4½ oz plain flour
- 1 tsp salt
- large pinch of paprika
- 1 large egg
- 125 ml/4 fl oz tepid water

Don't bother to clean fresh mullet (their insides are neatly avoided on the plate). Just scrape them from tail to head to remove the scales, then rinse. Tiny squid don't need cleaning either. In spring and early summer they are full of soft milky roe, which keeps them moist when fried. (The stiffener in them is like soft plastic and easy to discard.)

Make the batter: season the flour, adding paprika, and beat in the egg, then the water. If possible, leave to stand for 1 hour.

Heat plenty of oil for deep frying (top heat on an electric fryer). Dip fresh mullet into the batter and fry them, two at a time, for 4 minutes. Drain on kitchen paper and keep warm.

Let the oil reheat, then dip the squid in the batter and fry in two batches – also for about 4 minutes, as there are more of them. Fry pickled mullet (if using), then the fish in pieces. Arrange on a plate with lemon wedges and serve.

ANDALUSIA

Urta a la roteña

*Fish with onion, brandy and
tomato sauce from Rota*

~

Rota, which faces Cadiz across the bay, is famous for urta, a
bream that feeds on shellfish, which flavour its flesh. This recipe,
from a gipsy called Doña Pepa, was made in a deep paella pan.
The secret, she said, was to cook the onions very slowly till
they turn quite sweet. With brandy and wine they make
a wonderful sauce.

Fry the onions very slowly in 2 tsp oil in a casserole until they
melt. Add the garlic near the end. Turn up the heat slightly
and cook intil the onions caramelize and colour, stirring occasionally so the onions do not catch. Add the green pepper and
fry for 5 minutes. Add the chopped tomatoes, bay leaf, salt,
pepper and nutmeg and leave to reduce.

Meanwhile, if using monkfish, take the flesh off the bone
and cut it into fingers. Season them. Heat 3–4 tbsp oil in a
wide pan and colour the fish on both sides. Spoon off visible
oil. Warm the brandy in a ladle, then flame it and pour it over
the fish. Add the wine and stir to deglaze the pan. Stir in the
tomato sauce and simmer for a further 5 minutes.

SERVES 4

- 1 kg/2 lb urta in fillets, or
  monkfish on the bone
- 2 large mild Spanish onions,
  sliced very thinly
- 5–6 tbsp olive oil
- 3 garlic cloves, finely
  chopped
- 1 large green pepper, seeded
  and chopped
- 3 large ripe tomatoes,
  skinned and seeded
- 1 bay leaf
- salt and freshly ground black
  pepper
- freshly grated nutmeg
- 4 tbsp Spanish brandy or
  cognac
- 4 tbsp white wine

Merluza a la koxkera
Hake or cod with clams

~

SERVES 4

- 4 very fresh pieces of hake (or cod) fillet, 750 g/1 lb 10 oz together
- salt and freshly ground black pepper
- paprika
- 175 ml/6 fl oz olive oil, preferably Spanish
- 4 fat garlic cloves, sliced across in rings
- 250 g/8 oz small clams or cockles
- 250 g/8 oz small mussels, cleaned (see page 101)
- 125 ml/4 fl oz dry white wine, preferably txacolí
- 8 tbsp chopped parsley
- 1 hard-boiled egg, chopped

To be koxkera is to be truly Basque – born in the calle 31 de agosto, the last old street in the port of San Sebastián, an alley of golden houses between the churches of Santa Maria and San Vicente. Clams are traditional in this green sauce, for they trap a little seawater. The sauce is the famous pil-pil, a white emulsion (rather like a hot mayonnaise) thickened only by the natural gelatine which comes from the fish skin. It is one of Europe's great fish dishes, but rarely made correctly, because a bechamel sauce is much simpler to do.

Sprinkle the fish pieces with salt, pepper and paprika. Heat the and oil in a casserole into which all the fish will fit comfortably, preferably one made of flameproof earthenware. Add the garlic (to flavour the oil), frying until coloured, then remove and reserve. Add the fish pieces, skin up. Fry them briskly, 2–3 minutes on each side.

Meanwhile, put the shellfish and wine into a pan with a lid and heat to open the shells. Keep the lid on, to keep them warm until needed.

Pour half the oil in the hot dish back into the measuring jug. Grasp the casserole on both sides with gloves. Give it a steady swinging movement, in a small circle, to agitate the fish. The ideal place to do this is on the warm side of an Aga, but on a gas stove, I do it on the turned-off plate. After about five minutes the oil starts to cloud over, thickening and whitening as the sauce emulsifies.

Return the oil in dribbles, as though making mayonnaise, still shaking the casserole to work this in. It takes about 20 minutes to complete, so I hold the dish above a low gas flame every now and then, to keep the temperature up. Work in the stock which has accumulated under the shellfish in the same way, by swinging or agitating the dish.

Return the garlic, stir in a little parsley, check the seasonings and add the shellfish, removing some of the top shells. Garnish with chopped egg and the remaining parsley.

ARAGON AND NAVARRE

Truchas con serrano y hierbabuena

Trout with raw ham and mint

~

Trout with ham has become a Spanish classic. But I was surprised that mint and ham go so well together.

Ahead, extend the belly cavity of each trout, cutting up on one side of the backbone with a knife. Bending them makes the little rib bones pop up; snip these off with scissors. Stuff with several sprigs of crushed mint. Pack the fish head to tail into a dish where they fit closely and pour the wine over them. Leave in a cool place for at least 6 hours.

Pat the fish dry with kitchen paper (reserving the marinade) and season inside. Roll up the ham and stuff into the trout with a mint leaf on either side. Fry the trout over medium heat in the hot bacon fat, 5 minutes each side, when the skin will be crisp.

Serve accompanied by well-seasoned potatoes with the hot marinade poured over them, and sprinkled with good oil. Garnish with more mint if wished.

SERVES 4

○ *4 trout, cleaned*

○ *1 handful of fresh mint*

○ *125 ml/4 fl oz dry white wine*

○ *salt and freshly ground black pepper*

○ *4 thin slices of raw ham (or a 75 g/3 oz packet prosciutto)*

○ *2 tbsp bacon fat, from frying streaky rashers*

○ *boiled potatoes, in rounds, to serve*

○ *about 2 tbsp good olive oil*

MADRID

Besugo al horno

Baked whole fish with lemon and potatoes

~

SERVES 6 AS A LIGHT
MAIN COURSE

- 1.5 kg/2½–3 lb whole red bream, sea bass or salmon, cleaned
- 3 lemons
- 100 ml/3½ fl oz olive oil
- 2 bay leaves
- 350–700 g/12 oz–1½ lb potatoes, sliced (a long fish like salmon will need more)
- 1 onion, preferably purple, sliced in rings
- salt and freshly ground black pepper
- 1 garlic clove, cut in slivers
- a little dried guindilla chilli, seeded and chopped or a pinch of cayenne pepper
- 100 ml/3½ fl oz dry white wine
- 1 tbsp chopped parsley

Red bream, with a black spot on its shoulder (and the perfect shape) is cooked in many Spanish homes on Christmas Eve. This version is ideal for any whole fish. 'It is important to the dish,' said the retired diplomat's wife who gave it to me, 'that the potatoes are crisped round the edge and brown. They catch this from the lemon and oil. Be sure that the potatoes are pre-cooked, otherwise they will not be ready when the fish is done.'

Cut off the fins and rinse and dry the fish inside. Squeeze 1 lemon and sprinkle the juice and 4 tbsp oil inside. Leave to marinate for 2 hours. Then heat the oven to 200°C/400°F/Gas 6.

Reserve the marinade juices. With the point of a kitchen knife make slashes on the sides of the fish. Slice the second lemon, halve the slices and fit into the gashes, pointing backwards like fins. Oil an ovenproof oval dish and put in the fish with the bay leaves under it.

Cook the potatoes in salted water until just tender. Arrange round the fish, scattering with the rings pushed from the onion. Season lightly with salt and pepper and cover with thin slices of the third lemon.

Heat the remaining oil in a small pan with the garlic slivers and the *guindilla* chilli (if using), discarding them when they brown. Add the marinade juices, wine and cayenne (if using) and pour over the fish and potatoes. Cover with foil and put into the oven. Cook for 35–45 minutes (according to fish size).

Remove the foil and cook for a further 15 minutes to colour the potato edges. Sprinkle with a little parsley.

LEVANTE

Mújol a la sal

Whole fish baked in salt

~

One of the great recipes of the east coast, the fish is baked in a salt jacket, which keeps it very moist, without making it excessively salty. It's very easy too, and suddenly an accessible recipe, using granular salt sold for dishwashers. Two smaller fish work as well as one (about 600 g/1½ lb will serve two).

SERVES 6

○ *1 whole grey mullet, gilt-head bream or codling, about 1.25 kg/2½ lb, uncleaned*

○ *about 2 kg/4½ lb granular salt*

○ *lemon wedges or allioli (see page 149), to serve*

Make a bed of granular salt in a small roasting tin into which the fish just fits neatly – I saw this done in a small fruit box. Put in the fish, uncleaned (or it will leak), and build a snow mountain over it with salt, so there is no visible grey.

Heat the oven to top heat (240°C/475°F/Gas 9) and put in the fish. Cook for 25 minutes (20 minutes for smaller fish) – the salt will cohere into a solid mass, the sign that the fish is done. It will wait in a warm place for another 10 minutes.

Show it to the table as it is, cracking open the salt there. Best then to portion it on a side table. The skin and fins lift away with the salt crust. Take three portions off the top of the backbone. Turn it, discarding the stomach, and portion the other side. Serve with lemon wedges or *allioli*.

Note: Discard any coloured salt, then use the rest. Dishwasher detergent is a powerful cleaner and copes with all smells!

ASTURIAS AND CANTABRIA

Fabes con carabineros
Beans with giant prawns

SERVES 8

- 1 kg/2 lb fabes de la granja *or butter beans*
- 8 *large raw* carabineros, *or* scampi *with their claws, or* 1.5 kg/3 lb *big raw prawns*

ONION SAUCE

- 3 onions, *finely chopped*
- 2 tbsp olive oil
- 2 garlic cloves, *finely chopped*
- 2 dried guindilla *chillies, seeded and chopped, or a good pinch of cayenne pepper*
- 3 dried choriceros, *soaked for 2 hours, or 1 tbsp paprika*
- 5 tbsp chopped parsley
- 150 ml/5 fl oz fino *sherry or white wine*
- 1 bay leaf
- salt and freshly ground black pepper

One glorious carabinero *(huge scarlet prawn) is served on top of each portion. They have very rich heads, more so than langostinos; but use any raw prawn with a head. If this is a problem, make* fabes con almejas *(with clams) instead – see the note below.*

Starting a couple of days ahead, soak the beans for 24 hours. (With *fabes*, the skin will come off.) Cook in water to cover by 2 fingers for 4 hours: it must not bubble. Do this on the stove if you can manage a low heat, otherwise in the oven at 150°C/300°F/Gas 2. Don't stir them. Check occasionally; they must always be well covered with water. This is best done ahead as the beans will have a better texture.

Make the sauce by frying the onions in the oil in a flame-proof casserole. When they are nearly soft, add the garlic, *guindilla* chilli and pulp scraped from the *choricero* peppers (if using them), then purée with the parsley in a blender. Return to the pan and add the sherry or wine, bay leaf, a little salt, and the paprika and cayenne (if using). Taste: the sauce should be distinctly piquant.

Cook the *carabineros*, scampi or prawns in this sauce for 15–20 minutes, according to size. Take out the bay leaf. Stir the sauce and prawns carefully into the beans. Reheat slowly – 30 minutes in a low oven (150°C/300°F/Gas 2). Check the seasonings and serve with the *carabineros* on top.

Note: Clams are more traditional. Open 1.5 kg/3 lb clams, in batches, in a large covered pan with a small glass of white wine (or use 500 g/1 lb shelled clams). Shell them, saving the liquid, and add it to the sauce with 50 soaked saffron strands.

ASTURIAS AND CANTABRIA

Caldereta asturiana
Mixed shellfish and fish stew

SERVES 6

A stew of the fish that dart around the rocks, red mullet, grouper and many spiny members. Buy what is fresh, aiming at about 250 g/8 oz prepared fish per person. I bought a small grouper, a piece of cod fillet, a strip of monkfish and some conger eel. What is essential is to drink several culines of cider with it!

- 250 g/8 oz hake or cod fillet
- 250 g/8 oz monkfish fillet
- 1 red mullet, cleaned
- 250 g/8 oz conger eel steaks
- 250 g/8 oz small squid, cleaned (see page 143)
- 150 ml/5 fl oz dry white wine
- 250 g/8 oz mussels, cleaned (see page 101)
- 250 g/8 oz large clams, rinsed
- 1 onion, chopped
- 2 tbsp olive oil
- 3 garlic cloves, finely chopped
- 1 tbsp plain flour
- 2 tbsp brandy
- about 300 ml/½ pt fish stock
- 8 tbsp chopped parsley
- salt and freshly ground black pepper
- pinch of cayenne pepper
- 250 g/8 oz peppers, seeded and chopped
- 250 g/8 oz shrimps in their shells or raw prawns
- 1 bay leaf
- a strip of pared lemon zest
- juice of 1 lemon
- toasted bread, to serve

Prepare the fish, cutting it into pieces of even thickness. Cut the squid into 2–3 pieces.

Put the wine in a large saucepan and add the mussels and clams, in two batches. Put on the lid and cook over high heat for 2–3 minutes until the shells open. Discard the shells. Keep the liquor. Heat the oven to 180°C/350°F/Gas 4.

Fry the onion in the oil in a saucepan. Towards the end, add the garlic. Sprinkle with the flour and stir in, then add the liquor from the shellfish, the brandy, fish stock, parsley, and salt and black and cayenne pepper to taste.

Choose a small casserole, into which the fish will fit in two layers. Salt and pepper the fish and squid pieces and put in half of them. Add half the chopped peppers, mussels, clams and shrimps or prawns and cover with half the sauce. Repeat the layers and tuck in the bay leaf and strip of lemon zest. The top layer of fish should be just covered. If it is not, add a little more fish stock.

Cover and put into the oven for 30 minutes. Squeeze the lemon juice over the top and serve with toasted bread. The shrimps can be eaten unpeeled – though personally I discard the heads. Prawns will need peeling.

SERVES 6

○ *1.25 kg/2½–3 lb assorted filleted fish, plus their heads, bones and debris*

○ *1.2 litre/2 pt fish stock*

○ *about 6 tbsp plain flour*

○ *salt and freshly ground black pepper*

○ *2 tbsp olive oil (optional)*

○ *250 ml/8 fl oz dry white wine*

○ *2 sprigs of fresh thyme*

○ *2 sprigs of fresh oregano*

○ *500 g/1 lb scampi with their heads, or big raw prawns*

○ *250 g/8 oz small clams or 500 g/1 lb mussels, cleaned*

○ *4 small squid, cleaned (see page 143) (optional)*

○ *6 tbsp chopped parsley*

ROMESCO SAUCE

○ *25 g/1 oz almonds*

○ *25 g/1 oz hazelnuts*

○ *4 tbsp olive oil*

○ *1 slice of stale bread, crusts removed*

○ *2 garlic cloves, chopped*

○ *2 ñora chillies, or extra dried chilli*

○ *1 dried bitxo, guindilla or other chilli*

○ *2 tbsp chopped parsley*

○ *2 tbsp lemon juice*

○ *500 g/1 lb ripe tomatoes*

○ *salt and black pepper*

CATALONIA

Romesco de peix
Shellfish stew with hazelnut and chilli sauce

One of the great shellfish soup-stews of the Mediterranean, the romesco sauce is a subtle blend of chillies with hazelnuts and garlic. I used cod steak, small monkfish and flat fish, and a red mullet. Buy about 2.3 kg/5 lb whole fish if you can, and reckon to get 1 kg/2 lb heads and bones. Good fish stock is essential so, even if you start with a commercial stock, still simmer in it the prawn heads and unsightly fish trimmings (belly flaps etc.) for 30 minutes. Traditionally all the tomato is blended, but a little left sliced enhances the dish.

Simmer the fish heads, bones and debris in the fish stock for 30 minutes, to make a concentrated stock. Meanwhile, toast the nuts (see page 205), seed and chop the chillies and skin, seed and slice the tomatoes.

To make the sauce, heat the oil in a flameproof casserole to very hot and quickly fry the bread, garlic and chopped ñora chillies, if using. Pound the toasted nuts (or use a blender), adding the bread in pieces, the garlic, noras, other chillies, parsley and lemon juice. Blend in half the tomatoes and season.

Coat the fish pieces in seasoned flour. Add 2 tbsp oil to the casserole (if needed) and fry the fish over high heat, moving the pieces around. Pour the sauce over them and add the wine. Taste the stock and reduce if it is not good enough, adding more. Add enough stock to the casserole to cover everything and bring to simmering, adding the thyme and oregano.

Put in the scampi or prawns. (Scampi with heads go in whole: otherwise they should be shelled and deveined.) Bring back to simmering and then add the clams or mussels. When they open, add the squid and remaining tomato flesh. Simmer for 10 minutes. Taste for seasoning and add the parsley.

THE BASQUE COUNTRY

Gaſtaika

Ray or skate with chilli oil

~

A distinguished dish, because the flesh falls neatly from the wing bones in white strips, and the red sauce is minimal but very insistent. The bigger the flat fish the better.

Choose a wide flameproof casserole and put in just enough water to poach the wings. Add the onion, leek and parsley, season with salt and give it a headstart of 15 minutes cooking. Add the skate and poach – just 3–4 minutes if thin. Remove the fish to a big warm serving dish.

Put the vinegar in a small pan and boil to reduce by half. Throw it over the fish. Heat the oil in the same pan with the garlic cloves until they colour (seconds), then add the chilli pieces. Pour this over the fish. When the oil and vinegar have mingled, pour them back into the pan, reheat and pour them over the fish a second time. Serve at once.

Note: One of the best stocks for cooking fish – and one of the quickest! Afterwards, strain and keep as fish stock.

SERVES 6

- 1.5 kg/3 lb skate (or ray) wings, in 6 portions
- 1 onion, thinly sliced
- 1 leek with some green, sliced
- handful of parsley stalks, bruised
- salt

CHILLI OIL

- 5 tbsp sherry vinegar or wine vinegar
- 200 ml/7 fl oz olive oil
- 5 garlic cloves, finely chopped
- 1 dried guindilla or other chilli, seeded and finely chopped

CHAPTER SIX

Poultry
and Game

OLD CASTILE AND RIOJA

Menestra de pollo

Cauliflower, artichoke and chicken hotpot

SERVES 6

- ½ small free-range chicken (about 500 g/1 lb), in serving pieces
- 300 ml/½ pt light meat or good chicken stock
- 175 ml/6 fl oz dry white wine
- 1 small cauliflower, in florets
- bases of 4–6 large globe artichokes (see note)
- 2 tbsp diced ham fat or good chicken stock
- 175 g/6 oz raw ham or gammon, in small, thin slices
- salt and freshly ground black pepper
- 6 tbsp stale white bread-crumbs
- 4 tbsp chopped parsley
- 1 hard-boiled egg, chopped (optional)

CONDIMENT

- 2 tbsp olive oil
- 2 onions, chopped
- 6 garlic cloves, finely chopped
- 6 tbsp chopped parsley
- 2 tsp paprika

Menestras are spring vegetable dishes, with a handful of this and that, but usually containing fresh beans or peas and a little ham. Big fried artichoke bases give this one an interesting texture, though small ones, boiled whole, are quicker.

Cook the chicken in a small pan in the stock and wine for 30 minutes (originally it just came from the *cocido*, with some stock). Prepare the artichoke bases.

Next make the condiment: heat the oil in a frying pan and soften the onions, adding the garlic towards the end. Remove the onion to a mortar (or blender) and purée with the parsley and paprika.

Cook the cauliflower in boiling salted water in a flame-proof casserole for about 5 minutes, then drain. Fry the quartered artichoke bases for 5 minutes or so in the frying pan, with any ham fat, adding more oil as needed. Fry the ham, briefly.

Turn the chicken and stock into the casserole (removing unsightly bones) and stir in the condiment purée. Check the sauce seasoning. Gently mix in the cauliflower, ham and artichokes. Fry the crumbs in the frying pan, mix with the parsley and sprinkle on top, adding chopped egg if you wish. Eat with spoons and forks.

Note: To prepare artichoke bases snap off the stalks (if these are stringy, the artichokes are tough and will need an extra 5 minutes' cooking). Trim the bottom flat and cut through the top leaves just above the choke, leaving a base about 3 cm/1¼ in deep. Trim away the side leaves with a small knife until the white base shows. Cook in boiling salted water for

10 minutes, then drain upside down until cool enough to handle.

Flip off any soft leaf stumps with your thumb, revealing the hairy choke. Remove it with spoon and thumb, leaving a smooth cup base. This needs about 5 minutes' more cooking (braised or fried etc.) depending upon toughness.

NEW CASTILE AND LA MANCHA

Pollo con salsa de ajos
Chicken with saffron and garlic sauce

Old-fashioned fried chicken, with a saffron sauce which is thickened at the end with a typical picada *– a mash of mild garlic, seasoning and toast.*

SERVES 4

- *1.2–1.4 kg/2¾–3 lb free-range chicken, cut into 8 pieces*
- *salt*
- *1–2 tsp paprika*
- *4 tbsp olive oil*
- *1 slice of country bread, crusts removed*
- *1 bulb of garlic cloves, smashed and peeled*
- *50 strands saffron*
- *125 ml/4 fl oz white wine*
- *125 ml/4 fl oz hot water*
- *5 black peppercorns*
- *1 tbsp Spanish brandy or cognac*

Rub salt and paprika into the chicken pieces with your fingers. Heat the oil in a wide shallow flameproof casserole and fry the bread quickly on both sides, then reserve. Give the chicken pieces a turn in the hot oil with the whole garlic cloves. When the chicken starts to look golden, take out all the garlic and reserve with the bread, but continue frying the chicken (about 15 minutes in all).

Crumble the saffron with your fingers into the wine and add to the casserole with the water. Cover and reduce the heat to minimum. Simmer for 10 minutes.

Crush the black peppercorns in a mortar (or small blender). Add the garlic cloves with a pinch of salt and reduce to a paste. Add the fried bread in pieces and pulp it all. Stir this into the cooking liquid, spooning it over the chicken. When the chicken is cooked through, sprinkle with the brandy and serve.

Arroz a la vasca

Rice with everything from a chicken

~

SERVES 8 AS A
STARTER, 6 AS A
MAIN COURSE

- ½ large chicken
- 4 each of chicken livers, gizzards and hearts
- 125 g/4½ oz boneless lean pork
- 100 g/4 oz raw ham, bacon or streaky rashers
- 150 g/5 oz chorizo, *paprika* or smoked sausage
- 5 tbsp olive oil
- 3 garlic cloves, finely chopped
- 500 g/18 oz paella *or risotto rice, well rinsed*
- 150 g/5 oz shelled peas, fresh (preferably) or frozen
- 2 dried choricero peppers, soaked for 2 hours, or 2 tsp paprika (or more)
- pinch of cayenne pepper
- 3 tbsp sieved tomato (passata)
- salt and freshly ground black pepper
- 1.2 litre/2 pt good poultry stock, hot
- 200 ml/7 fl oz dry white wine or strong cider
- 2 red peppers, grilled and skinned (see page 110) or canned pimientos
- 3 hard-boiled eggs
- 2 tbsp chopped parsley

Simple and economical, this rice stew uses all the delicious extras that come with roasting chickens; collect them in the freezer. Four chicken wings (halved) can replace the giblets, or a little cold meat, even the leftover stuffing.

Take the chicken meat from the bones and cut it into small chunks. Save the better skin and cut it into shreds. Clean and quarter the chicken livers, and open the gizzards and wash them. Chop the giblets, pork and ham. Slice the sausage.

Heat the oil in a *paella* pan or large wide flameproof casserole, with any lumps of chicken fat, and crisp the chicken skin. Fry the chicken wings, larger chicken pieces and sausage over high heat, turning until starting to colour, then add the pork and ham, lastly the garlic and livers, and fry again.

Add the rice with the fresh peas, the pulp scraped from the *choricero* peppers (or sprinkle with paprika – 2 tbsp, if not using *chorizo*), cayenne and the sieved tomato, with salt and pepper to taste. Stir well.

Taste the hot stock and, if it is not well-flavoured, reduce, adding more. Add half to the pan with the wine or cider. When this is absorbed, add the remainder of the stock (and frozen peas if using). Cook the rice for a total of about 30 minutes until done and the liquid is absorbed. In a large flat pan this is easiest transferred to the oven to cook (at 180°C/350°F/Gas 4).

Decorate the top with strips of red pepper, slices of hard-boiled egg and parsley, then cover and stand for 5 minutes in a warm place, so the rice grains separate.

GALICIA

Gallina a la gallega

Buttered Galician chicken with noodles

A splendid end for a boiling hen, especially with a few yolks inside (added with the saffron) to give colour and richness to the sauce.

Cut the bird into 16 pieces (halving the backbone, breasts and thighs), removing or shredding any thick chicken skin, and season. Melt three-quarters of the butter in a large frying pan (with any lumps of chicken fat). Add the chicken pieces and fry them over the highest heat until well-coloured.

Move to a flameproof casserole with the butter from the pan and add the wine (or cider) and bouquet garni (include the bony extras from a boiling hen). Cook over a medium heat, basting regularly with the juices, until most of the wine has evaporated.

Melt the remaining butter in the frying pan and cook the onion till softened, frying the ham at the same time. Stir in the tomato concentrate and half the water or stock. Add a pinch of sugar and balance it with salt. Crumble in the saffron with your fingers. Bring to simmering, then pour over the chicken. (A boiling hen is simmered until tender at this point.)

Check the seasonings, adding nutmeg to taste, then more water or stock, judging enough to cook the noodles. Add these to the casserole.

Mash the garlic with ¼ tsp salt and pulverize with the parsley (or use the blender); add the paste to the pan. Cook until the noodles are ready (about 15 minutes) and the chicken falling off the bones. Remove the backbone, any bony extras and bouquet garni, and garnish with more parsley. Good with Brussels sprouts and plenty of cider to drink.

SERVES 4

- 1 boiling hen or 1.5 kg/3 lb free-range chicken
- salt and freshly ground black pepper
- 100 g/4 oz good butter
- 250 ml/8 fl oz dry white wine or strong cider
- 1 fresh bouquet garni of 2 sprigs each of thyme and parsley, plus bay leaf
- 1 onion, very finely chopped
- 100 g/4 oz raw ham or gammon, in small strips
- 1 tbsp tomato concentrate
- about 700 ml/1¼ pt vegetable water or light stock
- pinch of sugar
- 50 strands saffron
- freshly grated nutmeg
- 175–200 g/6–7 oz fideos, small elbow macaroni, or spaghetti broken into short lengths
- 2 tbsp chopped parsley, to garnish

CONDIMENT

- 2 garlic cloves, finely chopped
- 2 tbsp chopped parsley

LEVANTE

Pollo all y pebre
Peppered chicken

SERVES 4

- 1.5 kg/3½ lb free-range chicken, in bite-sized pieces, plus backbone
- 3 tbsp olive oil
- 6 garlic cloves, unpeeled but smashed
- 1 tbsp paprika
- salt and freshly ground black pepper
- 2 ñoras, or 1 cm/½ in pickled Mexican jalapeño pepper, seeded and chopped
- 1 dried guindilla *or other hot chilli, seeded and chopped*
- 350 ml/12 fl oz chicken stock, hot
- 20 strands saffron, crumbled and soaked in a little stock for 5 minutes
- freshly grated nutmeg
- 1 tsp lemon juice
- pinch of sugar

CONDIMENT

- 4 garlic cloves, unpeeled but smashed
- 50 g/2 oz almonds, toasted (see page 205)
- 1 tbsp pine nuts, toasted in a dry frying pan
- 2 tbsp chopped parsley

The 'garlic and pepper' of the title could just as easily be translated as 'brave and manly', for this red sauce can be very peppery. It was invented for the fat eels that used to swim in the Valencian rice paddies.

Heat the oil in a flameproof earthenware casserole with the garlic cloves until they colour, then discard them. Fry the garlic for the condiment and reserve. Season the chicken with paprika, salt and pepper and fry over a high heat (including the backbone) until coloured, then remove and reserve. Pour off all but 1 tbsp oil.

Add all the chopped chillies, stirring rapidly, then immediately add the hot stock, saffron and nutmeg. Boil for a couple of minutes, then return the chicken.

For the condiment, pound the garlic (discarding skins) with a little salt (or blend) to a paste with the nuts and parsley. Work in a little stock and add to the casserole. Cook gently for 15 minutes or so, then discard the backbone. Check the seasoning: it should be very piquant. A lack of Spanish peppers (which have a depth of flavour) can be balanced by adding the lemon juice and sugar. Plain rice makes the best accompaniment.

CATALONIA

Pechugas de pollo Villeroy

Chicken breasts in cream and crumb coating

~

Once French, this is now so well liked that Lhardy's in Madrid sells it ready-prepared, to cook at home. The sauce is also good for coating brochettes of mussels and other shellfish for grilling.

Make the sauce ahead: melt the butter, then stir in the flour and cook for 1 minute. Taste the stock and, off the heat, stir it in; simmer for 2–3 minutes, stirring gently. Add the milk, bring to simmering and then add nutmeg, salt and pepper to taste. Cool with a butter paper on the surface, then chill.

Coat the chicken breasts with the sauce using the back of a spoon, turn down on to a floured tray and dust lightly with flour. Then coat the chicken all over with beaten egg and breadcrumbs. Chill well.

Heat a generous quantity of olive oil in a wide pan. Fry the breasts for 10 minutes on each side, turning once, and serve with lemon wedges.

SERVES 4

- 4 boneless free-range chicken breast, without skin
- 3–4 tbsp plain flour, for coating
- 2 small eggs, beaten
- 8–10 tbsp stale breadcrumbs
- olive oil for frying
- 4 lemon wedges, to garnish

VILLEROY SAUCE

- 65 g/2 ¼ oz butter
- 50 g/2 oz plain flour
- 250 ml/8 fl oz good poultry stock (or fish stock, for shellfish), hot
- 250 ml/8 fl oz milk
- freshly grated nutmeg
- salt and ground white pepper

CATALONIA

Pollastre amb escamarlans o gambas

Chicken with scampi or prawns

~

SERVES 4

- 1.2–1.4 kg/2¾–3 lb free-range chicken
- 8 big scampi or 500 g/1 lb large raw prawns
- 5–6 tbsp olive oil
- 4 tbsp dry anis or liqueur, or Pernod
- 1 large onion, chopped
- salt and freshly ground black pepper
- 2 garlic cloves, finely chopped
- 500 g/1 lb ripe tomatoes, skinned, seeded and chopped
- 1 fresh bouquet garni of 2 thyme and 2 oregano sprigs, 1 bay leaf, 1 leek strip and bruised parsley stalks
- 150 ml/5 fl oz dry white wine (or dry oloroso sherry, but not with Pernod)
- about 100 ml/3½ fl oz chicken or fish stock, or water, if needed

CONDIMENT

- 2 garlic cloves, finely chopped
- 25 g/1 oz almonds, toasted (see page 205)
- 3 Marie (or Rich Tea) biscuits
- 2 tbsp finely chopped parsley

A delicious combination of delicate flavours. The dish needs raw shellfish to work, or 500 g/1 lb squid can be substituted.

Cut the chicken into bite-sized pieces, discarding unsightly skin and the worst bones. Heat 2 tbsp oil in a flameproof casserole and add the shellfish. Fry them over a medium heat for 4–5 minutes (or according to size). Move them to a warm dish. Warm the liqueur in a ladle, then flame it and spoon it over the shellfish until the flame dies. Reserve them (but don't put them in a warm oven!).

Add 3–4 more tbsp oil to the casserole and fry the onion and seasoned chicken over a medium-high heat. Move them fairly steadily so the onion doesn't catch, then add the garlic. When everything is coloured, add the tomato flesh and bouquet garni, and cook down to a sauce.

Add the wine, with a little stock or water if needed almost to cover the chicken. Cover and simmer for about 20 minutes.

For the condiment, pound the garlic cloves with a little salt (or blend), then work in the nuts and crumbled biscuits. Work in the parsley.

Discard the bouquet garni and stir the condiment paste into the sauce. Return the shellfish (peel them at this point if you feel you must) and their juices and warm through. Check the seasonings.

Note: It isn't orthodox, but one woman finished the dish with a little cream and cayenne, instead of the nuts and biscuits.

THE BALEARIC ISLANDS

Escaldums d'indiot o de pollastre

Turkey or chicken fricassée

~

Turkey fricassée takes on Spanish identity with a sauce of puréed nuts enriched with a little of the smooth local sausage. It is served with roast potatoes as a New Year dish in the islands.

Season the poultry pieces with salt, pepper and 1 tsp paprika. Heat the oil (and fat) in a wide flameproof casserole and fry them over a medium-high heat, in two batches, moving them around and removing when coloured.

Fry the onion and celery, adding the whole garlic cloves towards the end (these mellow with cooking). Add the chopped tomato flesh, bay leaf, oregano and ground cloves and cook gently to reduce the tomato to a sauce. Add the *amontillado* and stock, and return the poultry – it should just be covered. Simmer for 30 minutes. This can be done ahead, so flavours blend.

For the condiment, pound the nuts in a mortar (or blend), adding the *sobrasada*. This is a raw pork and paprika sausage, very soft and fatty, and it both thickens and enriches the final sauce. Add a little stock from the casserole and stir into the sauce. Taste for seasoning and simmer for 10 minutes. Serve sprinkled with a little parsley.

Note: As a substitute for the sausage, use a 50 g/2 oz smooth liver pâté (such as Brussels), worked to a paste with 1 tsp paprika and 1 tbsp melted butter.

SERVES 5–6

- 1.2 kg/2½ lb boneless turkey breast, or free-range chicken, in frying pieces
- salt and freshly ground black pepper
- 1 tsp paprika
- 3–4 tbsp olive oil (or half lard)
- 1 large Spanish onion, finely sliced
- 1 celery stalk, sliced
- 1 bulb of garlic, cloves smashed then peeled
- 350 g/12 oz ripe tomatoes, skinned, seeded and chopped
- 1 bay leaf
- 5 sprigs of fresh oregano, leafy tips
- 3 cloves, ground to powder, or a good pinch of ground cloves
- 75 ml/3 fl oz amontillado sherry
- 150 ml/5 fl oz poultry stock
- 2 tbsp chopped parsley, to garnish

CONDIMENT

- 25 g/1 oz pine nuts, toasted in a dry frying pan (or toasted almonds – see page 205)
- 2 slices of sobrasada sausage (see note)

Caracoles Lola
Snails with piquant sauce

SERVES 4

- 60 snails
- plain flour
- salt
- vinegar
- handful of fennel stalks or parsley stalks

SPICY TOMATO SAUCE

- 350 g/12 oz onions, chopped
- 3 tbsp olive oil
- ½ bulb garlic, finely chopped
- 1 leek, chopped
- 1 green pepper, seeded and chopped
- 500 g/1 lb ripe tomatoes or 400 g/14 oz canned tomatoes, chopped
- 3 guindilla *chillies* or *dried chillies, whole*
- 1 bay leaf
- freshly ground black pepper
- 1 tsp lemon juice
- 2 tbsp chopped parsley

Hunters, out with a gun and a dog, often collect snails in their knapsacks too. They are free food – and so a gift from God. Snails are deeply embedded in the Spanish psyche and are eaten in many regions, usually as a tapa or first course. This spicy tomato sauce is also used for tripe, and is excellent for heating cooked prawns.

Snails should be purged for a week in case they have eaten something toxic to humans. Shut them up in a box or bucket with a lid to prevent them walking away. Weight it – there is snail power! After 3 days feed them by sprinkling flour into the bucket.

The day before cooking moisten them by splashing a little fresh water into the bucket. The ones that climb up the sides are alive. Any motionless ones in the bottom are probably dead: discard them.

Clean the snails with salt and vinegar to get rid of the black spittle which they usually have. After half an hour, rinse them under fast-running water for several minutes, or wash them in several waters. When the black has all gone, drain them well.

For easy eating, they must be tricked into expiring with the maximum of body outside the shell. Put them into a pot with very lightly warmed water. Bring slowly to the boil and they seem to get caught unwares. Discard this water, which will be scummy.

Drain them and put again to boil in salted water with handfuls of herbs: wild fennel, or bruised parsley stalks will do. Cook for a good 30 minutes.

Make a tomato sauce in a big saucepan: fry the onions in the oil until soft. About halfway through, add the garlic, leek and green pepper. When the onions are ready, add the tomatoes and the whole chillies (seed and chop one if you really like things hot!). Add the bay leaf and a little salt. Cook gently for 10 minutes, then add a ladleful of stock from the snail pan and cook down to a sauce.

Sieve the sauce (or not, in which case the tomatoes must be skinned at the beginning, and the chillies and bay leaf removed): a blender produces the wrong consistency. Return to the saucepan, taste, add the lemon juice and correct the seasoning. If the sauce is not piquant enough, the chillies can be returned, and then removed before serving.

Add the snails and simmer for a further 30 minutes. Serve in individual casseroles, sprinkled with the parsley, and accompanied by bread.

Pato con aceitunas a la antigua

Duck with olives the old-fashioned way

SERVES 4

- 2 kg/4 lb duck, with its liver or 3 chicken livers (75 g/3 oz)
- 50 g/2 oz pork fat (back or belly) or bacon fat, cubed
- 1 tbsp olive oil
- 1 slice of stale bread
- salt and freshly ground black pepper
- 125 g/4 oz raw ham or gammon, cut into strips
- freshly grated nutmeg
- 24 green olives, stoned (200 g/7 oz jar)
- 1 bay leaf, crumbled
- 150 ml/5 fl oz red Rueda, or fino sherry
- 250 ml/8 fl oz stock, from the neck and giblets
- 1 tbsp chopped parsley

A sister recipe to duck with orange, this one is much older. But the olives serve the same function as bitter Seville orange juice: to cut the fat.

Sweat the fat cubes in the oil in a flameproof casserole, then remove. Fry the bread and cook the liver lightly, then reserve. Remove the wing tips from the duck. Cut off the excess neck skin, then use a little knife to remove the wishbone. Cut off the parson's nose, then the pad of fat on either side of the tail. Rinse and pat dry with kitchen paper. Prick all fatty pads and season inside and out.

Put the duck, breast down, in the casserole, then turn it, propping it against the side, so that it colours on all sides – 15–20 minutes. On the last turn, add the ham strips.

When the duck is golden, remove it and drain all the fat from the casserole. Quarter the duck and cut the backbone free. Sprinkle the meaty sides well with nutmeg. Return the duck, backbone, pork cubes and ham to the casserole and add the olives, bay leaf, Rueda or sherry and enough stock almost to cover. Cook over a gentle heat, covered, for about 45 minutes or until tender.

Pound (or blend) the liver and the bread with the parsley. Remove the backbone from the casserole and stir the liver mixture into the sauce to thicken it, seasoning as necessary with salt, pepper and nutmeg. Use a slotted spoon to move duck and garnish to a serving plate and pass the sauce in a sauce boat.

NEW CASTILE AND LA MANCHA

Perdices estofadas
Partridges in wine and vinegar

~

Spain's favourite bird is set off here by the wine and vinegar sauce. This type of dish is called an escabeche, *and was first introduced by the Arabs. The sauce can also be used to give character to a small chicken. Easy, successful – and also good cold.*

SERVES 6

- 3 partridges
- salt and freshly ground black pepper
- 3 tbsp olive oil
- 1 large mild Spanish onion, chopped
- 1 tender celery stalk, finely diced
- 3 garlic cloves, finely chopped
- 1 bay leaf
- 2 cloves
- 175 ml/6 fl oz dry white wine
- 4 tbsp sherry vinegar or red wine vinegar
- about 200 ml/7 fl oz chicken stock
- boiled potatoes (to serve hot)

Reach into the neck of each bird and run finger and thumb nails up the wishbone to the top and pull it out. Salt and pepper the birds inside and out. Choose a flameproof casserole into which they fit snugly. Heat the oil and fry the birds, turning them over and propping them against the sides of the pan, until they are coloured on all sides. Remove the birds and keep warm.

Fry the onion and celery in the same oil, adding the garlic when they soften. Return the birds. Add the bay leaf, cloves, wine, vinegar and sufficient stock to cover the legs. Simmer, covered, over a low heat until cooked – about 30 minutes.

Remove the birds to a hot serving platter. Strain the stock, pressing the solids through back into the casserole. Alternatively blend the solids, discarding the bay leaf. Skim the stock and add about half to the blender. Purée, then reheat in the casserole. Check the seasoning. The Spanish like their potatoes soggy and often reheat them in the sauce.

Divide the birds in half, surround with potatoes and pass the sauce in a sauce boat.

ASTURIAS AND CANTABRIA

Perdices con verduras

Partridges in wine with cabbage

~

SERVES 4

○ *2 plump partridges*

○ *100 g/4 oz raw or cooked ham and unsmoked bacon*

○ *freshly grated nutmeg*

○ *salt and freshly ground black pepper*

○ *about 2 tbsp melted ham or bacon fat (or more oil)*

○ *2 tbsp olive oil*

○ *2 onions, chopped*

○ *1 large carrot, diced then chopped*

○ *2 garlic cloves, finely chopped*

○ *2 tbsp chopped parsley*

○ *1 small green-hearted cabbage*

○ *1 fresh bouquet garni of 2 sprigs each of oregano and thyme, plus 1 bay leaf*

○ *about 300 ml/½ pt red wine*

○ *about 300 ml/½ pt good poultry stock*

Partridges are served with wedges of cabbage that imitate their shape. The wine in the sauce makes the vegetable slightly acidic, and so the perfect complement to rich game. The casserole is good newly made, and even better reheated.

Heat the oven to 200°C/400°F/Gas 6. Cube the ham or bacon, seasoning on the board with nutmeg. Tweak out the wishbones from the partridges, running finger and thumb up them, inside the neck skin. Salt and pepper inside and stuff the birds with the ham or bacon. Spread the birds well with fat and put them to roast until they are lightly golden, 15–20 minutes.

Choose a small flameproof casserole (of a size to take 4 partridges) and fry the onions and carrot in the oil until softened, adding the garlic and parsley towards the end. Cut the cabbage into quarters – each wedge should be bird-sized. Blanch the wedges in boiling salted water for 3–4 minutes and drain.

When the onion is soft, put the partridges and their juices into the casserole. Pair the cabbage wedges, curves outwards, and fit them between the birds. Add the bouquet garni. Pour in an equal amount of wine and stock, adding them alternately, until everything is well covered. Bring gently to simmering, cover and cook in the oven for 1–1½ hours.

Remove the cabbage wedges and split the birds. Discard the bouquet garni and sieve (or blend) the sauce, then reheat, check seasoning and serve in the casserole.

ARAGON AND NAVARRE

Pichones con pasas y piñones

Pigeons with raisins and pine nuts

~

Pigeons fly low over the massive Pyrenees and are trapped in nets in the valleys. I ate this rich dish in the hidden Vall d'Arán, which has a reputation for gourmet food.

Pour boiling water to cover over the raisins. Reach into the neck of each bird and run finger and thumb nails up the wishbone to the top; pull it out. Salt and pepper the birds inside and out. Choose a flameproof casserole into which they fit snugly. Heat the oil and spend 20–25 minutes browning the birds on all 3 sides. Remove and keep warm.

Add the chopped onions to the pot, and fry gently until soft, adding the garlic towards the end. Sprinkle with the flour and cook for 1 minute. Stir in the chopped tomatoes, parsley, wine, stock, brandy and bay leaf, and season with a little nutmeg.

Snug the birds back into the casserole and simmer until tender, about 1½ hours, though tough wild birds in Spain may need 2 hours. Keep an eye on the liquid level – spare liquid from the raisins can be used to top up the pan. Meanwhile dry-fry the pine nuts over a low heat in a frying pan for 2–3 minutes.

Remove the birds and sieve the sauce (or blend, first discarding the bay leaf). Return the birds and sauce to the pot, adding the drained raisins (seeded if necessary) and pine nuts. Simmer for 10 more minutes, then check the seasonings. Green cabbage is the best accompaniment.

Note: Made with 4 partridges, this serves 8.

SERVES 4

- 4 pigeons, cleaned
- 125 g/4 oz muscatel raisins, preferably from Malaga
- salt and freshly ground black pepper
- 4 tbsp olive oil
- 2 onions, chopped
- 3 garlic cloves
- 1 tbsp plain flour
- 2 ripe tomatoes, skinned, seeded and chopped (or 4 canned ones)
- 2 tbsp finely chopped parsley
- 200 ml/7 fl oz Cariñena or red Côte de Rhône
- 200 ml/7 fl oz good meat or poultry stock
- 4 tbsp Spanish brandy or cognac
- 1 bay leaf
- freshly grated nutmeg
- 50 g/2 oz pine nuts

ANDALUSIA

Conejo en ajillo pastor

Rabbit with aromatics and saffron

～

SERVES 4–5

- 2 wild rabbits, with kidneys and liver, or 1.3 kg/2½ lb farmed rabbit
- 2 large mild Spanish onions, chopped
- 7 tbsp olive oil
- 1 garlic clove, finely chopped
- 50 strands saffron
- 4 tbsp hot water
- salt and freshly ground black pepper
- 4 tbsp Spanish brandy or cognac
- 250 ml/8 fl oz white wine
- 15 black peppercorns, lightly crushed
- 6 sprigs of fresh thyme or ½ tsp dried thyme
- 1 bay leaf
- about 125 ml/4 fl oz cold water

Ampara Moreno in Coín gave me this recipe, which she learned from her mother. When I asked if it was written down, there was a smiling 'no': she cannot read.

Fry the onions slowly in 2 tbsp oil in a wide, deep pan until soft, then add the garlic. Meanwhile, wash the cleaned rabbit to remove any blood inside. Pat dry and split the front legs from the ribs. Cut free the flaps from the saddle. Cut the meaty back legs in half through the joint and halve the saddle with a heavy knife. Cut the thin pieces so they are flat.

Crumble the saffron stamens in your fingers and put to soak in the hot water for 5 minutes.

Remove the onion from the pan and add about 4 tbsp more oil (there should be enough to coat the bottom and just float the rabbit). Salt and pepper the rabbit and fry the meaty portions – back legs and saddles – for 10 minutes. Tuck in the remaining rib pieces and flaps (and the liver and kidneys later, if present) and fry for about another 10 minutes until everything is golden. Remove the pieces of meat and spoon off all the oil.

Add the brandy and wine and stir to deglaze the pan. Pack in the rabbit pieces neatly and return the onion. Add the saffron liquid and peppercorns, and tuck in the thyme and crumbled bay leaf. Add the cold water, almost to cover the meat. Put on the lid and simmer very gently for about 1 hour, until the rabbit is tender, making sure it does not get dry. Check the seasonings and serve from the pan.

ARAGON AND NAVARRE

Conejo con patatas
Rabbit stewed with potatoes

We climbed the Col de Leyre, which edges the Pyrenees, and slept on a thyme bank at the top. There were rabbits aplenty. How good they would be coooked with that, I thought.

Ahead, wash the cleaned rabbits free of any blood inside and soak in water and vinegar overnight. Pat dry and split the front legs from the ribs. Cut free the flaps from the saddle and cut all the thin end pieces into flat portions. Put all the pieces in a flat dish and sprinkle with brandy. Marinate for 2 hours or till ready to cook.

Heat the oil in a wide frying pan (there should be enough to float the rabbit, as it is wettish). Salt and pepper the rabbit and fry the back legs and saddles until golden on all sides – 15–20 minutes. Remove from the pan to an earthenware casserole and heat the oven to 180°C/350°F/Gas 4. Fry the remaining rabbit pieces more briefly and add to the casserole with any remaining marinade. Tuck in the thyme and break up the bay leaf and add.

Fry the onions slowly in the frying pan until soft, then add the chopped garlic. Add the tomatoes, breaking them up, with the wine. Bring gently to the boil and pour over the rabbit. Cook in the oven for about 1 hour until it is approaching tender.

Cut the potatoes into chip shapes and add to the casserole, distributing them, and pushing them under the sauce. Return to the oven to cook for another 30 minutes or longer until the potatoes are tender. Covering helps if the liquid is low.

SERVES 6

- *2 wild rabbits, about 800 g/ 2 lb 10 oz each*
- *250 ml/8 fl oz water*
- *2 tbsp wine vinegar*
- *4 tbsp Spanish brandy or cognac*
- *6 tbsp olive oil*
- *salt and freshly ground black pepper*
- *2 sprigs of fresh thyme*
- *1 bay leaf*
- *500 g/1 lb onions, thinly, sliced*
- *2 fat garlic cloves, finely chopped*
- *400 g/14 oz canned tomatoes*
- *250 ml/8 fl oz red wine*
- *600 g/1¼ lb potatoes*

Liebre guisada
Hare in red wine

<hr/>

SERVES 6

- *1 hare, 1.5 kg/3½ lb after cleaning*
- *100–200 g/4–7 oz streaky pork belly, fresh or salt, such as Italian pancetta*
- *4 tbsp olive oil*
- *6–8 tbsp plain flour*
- *1 onion, finely chopped*
- *1 celery stalk, finely chopped*
- *salt and freshly ground black pepper*

MARINADE

- *6 parsley stalks, bruised*
- *2 sprigs of fresh thyme*
- *1 bay leaf*
- *1 inner celery stalk with leaves*
- *1 cinnamon stick*
- *6 black peppercorns, roughly chopped*
- *1 tbsp olive oil*
- *75 cl bottle of red wine*

CONDIMENT

- *3 garlic cloves, smashed*
- *¼ tsp salt*
- *25 g/1 oz almonds, toasted (see page 205)*
- *25 g/1 oz pine nuts*
- *2 tbsp Spanish brandy or cognac*
- *2 tbsp fino sherry*

A rich dish, and so associated with parties. In Salamanca, in neighbouring Castile, a similar dish is nicknamed liebre pregonoas, 'the announcement hare', because it is often served at engagement parties, when the young couple announce their intention to wed.

The dish below originally cooked with hot charcoal on top of a heavy iron lid. At the end of the cooking the sauce was thickened with some of the hare's blood. When I explained blood was a problem here, I was given the tip to replace this with a small glass of mixed brandy and sherry.

Two or three days ahead, rinse and dry the hare well. Cut it into serving portions, severing the flaps and taking the ribs off the front legs. Put it in an earthenware casserole – of the kind that can be used for cooking. Make a bouquet garni with the herbs, celery and cinnamon and add this and the peppercorns (but no salt, because this would make the meat tough.) Add 1 tbsp of oil and the pork belly and pour in the wine to cover. Leave this for 2–3 days, covered.

Take the hare and pork out, blotting them well with kitchen paper. Cube the pork. Heat the oil in a frying pan and, just before putting the meat in the pan, sprinkle with flour. Brown the meat on all sides and return to the empty casserole, packing it tightly.

Fry the onion and celery in the fat remaining in the pan and add to the casserole. Pour the marinade and bouquet garni over the hare pieces. Cover and bring to simmering (I started with the oven at 170°C/325°F/Gas 3, turning it down after 30 minutes). Cook the hare at 140°C/275°F/Gas 1, barely simmering, for about 2½ hours.

The condiment will also thicken the sauce. Briefly dry fry the pine nuts in a frying pan over a low heat for 2–3 minutes. Purée the garlic with the salt in a mortar (or small blender) and add the toasted almonds and pine nuts. Reduce to a paste and dilute with the brandy and sherry. Check the amount of sauce (remove the hare and boil if necessary). Stir the paste into the sauce and simmer briefly to thicken. Check the seasoning, and serve from the casserole. Serve with boiled potatoes.

Note: Another traditional gravy ingredient, replacing blood, is chocolate – 15 g/½ oz is needed here. The Spanish introduced it to Europe from America with the Mexican idea attached, of using it as a sauce thickener and seasoner. Chocolate is not, of course, naturally sweet.

CHAPTER SEVEN

Meat

Arròs amb forn

Oven rice with pork and tomato

~

SERVES 4

- 4 pork belly ribs, cut with the meat
- salt and freshly ground black pepper
- 1½–2 tbsp paprika
- 6 tbsp olive oil
- 8 thickish rounds of potato
- 350 g/12 oz morcilla or black pudding
- 1 whole bulb of garlic, loose skin removed
- 200 ml/7 fl oz fino sherry
- 1 litre/1¾ pt good stock (taste before use)
- 1 tsp best Manchego saffron strands
- 1 large onion, chopped
- 1 garlic clove, finely chopped
- 4–6 fat tomatoes
- 400 g/14 oz paella or risotto rice

You won't find this recipe in any book, but it is the forerunner of paella – and much easier to make, for it is made in a flat casserole in the oven. It never contains fish, but it is made with pork, except in Lent, when it features garlic!

Rub the pork ribs well with salt, pepper and some of the paprika. Heat 2 tbsp of oil in a large pan and fry the potato rounds and meat until golden on all sides. Sausages and potatoes will take about 25 minutes, ribs and black pudding (in 4 chunks) about 15 minutes.

Heat the oven to 180°C/350°F/Gas 4 with the garlic bulb in it. Warm the sherry with the stock, and put the crumbled saffron to soak in 4 tbsp hot stock for 5 minutes or so.

Meanwhile, heat 3 tbsp of oil in a saucepan and soften the onion, adding the chopped garlic towards the end. Cut 4 tomatoes in half across the middle, taking a good slice off each side. Dice the ends and the other tomatoes, add them to the saucepan and cook gently to a sauce. Add 1 tbsp paprika plus the saffron and its liquid.

Rinse the rice in a colander, stir it into the sauce and heat gently. Turn into a wide flat earthenware casserole and spread it out, seasoning generously. Bed the pork and black pudding or sausages down into the rice, slicing them when in position. Press the potato and tomato slices into the spaces and put the garlic bulb in the middle, opening it out a bit. Pour in the stock and put the dish into the oven for 30 minutes.

When the rice is tender, cover the pan with foil, turn off the oven and leave, with the door open, for 10 minutes, so the rice can absorb the last drop of moisture.

To serve, give everyone their share of pork, sausage, tomato and potato, then stir the rice before spooning it out. If you like garlic, mash a cooked clove or two into the rice as you eat.

EXTREMADURA

Costillas con níscalos
Pork ribs with wild mushrooms

The pig's ribs are often eaten the day it is killed, either baked with cinnamon, black pepper and salt or, as here, in sauce. Crude food, it is the kind enjoyed by men and boys. Níscalos (saffron milkcaps; see page 78) are in season in late November. I think them overrated and that brown mushrooms have the better flavour.

Rub the ribs well with salt and pepper. Heat the oil in a big frying pan and fry them until browned. Pack them into a flameproof casserole and add the cinnamon stick, chilli, wine and water to cover. Simmer gently for 20–30 minutes until tender.

In the oil remaining in the frying pan, fry the onion slowly until soft, adding the garlic towards the end. Sprinkle with the paprika and flour. Stir and then add the mushrooms. Cook gently.

When the ribs are tender, add a ladleful or so of their liquid to the frying pan and stir until thickened. Bed the ribs down into the frying pan, adding as much of their cooking liquid as needed to make a sauce. Cover the frying pan and simmer 5 minutes more: it will wait without harm. This is a messy finger-and-bread dish, so serviettes are needed.

SERVES 4

- 1 kg/2 lb meaty pork belly ribs
- salt and freshly ground black pepper
- 2 tbsp olive oil
- 1 cinnamon stick
- ½ dried chilli pepper, seeded and chopped
- 150 ml/5 fl oz red wine
- about 250 ml/8 fl oz water
- 1 onion, chopped
- 1 fat garlic clove, finely chopped
- 1 tsp paprika
- 1 tbsp plain flour
- 350 g/12 oz níscalos or brown mushrooms, cleaned and thickly sliced

Calderillo bejarano

Potato, green pepper and rib stew

SERVES 8 OR MORE

- 6 pork ribs, cut through the belly
- 2 kg/4 lb potatoes
- 500 g/1 lb green peppers, seeded and chopped
- 4 tbsp olive oil
- 2 Spanish onions, chopped
- salt and freshly ground black pepper
- ½ tsp paprika
- 4 garlic cloves, peeled
- 6 tbsp chopped parsley
- 2 tbsp white wine
- pinch of cayenne pepper
- 2 bay leaves
- 800 ml/1 pt 7 fl oz water
- 6 tbsp (or to taste) virgin olive oil, if eating cold

A filling potato pot from the snow-covered Sierra de Bejar in the west, the recipe was made with veal ribs (unobtainable elsewhere) in a copper pot, and it is normally eaten hot. It also makes one of the nicer potato salads, before barbecued sardines.

Heat 2 tbsp of oil in a wide flameproof casserole and fry the onions over low heat. When they begin to soften, push them to the sides and add 2 more tbsp of oil. Put in the ribs, well seasoned with salt, pepper and paprika. Turn up the heat a little and fry them, stirring occasionally to make sure the onion doesn't catch. Add the chopped peppers as the ribs are browned.

Pound the garlic with the parsley (or blend), adding the wine. Add this paste, plus any remaining paprika and a little cayenne, to the casserole with the bay leaves and water. Let this simmer while you peel and dice the potatoes.

Add the potatoes to the casserole with a little extra water if absolutely necessary to cover. Simmer for 30 minutes, or until the potatoes are ready. (If there seems to be too much liquid, ladle out, boil to reduce and return.) Season with salt, turn the stew over gently and serve hot with the ribs on top.

To serve cold, shred the meat, discarding the bones. Check the seasonings again and dress with a little virgin oil.

Castañas con berza

Chestnut, cabbage and sausage pie

~

A simple country dish of the kind I like best. The sausages in Galicia had a touch of anis, so I have included this as the alcohol ration.

Slightly undercook the chestnuts, boiling them for about 15 minutes, then peel, removing all the skin. Meanwhile, oil an earthenware dish and put it to heat with the oven at 170°C/325°F/Gas 3.

Wash the good outer cabbage leaves, about a dozen of them, and cut out the hard end in a V. Blanch the leaves briefly in boiling water, drain and run cold water over them. Cut up the cabbage heart roughly and cook for 5 minutes. Drain well, then turn on to a board and chop.

Slice the sausages and give them a brief turn in hot oil in a frying pan – which gives a chance to judge their seasoning.

Spread the chopped cabbage in the earthenware dish, then top with the sausages and chestnuts. Season well, sprinkling with the paprika if not using *chorizo*. Cover with the cabbage leaves and press down gently. Heat the stock and anis in the frying pan and throw over the top (which glazes the cabbage). Bake for about 1 hour.

SERVES 4

- 1 kg/2 lb chestnuts
- 2 tbsp oil or lard
- 1 small green-hearted cabbage, about 700 g/1½ lb
- 600 g/1¼ lb chorizos, paprika sausage or fresh garlic sausage
- salt and freshly ground black pepper
- 1 tbsp paprika (if using garlic sausage)
- 150 ml/5 fl oz stock
- 2 tbsp anis liqueur

Callos con garbanzos y costillas
Tripe with chick peas and pork ribs

SERVES 4

- 400 g/14 oz chick peas, soaked overnight
- 3 pork belly ribs, with meat, chopped by the butcher into squares
- 150 g/5 oz raw ham or smoked gammon, cubed
- 500–700 g/1–1½ lb tripe, par-cooked (see note)
- 175 ml/6 fl oz white wine
- 100 g/4 oz chorizo, or any smoked paprika sausage such as kabanos, sliced
- 1 tbsp lard or oil
- 1 tsp paprika
- pinch of freshly grated nutmeg
- pinch of ground cloves
- salt and freshly ground black pepper

Tripe, callos a la gallega, *is popular on Sundays in Galician taverns. Here is an intelligent modern version of the recipe. Nutty chick peas contrast perfectly with the meat and the smooth, creamy texture of tripe. The tripe almost disappears – an angel passing! Pork ribs replace the traditional calf's foot; buy meaty ones, cut through the belly, not spare ribs.*

Put the drained chick peas in a pot with the ribs and ham and just cover with cold water. Bring to simmering, then skim off the scum. Add the whole onions and bulbs of garlic. As soon as these are cooked – about 20 minutes – remove and reserve them.

Add the tripe and continue to cook over a very low heat, or in a low oven (150°C/300°F/Gas 2), until the meat falls from the rib bones and the chick peas are tender, 2–2½ hours longer. Check occasionally that the chick peas are not drying out and add the wine about three-quarters of the way through, when you can judge liquid levels – the final dish should not be too sloppy.

For the condiment, crush the cumin and *guindilla* in a mortar. Peel the cooked garlic and mash in the mortar (or blend everything), adding the onions in pieces. Reduce to a paste with the parsley and toasted bread, adding liquid from the pot as needed.

Fry the sausage in lard or oil. Add the sausage with its juices and the condiment to the pot. Taste and season, adding the paprika, cayenne (if using), nutmeg, cloves, salt and pepper; the spicing should be quite discreet or it will distract attention from the texture. Cook it all together for 30 minutes before sending it to the table. The dish reheats well, and we ate it from individual casseroles, heated in the oven from a big family stewing pot.

Note: The recipe as given to me started: first wash the tripe well, both in cold water and in warm water. Rub it with lemon juice and vinegar. Cut it into bite-sized pieces and put in a pot with cold water. When it boils, throw away the water and start again, simmering (usually with calf's foot) until tender. However, because tripe is more often sold par-cooked, I have started at a suitable point. Check cooking times when you buy it.

CONDIMENT

- 3 small onions, peeled (250 g/8 oz)
- 2 bulbs of garlic
- 12 cumin seeds
- 1–2 dried guindilla chillies, seeded and chopped or a good pinch of cayenne pepper
- 2 tbsp chopped parsley
- 1 slice of stale bread, crusts removed, toasted

EXTREMADURA

Prueba de cerdo

Fried pork with paprika and vinegar

~

The dish that 'tests' the meat of a newly killed pig. My guess is that the vinegar was once the lees of wine. This simple dish becomes an elegant one when made with two whole pork fillets or tenderloins, cut into rounds.

Season the pork with paprika, salt and black pepper. Heat the oil in a flameproof casserole on your hottest burner. Put in the pork in handfuls, turning it and keeping it moving with a wooden spoon, adding more when it is sealed. Add the onion, garlic, *guindilla* or cayenne, thyme and bay leaf and fry, stirring every now and then as the onion softens.

Add half the water and 2 tbsp vinegar. Cook until this is gone, then add more water and vinegar. When the liquid has reduced to a couple of spoonfuls of sauce, sprinkle with the parsley and serve.

SERVES 4

- 800 g/1¾ lb boneless pork, diced
- 2 tsp paprika, preferably from Jarandilla
- salt and freshly ground black pepper
- 4 tbsp olive oil
- 1 onion, chopped
- 3 garlic cloves, finely chopped
- 1–2 guindilla chillies, seeded and chopped, or a pinch of cayenne pepper
- 4–5 sprigs of fresh thyme
- 1 bay leaf
- 175 ml/6 fl oz hot water
- 4 tbsp red wine vinegar
- 2 tbsp chopped parsley

Lomo de cerdo con castañas

Roast pork with chestnuts and cognac

SERVES 6

*The ideal winter roast – easy to do, but with a rich sauce and
satisfyingly crunchy garnish.*

- ○ *1 kg/2 lb boned pork loin
  (6-chop loin, skinned and
  tied)*
- ○ *salt and freshly ground black
  pepper*
- ○ *2 garlic cloves, smashed and
  peeled*
- ○ *1 bay leaf, crumbled*
- ○ *50 ml/2 fl oz fino sherry*
- ○ *2 tbsp lard or olive oil*
- ○ *50 ml/2 fl oz Spanish brandy
  or cognac*
- ○ *750 g/1½ lb peeled, cooked
  chestnuts (see page 51)*
- ○ *2 tsp paprika*

A few hours ahead, rub the pork with salt and pepper and put
it in a crock (or better, a plastic bag) to marinate with the
garlic, bay leaf and sherry. Turn once.

Heat the oven to 200°C/400°F/Gas 6. Spread the pork
with lard, or rub with oil, and put it in an earthenware dish
with the marinade juices. Add ½ glass of water. Roast for 1½
hours, keeping an eye on the juices so they don't burn.

Fifteen minutes before the end, baste with the brandy, and
again after 10 minutes. Remove the meat and leave to rest for
10 minutes before carving. Meanwhile, add the chestnuts to
the dish, sprinkle with the paprika and toss in the juices. Carve
the meat thinly and serve with the juices, surrounded by the
chestnuts.

OLD CASTILE AND RIOJA

Jamón asado con pasas
Roast pork with red wine and raisin sauce

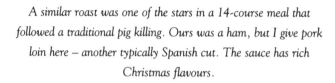

A similar roast was one of the stars in a 14-course meal that followed a traditional pig killing. Ours was a ham, but I give pork loin here – another typically Spanish cut. The sauce has rich Christmas flavours.

A day ahead, rub salt and pepper into the pork and marinate it with the garlic, bay leaf and wine (a plastic bag is easiest). Turn the meat over once.

Heat the oven to 200°C/400°F/Gas 6. Stand the joint on a rack in a small roasting tin. Add the garlic and bay leaf from the marinade to the tin and pour in a glass of water. Roast for 1½ hours, keeping an eye on the juices so they don't burn. Add the marinade after 1 hour and baste twice. Leave the joint to rest for 10 minutes.

Meanwhile, make the sauce. Cook the raisins (seeded if you wish) and prunes with the red wine, sugar, orange zest, nutmeg and cloves until they are well plumped – 20–30 minutes. The wine should reduce well at this point.

Turn into the roasting tin and stir to deglaze. Discard the garlic and zest and add the candied orange peel and orange juice. Mix the cornflour with the lemon juice and a little of the hot sauce, and stir back into the sauce to cook this. Taste and add salt and pepper (and more lemon) if needed. The trick is to balance the sweet and sour with salt and pepper – but don't overdo any of them.

Carve the joint thinly and pass the wine and raisin sauce separately in a jug.

SERVES 6

- 900 g/1 lb 14 oz eye of pork loin (6/7-chop loin, boned, skinned and flaps removed)
- salt and freshly ground black pepper
- 2 garlic cloves, smashed and peeled
- 1 bay leaf, crumbled
- 100 ml/3½ fl oz red or white wine

RED WINE AND RAISIN SAUCE

- 75 g/3 oz muscatel raisins, preferably from Malaga
- 8–10 prunes
- 250 ml/8 fl oz red wine
- 2 tbsp sugar
- zest of 1 orange, pared in a spiral, plus juice
- pinch of freshly grated nutmeg
- pinch of ground cloves
- 1½ tbsp chopped candied orange peel
- 2 tsp cornflour
- 1 tbsp lemon juice

Menestra de ternera
Veal with new vegetables

SERVES 6

Stews are a favourite form of food in Spain, even in the heat.
Use fresh peas if you can, or fewer frozen ones if you can't.
The potatoes can be included, or served as an accompaniment.

- 1.5 kg/3 lb boneless pink veal, cubed
- 4–6 tbsp plain flour
- salt and freshly ground black pepper
- 4–6 tbsp olive oil
- 2 onions, chopped
- 2 garlic cloves, finely chopped
- 1 tsp paprika
- 175 ml/6 fl oz white wine
- 300 ml/½ pt meat stock (or more)
- 500 g/1lb chard (or 250 g/ 8 oz spinach or lettuce)
- 250 g/8 oz tiny new potatoes
- 300 g/10 oz fresh shelled peas (or 150 g/5 oz frozen peas)
- 250 g/8 oz fresh broad beans (or frozen)
- 2 large carrots, sliced
- 4 small globe artichokes, halved or 2 artichoke bases (see page 164)
- 1 leek, sliced
- 2 tbsp chopped parsley
- ½ lemon

Heat the oven to 170°C/325°F/Gas 3. Coat the meat with seasoned flour. Heat the oil in a frying pan and fry the meat in batches, then remove to a large earthenware casserole. Fry the chopped onions in the frying pan, adding the garlic near the end. Sprinkle in 2 tbsp flour and cook, stirring, until darkened. Add the paprika, a little salt and pepper and, stirring slowly, the white wine and stock. Pour over the meat in the casserole and cook, covered, for 1 hour. (It can also be cooked, covered, on the top of the cooker.)

Meanwhile prepare and cook the vegetables. Remove the stalks from the chard and cut them into lengths (like celery). Tear up the leaves. Bring a large pot of water to the boil and add the potatoes, fresh peas and beans, carrots, halved artichokes and chard stalks. Small potatoes and summer peas can take up to 15 minutes, though 10 minutes is average, so judge the cooking sequence by size. In a second pan of boiling water cook the leek and chard leaves for 5 minutes. If using spinach or lettuce, simply pour boiling water over it, then drain.

Drain all the vegetables and add to the meat with parsley and a couple of ladlefuls of vegetable water (or stock) as needed. Check the seasoning and give the dish 10 more minutes' cooking.

To lift the flavour, grate a good pinchful of lemon zest on your smallest grater and stir it in with the juice of the lemon half. Do not boil after this, to keep the savour of fresh lemon oil.

OLD CASTILE AND RIOJA

Carne con chocolate
Beef stew with chocolate

~

Another rich, all-meat recipe, the chocolate gives the sauce gloss and thickness. Of course it's not sweet! The recipe comes from Guadalajara and the cook who gave it to me said it was the way her mother used to cook quails.

SERVES 4

- *1 kg/2 lb braising beef, cut into short fingers*
- *about 6 tbsp olive oil*
- *2 onions, chopped*
- *3 garlic cloves, finely chopped*
- *2–3 tbsp plain flour*
- *1 tsp paprika*
- *salt and freshly ground black pepper*
- *2 big carrots, cut into short sticks*
- *1 bay leaf*
- *175 ml/6 fl oz red wine*
- *150–175 ml/5–6 fl oz meat stock*
- *25 g/1 oz dark chocolate, in pieces*
- *1–3 tsp vinegar*

Heat 2 tbsp of the oil in a casserole and fry the onions until soft, adding the garlic towards the end. Season the flour with paprika, salt and pepper and lightly coat the beef. (Putting it in a bag and shaking, in two batches, is the easiest way. This controls the amount of flour in the sauce.)

For speed heat more oil in a frying pan and fry the beef, in two batches, until well coloured. Transfer to the casserole. Add the carrots and bay leaf and pour in the wine and enough stock to cover. Put on the lid and simmer for 40 minutes. The sauce should just clothe the meat. If there seems to be too much, remove some, boil to reduce it and then return to the casserole. Add the chocolate and stir until melted. Add the vinegar to taste (stirring it in well): the amount will depend on the wine used and the brand of chocolate. Check the seasoning. Simple boiled potatoes go well with the rich sauce.

Redondo de ternera mechada
Pot-roast beef larded with ham

~

SERVES 6

- ○ *1.3 kg/2½ lb beef rump in a long shape, tied*
- ○ *100 g/4 oz ham fat or pork back fat*
- ○ *4 garlic cloves, cut in slivers*
- ○ *200 g/7 oz jar or can pimiento-stuffed olives*
- ○ *salt and freshly ground black pepper*
- ○ *4 tbsp olive oil*
- ○ *2 big ripe tomatoes, skinned, seeded and chopped*
- ○ *freshly grated nutmeg*
- ○ *1 bay leaf*
- ○ *125 ml/4 fl oz good meat stock*
- ○ *400 g/14 oz green beans, in short lengths, to serve*

MARINADE

- ○ *good olive oil*
- ○ *2 onions, chopped*
- ○ *2 garlic cloves, finely chopped*
- ○ *125 ml/4 fl oz dry white wine*
- ○ *125 ml/4 fl oz Spanish brandy or cognac*

Watching the layer of fat being carved from the outside of an exquisite Jabugo serrano ham, I commented on the enormous cost of something that was to be discarded. 'Oh, we keep it all, to lard Mama's pot-roast beef,' was the response. Now I save the fat from Christmas hams – brown-sugared and clove-scented – for this, and own a larding needle. But I give the recipe by the hand method as I first tried it. It sounds tricky but was fun to do. It is a very Spanish thing to cook beef in a liquid. Only young animals are roasted.

A day ahead, cut the fat into thin strips, each about 4 cm/ 1½ in long. Lay them in a metal tray and freeze until stiff. Working on one cut end, jab a thin knife blade into the beef, a finger's width from the meat edge (and parallel to it). Go halfway through. Then jam in the handle of a wooden spoon.

Push in a sliver of garlic, then a stiff strip of fat, then another garlic sliver. Work round the outside – I repeat the holes nearer the middle, pushing in olives. Then more fat in the centre. Repeat at the other end of the beef. Allow time, as this is fiddly.

Rub the beef all over with plenty of black pepper and olive oil. Put it in a small deep bowl with the marinade ingredients and leave for 24 hours, turning.

Heat the oven to 150°C/300°F/Gas 2. Dry the beef with kitchen paper and salt lightly. Heat the oil in a small flame-proof casserole and turn the meat until browned on all sides. Add the drained onions from the marinade and fry until soft-ened. Add the chopped tomatoes, a good sprinkling of nutmeg, bay leaf, half the marinade juices and the stock. Cover and cook in the oven until tender, about 2½ hours. Check occasionally that the liquid is just barely simmering and turn the beef over halfway through.

Remove the beef from the casserole and leave to rest for 10–20 minutes. Meanwhile, discard the bay leaf and purée the remaining solids. Skim the pan juices, add half to the purée and season the sauce.

Cook, drain and season the green beans. Carve the beef and arrange overlapping slices on a hot platter. Garnish with the beans and pour a little sauce over the meat. Heat the remaining marinade juices and add to the rest of the sauce; pass in a sauce boat.

THE BASQUE COUNTRY

SERVES 4

Solomillo con salsa de berros
Steak with watercress sauce

Steaks in the Basque country are enormous, well-hung and well-grilled. Cream sauces are popular: Roquefort (see page 137) and this one, with peppery watercress.

- ○ *4 rump steaks or entrecôtes*
- ○ *40 g/1½ oz butter*
- ○ *salt and freshly ground black pepper*
- ○ *4 tbsp Spanish brandy or armagnac*

WATERCRESS SAUCE

- ○ *15 g/½ oz butter*
- ○ *2 shallots, finely chopped*
- ○ *150 ml/5 fl oz white wine or 100 ml/3½ fl oz dry white vermouth*
- ○ *300 ml/½ pt meat juice or well-reduced meat stock*
- ○ *bunch of watercress, picked over and chopped*
- ○ *125 ml/4 fl oz thick cream*

Make the sauce first. Melt the butter in a saucepan and cook the shallots. When soft, add the wine, meat stock and water-cress and boil to reduce by half. Purée (in a blender), then add the cream and reduce again. Add salt to taste.

Heat the butter and fry the well-seasoned steaks to your taste. Pour the brandy over and flame it, scooping the juices back over the steaks. Serve at once, with the sauce.

ARAGON AND NAVARRE

Cochifrito
Fried lamb with lemon juice

SERVES 4

- 800 g/ 1¾ lb very well-trimmed, tender lamb, in strips
- salt and freshly ground black pepper
- 2 tbsp olive oil
- 1 onion, chopped
- 2 garlic cloves, finely chopped
- 2 tsp paprika
- 250 ml/9 fl oz stock or water
- juice of 1 lemon
- finely chopped parsley

One of the easiest of meat dishes, it a classic in the uplands of Navarre and round Soria. I believe the name means 'our little one, fried'. Similar recipes are made by frying pork with seasoning and a little acid, such as vinegar (see prueba de cerdo, page 189). In Extremadura these pig versions are often called cuchifrito – 'cuchi-cuchi' is a common way there of summoning small pigs to the feeding bucket.

Season the lamb strips with black pepper and salt. Heat the oil in a casserole on the hottest burner and add the meat in handfuls. Add the onion too and keep pushing the meat around with a wooden spoon. Add more as each batch is sealed. Add the garlic, with more oil if necessary.

When the meat is golden and the onion soft, sprinkle with paprika and add the stock or water. Continue over medium heat until the liquid has virtually gone. Sprinkle with the lemon juice and parsley, cover and simmer for 5 minutes. Check the seasonings.

MADRID

Chuletas de cordero con pimientos asados

Lamb cutlets with soft red peppers

~

*Lamb is the festive choice in Spain and the cutlets are
often very small and numerous. These have a simple
garnish of sweet red pepper.*

SERVES 4

- 12 best-end lamb cutlets,
  50 g/2 oz each, the bones
  cleaned of fat down to the
  eye of meat
- 4 red peppers
- paprika
- salt and freshly ground black
  pepper
- 2–4 tsp olive oil

Grill the peppers for about 20 minutes, giving them a quarter turn every 5 minutes, until they are charred on all sides. Put them in a plastic bag for 10 minutes, then strip off the charred skins and pull out the stalks and seeds. (Do this on a plate to catch all the sweet juices.) Open the peppers to remove the last seeds and cut them into strips. Save them in a saucepan with their juices.

Rub the cutlets with paprika, salt and black pepper. Brush lightly with oil and grill them for 3–4 minutes on each side. Arrange them with the bones overlapping in threes on a big serving plate. Reheat the pepper strips in their liquid, with a little oil if needed, and garnish the dish.

Note: This is very popular grilled *al sarmiento*, over vine prunings. These give an intense heat, very different from the charcoal normally used for barbecuing and for *paella*.

Caldereta extremeña

Extremaduran stewed lamb

When Spaniards splurge they do it thoroughly. This rich stew – from a poor country district – is almost pure meat, so portions are quite small. Watercress grows abundantly in all the local streams and makes a good side salad.

SERVES 4

- 700 g/1½ lb boneless young lamb, in large cubes
- 200 g/7 oz lamb's liver, in 2 slices
- 2–3 tbsp olive oil
- 6 garlic cloves, unpeeled but smashed
- 2 tbsp lard (or more oil)
- salt and freshly ground black pepper
- 1 onion, finely sliced
- 1 dried guindilla chilli, seeded and chopped, or a big pinch of cayenne pepper
- 1 bay leaf
- 2 sprigs of fresh thyme
- 1 tbsp paprika, best from La Vera
- 200 ml/7 fl oz pitarra wine or Beaujolais Villages
- 175 ml/6 fl oz meat stock, warmed
- 6 black peppercorns
- 1 big red pepper, grilled and skinned (see page 197) or canned pimiento
- 1 tbsp vinegar

Heat the oil in a small flameproof casserole and fry the whole garlic cloves, then reserve them. Fry the liver quickly until stiffened, then reserve it.

Add the lard and the lamb, seasoned with salt and pepper, the onion, *guindilla* or cayenne, bay leaf, thyme and paprika. Fry until the lamb is golden all over, stirring every now and then. Add the wine and, as soon as it reaches boiling, a little warm stock. As this reduces add more stock, in 2–3 stages, letting it boil down to a sauce – about an hour.

Meanwhile slip the skins off the garlic cloves and pound them with the black peppercorns (or use a blender), working in the chopped liver and red pepper. When reduced to a paste, thin it with the vinegar. Add this to the lamb and simmer for 10 minutes. Remove the thyme and bay leaf and serve.

ARAGON AND NAVARRE

Chilindrón de cordero

Lamb stewed with peppers

Named after a card game, this dish has a long and famous history
in Navarre, and is about what peppers – the queen of hearts – will
do for lamb. Old recipes use only dried choricero peppers. 'No
tomato,' I was told. 'This is a stew of lamb and peppers – about
two dried peppers each. Extract the pulp after soaking them. And
no water. There's lots of onion and this gives all the liquid needed.'
I love these spare recipes with tightly balanced seasoning.
Impossible, though, to get the right dried peppers outside
Spain, so I have used fresh ones.

Heat 2 tbsp of oil in a flameproof casserole and fry the seasoned
lamb, in two batches, over a high heat until browned on all
sides, then remove from the pan.

Fry the onions, adding more oil if needed, adding the garlic
at the end. Chop the tomatoes and red peppers finely (or
process), then add to the pan with the parsley, bay leaf and
cayenne. Cook for a few minutes to make a sauce, then season
and return the lamb. Simmer for 1 hour, covered, over a very
low heat. It makes its own liquid, but check occasionally that
the heat is low enough.

Taste for seasoning, thinking particularly about pepper and
cayenne: it should be just spicy. Surprisingly, you may even
have to boil off a little liquid – it's pure lamb essence.

Note: Also good made with chicken. Diced raw ham (or bacon) –
about 100 g/4 oz – is usually included with it.

SERVES 4–5

- 1.5 kg/3 lb boneless shoulder of lamb, cubed
- 2–4 tbsp olive oil
- salt and freshly ground black pepper
- 2 onions, chopped
- 2 garlic cloves, finely chopped
- 4–6 big ripe tomatoes, skinned and seeded
- 2 big red peppers, grilled and skinned (see page 197), or canned pimientos
- 2 tbsp finely chopped parsley
- 1 bay leaf
- good pinch of cayenne pepper

CHAPTER EIGHT

Sweets
and Drinks

ANDALUSIA

Pestiños

Fritters in honey syrup

Sweet fritters date from Arab frying pans and are associated with festivals. Nowadays they are often made and sold by nuns. These ones are shaped like tubes, and I was told they were once fried round pieces of bamboo.

MAKES ABOUT 18

- 2 tbsp sunflower oil
- thinly pared zest of 1 lemon
- ½ tsp aniseeds, crushed
- 25 g/1 oz butter
- 75 ml/3 fl oz white wine like Diamante (not too dry), moscatel or amontillado sherry
- 175 g/6 oz plain flour, plus extra for rolling
- ¼ tsp salt
- 100 g/4 oz thick orange-flower honey
- 4 tbsp water
- sunflower oil for deep frying
- sugar for sprinkling

Flavour the sunflower oil by heating it in a small pan with the strip of zest until the latter browns. Discard the zest then, off the heat, add the aniseeds to toast them followed by the butter and wine.

Immediately add the flour and salt and beat them in to make a smooth dough. Turn on to a floured surface and knead briefly. Rest the dough briefly.

Make the syrup by melting the honey with the water. Heat the clean oil for frying in a deep pan, enough oil to float the fritters.

Roll out the dough as thinly as you can on a floured surface and cut into squares about 7 cm/3 in. Fold two corners across diagonally, moistening and pinching to seal.

Lift the pastries on a wooden-spoon handle and slide them into the hot oil, 4 or 5 at a time. They will bob to the surface as they start to expand. Spin them over with a slotted spoon and fry until golden. Drain on kitchen paper while you fry the next batch.

Dip the fritters in honey syrup, then drain on a wire rack. Serve the same day, sprinkled with sugar.

LEVANTE

Paparajotes
Fritters with lemon or bay leaves

~

The lovely lemon tree has deliciously scented leaves as well as fruit and these are used to flavour simple fritters. You can do the same thing with bay leaves (even dried ones). At teatime children can easily devour a dozen fritters each – the best way to eat them – but an adult portion for dessert is about 8.

SERVES 8

- about 70 fresh lemon or bay leaves
- 250 g/8 oz plain flour
- 50 g/2 oz caster sugar
- 250 ml/8 fl oz milk
- 2 tbsp not-too-dry white wine or (better) moscatel
- 3 small egg whites
- fresh sunflower oil for deep frying
- vanilla sugar for sprinkling

Wash and dry the leaves. Mix the flour and sugar together in a bowl, and make a well in the middle (or use a food processor). Pour in the milk and wine and beat in the flour to make a smooth cream. Whisk the whites to soft peaks and fold them into the batter.

Heat clean oil for deep frying. Hold each leaf by the stalk and quickly dip it in the batter. Fry about 8 at a time (a portion), flipping them over with a slotted spoon when they start to colour round the edges – about 2 minutes overall. They puff like cigars. Drain on kitchen paper. If serving a batch at a time – the best way – take the oil off the heat, until you are back to cooking. (Otherwise it overheats and the first fritters of the new batch overbrown before the last ones are dipped.)

Sprinkle with vanilla sugar and eat by picking them up by the stalk and pulling the fritter off the leaf (discard it) with your teeth.

Bunyols de vent

Hot orange puffs a wind could lift

~

SERVES 4

- 75 ml/3 fl oz milk
- 50 ml/2 fl oz water
- 1 tbsp strong black coffee (the end of a solo cup, usually sweet)
- 15 g/½ oz butter
- 1 tbsp sunflower oil
- pinch of salt
- 75 g/3 oz plain flour, sifted
- finely grated zest of ½ orange
- 2 small eggs
- 1 tsp orange-flower water
- oil for deep frying
- caster sugar for sifting

'This recipe is a gift!' I was told, with Spanish enthusiasm. They are the lightest of little choux puffs with very Spanish ingredients.

Put the milk, water, coffee, butter, oil and salt in a saucepan over heat. When boiling point is reached, shoot in the sifted, measured flour. Beat vigorously with a wooden spoon to obtain a fine dough. When it comes away clean from the sides of the pan (about a minute) take from the heat. Don't skimp here – it must be reasonably dry.

Beat in the grated orange zest. Let it cool a minute, then beat in the eggs in turn, to make a smooth paste. Lastly beat in the orange-flower water.

Heat clean oil for deep frying. Make small balls with 2 teaspoons, using one to scrape the mixture off the other into the fat, 6–7 together, as quickly as you can. Fry them, rolling them over with a slotted spoon, so they expand evenly – 1–2 minutes. Drain on kitchen paper, while you fry the rest. Don't keep them waiting long. Eat powdered with sugar.

ANDALUSIA

Soplillos de Granada

Granada almond meringues

～

A home-made version of the Christmas candy, turrón. The name suggests a gust of wind will blow them away, but they are actually the chewy rather than the melt-in-your-mouth variety of meringue. It is the just-perceptible amount of lemon that makes them such a success.

Toast the almonds in the oven at 150°C/300°F/Gas 2 until biscuit-coloured and smelling pleasantly – about 30 minutes. Leave the oven on. Chop one-third of the nuts coarsely and grind the rest (in a food processor).

Whisk the egg whites in a large bowl until stiff, then fold in the lemon zest with two-thirds of the sugar, shaking in a spoonful or so at a time. Add the lemon juice and whisk until stiff and shiny. Mix together the remaining sugar and ground nuts and fold into the meringue. Fold in the chopped nuts.

Spoon the meringue into tall heaps on greased foil on two baking trays, spacing them out well. Put into the oven and immediately turn it down to 125°C/225°F/Gas low. Leave to puff and dry out for 1–1½ hours.

MAKES ABOUT 30

- ○ *150 g/5 oz blanched almonds*
- ○ *2 large egg whites*
- ○ *grated zest of ½ lemon*
- ○ *200 g/7 oz vanilla caster sugar*
- ○ *2 tsp lemon juice*

LEVANTE

Tocino de cielo

Sweet temptation

SERVES 8–10

- ○ *75 g/3 oz granulated sugar for the caramel*
- ○ *175 g/6 oz caster sugar*
- ○ *½ cinnamon stick*
- ○ *pared zest of ½ lemon*
- ○ *150 ml/5 fl oz water*
- ○ *6 yolks plus 1 whole egg*

One dessertspoon is the most you should eat, so it doesn't matter that everything about this dessert is sinful! It is one of those sweets that one has no curiosity to try, but then proves to be irresistible. The name means, literally, a slab of heaven.

Put the sugar for the caramel in a small saucepan with 1 tbsp of water and heat until it caramelizes, pulling the toasted sugar in from outside to middle. When the syrup is a good toffee colour, pour it immediately into an 18 cm/7 in ring mould: it helps if this is warm. Using gloves, quickly tip the mould to and fro until coated.

Put the caster sugar in the same pan with the cinnamon stick, lemon zest and water. Dissolve the sugar slowly, then boil – for about 10 minutes – until it will make a weak thread when dropped from a spoon (102°C/215°F on a sugar thermometer). Remove the cinnamon stick and zest.

Whisk the yolks with the whole egg until creamy, then slowly pour in the hot syrup, whisking all the time. Strain the custard into the mould.

The cooking operation is very delicate, and even a bain-marie in the oven risks splitting the custard. Stand the mould on a trivet (of the type used for steaming vegetables) in a saucepan and pour boiling water beneath it. Cover the pan with foil, then a lid and steam for 20 minutes. Cool then chill. Run a knife round the custard, invert a plate over the top and turn out to serve. Cut small portions.

ASTURIAS AND CANTABRIA

Arroz con leche requemado
Rice pudding with caramel topping

~

With its subtle Arab flavouring and the creaminess of good ice cream, the old way to make this milk pudding was to simmer the milk for several hours, to reduce it. The modern version adds butter. I own a quemador to glaze the sugar top, a round metal plate with a long wooden handle, which is heated on the stove. But outside Spain, I use the blow-torch bought for stripping paint!

SERVES 6

- 1 litre/1¾ pt full-fat milk
- 1 cinnamon stick
- thinly pared zest of 1 lemon
- 4 tbsp medium-grain or short-grain rice
- 75 g/3 oz sugar
- 25 g/1 oz unsalted butter
- 2 tbsp Anís de la Asturiana dulce or another anis liqueur

TOPPING

- ground cinnamon
- 12–15 tbsp sugar

Heat the milk with the cinnamon stick and the lemon zest loosely attached together by a cocktail stick. When hot, add the rice and leave to cook on the lowest possible heat, with a wooden spoon in, stirring occasionally to make sure the bottom doesn't catch. Cook for about 50 minutes, when the rice should start to be visible above the surface of the milk.

Add the sugar and butter and cook for 10 minutes longer. The whole thing should be fairly liquid, as it will thicken when cold. Remove the cinnamon and zest, stir in the anis and ladle into 6 individual bowls or ramekins. Sprinkle with cinnamon, then chill.

Not more than an hour before serving, cover each top with 2–3 tbsp of sugar and give them a blast of heat to glaze: some grills are hot enough for this. (The glaze melts into the pudding if left too long.) Then re-chill until ready to serve.

ASTURIAS AND CANTABRIA

Casadielles
Walnut puff pastries

MAKES 18

- 200 g/7 oz shelled walnuts
- 75 g/3 oz caster sugar
- 2 tbsp Anís de la Asturiana dulce *(see note)*
- 25 g/1 oz butter, plus extra for greasing
- 50 g/1 lb prepared puff pastry
- 1 large egg, beaten for glazing

The Christmas cracker shape of these pastries is distinctive. In the old days they used to be deep-fried in clean oil, then sugared, but nowadays they are usually baked.

Heat the oven to 230°C/450°F/Gas 8. Crush the nuts. (Angelina, who gave me the recipe, does it with a rolling pin, but at home a food processor was perfect.) Work in the sugar, anis and butter, then divide in half.

Roll out half the puff pastry (keeping the rest in the fridge) to a 30 cm/12 in square and cut it into 9 squares. Portion half the filling, making a bullet shape on each square. Brush the edges to left and right with beaten egg. Fold the top edge over the filling, brush with egg and then cover with the bottom edge. Press the ends together to make a little pillow shape.

Arrange on a greased baking tray, seam down, pressing gently to seal. Seal the free ends by pressing with a fork, then glaze the tops with beaten egg. Bake in the oven for 9–10 minutes until well puffed and brown, while you prepare the second batch. Eat warm, on the day they are baked.

Note: Anís is an *aguardiente* (eau-de-vie) that turns up constantly in Spanish cooking. This one is a sweet liqueur; others, like Anís de Chinchón and Anís de Mono, are dry and are drunk with water like pastis. Pernod is the easy substitute.

THE BASQUE COUNTRY

Helado Nelusko

Chocolate and toasted almond ice cream

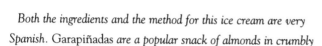

Both the ingredients and the method for this ice cream are very Spanish. Garapiñadas are a popular snack of almonds in crumbly sugar, toasted but not caramelized.

SERVES 8

- 200 g/7 oz dark chocolate
- 75 g/3 oz caster sugar
- 250 ml/8 fl oz milk
- 125 g/4½ oz toasted almonds (see page 205), garapiñadas *or* guirlache (see page 212)
- 6 large egg yolks
- 4 tbsp curaçao *or* Cointreau

MERINGUE

- 3 large egg whites
- 2 tbsp caster sugar

Ahead, make hot chocolate by stirring the chocolate and sugar together in the hot milk. Let this chill.

Pound the almonds (they must be very dry) or process – I used half toasted almonds and half *guirlache* very successfully. Beat the egg yolks until very fluffy and incorporate the almond powder with the chocolate milk. Freeze this – it remains soft.

Whisk the egg whites to soft peaks in a big bowl. Sprinkle with the sugar and whisk until glossy. Fold the frozen custard and liqueur into the meringue. Put it into a mould (1.5 litre/ 2½ pt) if you like, then freeze until firm. This can be portioned directly from the freezer.

Note: Raw egg yolk custards used to be more common in ices than they are now. Freezing thickens egg yolks and they never liquefy completely again. However, cook over simmering water, if you prefer, for safety reasons.

THE BASQUE COUNTRY

Reinetas en salsa de limón
Baked apples with lemon sauce

~

SERVES 6

- 6 reinetas or Cox's apples
- about 100 g/4 oz caster sugar
- butter for greasing
- about 175 ml/6 fl oz thick cream, whipped

TART LEMON SAUCE

- 75 g/3 oz sugar
- 75 ml/3 fl oz water
- 2 strips of lemon zest and juice of 2 lemons
- 2 tsp cornflour
- 25 g/1 oz unsalted butter
- 1 egg yolk

A pleasant contrast of hot, slightly caramelized apple pieces and a rather tart lemon sauce. Thick cream is served as an accompaniment – a reverse of the usual truth that lemon juice cuts the fat!

Heat the oven to 220°C/425°F/Gas 7. Peel and core the apples and cut into 6–8 wedges according to size. Toss them in sugar and arrange (core side upwards) on a heavy baking sheet greased with butter. Sprinkle more sugar over them, then bake in the hot oven for 10 minutes, until the sugar starts to caramelize on the sheet. Give the apples a stir to coat well.

Meanwhile put the sugar and water for the sauce in a pan with the strips of lemon zest. Bring slowly to the boil, then boil for 5 minutes. Leave off the heat to infuse. Dissolve the cornflour in a little lemon juice. Pour the hot lemon syrup on to it and return to the pan. Stir over a low heat until thickened. Discard the zest pieces and add the remaining lemon juice. Bring back to the boil, then add the butter and egg yolk. Stir off the heat.

Centre the apple wedges on 4 plates, pour the lemon sauce round and pass whipped cream.

NEW CASTILE AND LA MANCHA

Alajú

Arab honey and nut sweetmeat

~

An old, old Arab sweetmeat, famous in Cuenca and clearly related to Sienese panforte. It is very moreish, despite simple ingredients. The touch of orange lends it magic.

Put the honey in a saucepan with the orange zest, grated on a coarse cheese grater. Leave to simmer for a couple of minutes. Grate the bread into crumbs – grating on the same grater as the zest to pick up all the orange oil. Add the toasted almonds (plus walnuts – recommended!) to the honey, then the crumbs. Stir continuously for about 5 minutes; the mixture will stiffen and come away from the side of the pan. Off the heat add the orange-flower water (it otherwise evaporates during cooking) and stir it in.

Turn on to the rice paper and pat into a disc, or make 2 smaller discs. Cover with another piece of rice paper and press down gently, to less than a finger thickness. Work round the edge with a table knife, to neaten it. When the sweetmeat is cold, trim the rice paper to fit. Keep in an airtight tin and slice off chunks then cut into pieces to serve.

MAKES 18–24 PORTIONS

- 250 g/8 oz honey, warmed by standing in hot water
- grated zest of 1 orange
- 150 g/5 oz stale bread without crusts
- 150 g/5 oz almonds, toasted (see page 205), or part of the weight in walnuts
- ½ tsp orange-flower water
- 2 sheets of rice paper, each 24 cm/9 in square (or 4 smaller sheets)

Guirlache

Almond and aniseed candy

MAKES 48

- 250 g/8 oz almonds, half blanched, half unblanched
- 250 g/8 oz sugar
- 1 tbsp lemon juice
- ½ tsp aniseeds, roughly crushed
- 1 tsp almond oil or a flavourless oil

Almonds and honey make the hugely popular Christmas candy, turrón. Guirlache is a much less sweet version, hardly known outside Spain. It is sold in a bar, but I make it in little rounds to serve with ice cream.

Toast the almonds – 30 minutes in an oven at about 150°C/300°F/Gas 2 – shaking the pan occasionally. They should become biscuit-coloured, smell pleasantly and be very dry.

Put the sugar and lemon juice in a small pan over a high heat. As the sugar melts and colours round the edges, pull it towards the middle with a wooden spoon. Continue until it is all coffee-coloured. Tip in the almonds and stir once, then add the aniseeds. Spoon on to oiled foil, four nuts at a time (mixing the colours) to form little rounds.

Alternatively, spread out on the foil, keeping the nuts close together. Let it set for a couple of minutes, then use the foil to fold it over lengthways. Press it together with a rolling pin and pat with the side of the pin to make straight edges all round. Wrap the spare foil round and store as it is, in an airtight box. Chop off strips to eat.

GALICIA

Tarta de Santiago
St James's almond tart

~

Not the cake you find in Madrid, but the real thing, as served in Santiago on St James's Day. The almond flavour is set off by sherry. The top is dusted with icing sugar, with a stencil of St James's two-handled sword. The layer of quince paste under the almond was suggested by a friend.

Make a sweet pastry dough by combining the flour, cinnamon, sugar, butter and egg yolk in a food processor. Chill it for 20 minutes while the oven heats to 200°C/400°F/Gas 6 with a baking sheet in it.

Grease a 22 cm/9 in flan tin with removable bottom. Roll out the dough on a floured work surface to just larger than the flan tin (this is best done between 2 sheets of cling film). Remove the top film and turn the dough face down in the tin, then remove the rest of the film and press the dough into position.

Mix 50 g/2 oz ground almonds with the quince paste or jam and spread over the bottom of the pastry case. Mix the remaining almonds with the caster sugar, cinnamon, lemon zest, eggs, melted butter and sherry. Turn into the pastry case and smooth.

Put the tart on the hot baking sheet in the oven and bake for 10 minutes. Then turn down the heat to 170°C/325°F/Gas 3 and cook for 15–20 minutes longer, until lightly browned. Let it stand for 5 minutes then remove the tin and cool on a wire rack. Dust the cold tart with icing sugar.

SERVES 8

- 150 g/5 oz plain flour, plus extra for sprinkling
- ½ tsp ground cinnamon (optional)
- 2 tbsp caster sugar
- 100 g/4 oz butter, finely diced
- 1 small egg yolk, beaten
- 200 g/7 oz dulce de membrillo, *sweet quince paste (sold in Italian delicatessens as* cotogna*), or apricot jam*
- icing sugar for dusting

ALMOND FILLING

- 200 g/7 oz ground almonds from a sealed packet
- 100 g/3½ oz caster sugar
- ½ tsp ground cinnamon
- finely grated zest of ½ lemon
- 3 small eggs
- 75 g/3 oz butter, melted
- 75 ml/3 fl oz oloroso sherry

Tarta de manzanas
Apple batter cake

~

A cake from apple-and-dairy country in the north, with the typically Spanish flavouring of cinnamon.

SERVES 6–8

- 175 g/6 oz unsalted butter
- 150 g/5 oz plain flour
- 6 small tabadillas or Cox's apples, peeled, cored and cut in 10–12 segments
- 2 tbsp apple brandy or Calvados
- 2 tsp baking powder
- 1 tsp ground cinnamon
- 175 g/6 oz caster sugar
- 3 large eggs
- 3 tbsp full-fat milk

GLAZE

- 4 tbsp apricot jam
- 1 tbsp apple brandy or Calvados
- 1 tsp cornflour mixed with 2 tsp water

Heat the oven to 180°C/350°F/Gas 4. Use a little of the butter to grease a 22 cm/9 in spring-release cake tin, then dust with flour. Heat the remaining butter in a frying pan, add the apples and stir to coat. Cover and cook gently for 10 minutes, stirring once. Chop one-third of the apples (or process roughly) and add the apple brandy.

Combine the sifted flour, baking powder, cinnamon and sugar (adding them to the processor, if using), then add the apple mixture. Work in the eggs and milk and pour into the tin. Arrange the remaining apple slices on top, then bake in the oven for about 50 minutes, or until slightly shrunk from the edge of the tin, risen and golden.

For the glaze, warm the jam and apple brandy, and stir in the cornflour mixture. Cook for 2–3 minutes until clear. Brush the cake top with some glaze. Leave to cool for about 30 minutes, then remove the sides of the tin. Rewarm the remaining glaze and brush on the cake. Eat warm or cold, with cream, egg custard or on its own.

THE BALEARIC ISLANDS

Ponx d'ous

Rum and milk punch

~

A milk and rum punch with overtones of the English navy, it is served in Majorca at Carnival balls and grand occasions. Some older families have beautiful china punch bowls and fine silver spoons with long mother-of-pearl handles to ladle it.

Beat the yolks and sugar until the sugar has completely dissolved and the mixture is white. For a hot punch, stir in the hot milk and rum to form a cream. Strain into 2 glasses and serve at once.

For cold punch, use cold milk and serve the drink in wine glasses over ice.

MAKES 2 GLASSES

- *2 small egg yolks*
- *2 tablespoons caster sugar*
- *250 ml/8 fl oz milk, hot or icy*
- *2 tablespoons dark rum (or brandy)*

THE BALEARIC ISLANDS

Ponche de sanguineas

Iced white rum with blood oranges

~

A beautiful pink summer punch, made with the local white rum.

Put the water and sugar into a punch bowl. Add the thinly pared citron (or lemon) zest and the fruit, sliced very thinly. and stir to dissolve the sugar. Leave for 24 hours to infuse, chilling thoroughly.

Strain, pressing the fruit slices well. Add the orange-flower water with lemons, because citrons are highly perfumed. Add the orange juice and rum from a bottle in the fridge before serving. Serve in a wine glass over a couple of ice cubes.

MAKES 16 GLASSES

- *250 ml/8 fl oz white rum or Bacardi, chilled*
- *juice of 4–6 blood oranges*
- *1 litre/1¾ pt water*
- *350 g/12 oz sugar*
- *3 ripe citrons (or lemons)*
- *1 tsp orange-flower water (with lemons)*
- *ice cubes*

Granizado
Iced lemonade

MAKES 20 GLASSES

- ○ *10 juicy lemons*
- ○ *1 litre/1¾ pt boiling water*
- ○ *350 g/12 oz sugar*
- ○ *ice cubes*

In the glare of the day, or sitting out under the trees at night waiting for the first breeze to break the heat, nothing is more refreshing than ice tinkling in a glass. Unlike the Italian granità, this is not frozen lemonade, but is poured over slushed ice.

Wash the lemons and thinly pare off strips of zest with a potato peeler. Pour boiling water on to the zest in a bowl and leave to infuse until cold.

Remove the zest strips and stir in the sugar with the lemon juice. Keep this base in the fridge. Dilute with an equal amount of water.

Break ice cubes inside a towel by hitting with a rolling pin, then put in the processor, to reduce to slush. To serve, fill a tall glass with ice slush, then top up with lemonade and add straws.

Carajillo
Brandied coffee

SERVES 1

- ○ *1 solo (small black) cup of coffee*
- ○ *sugar to taste*
- ○ *Spanish brandy or Anís de Chinchón*

'The perfect drink to start an evening when you are rather tired,' said a Valencian friend, 'because it gets you drunk and wakes you up at the same time.' It is also provocative – the name means a 'willy'.

Sweeten the coffee and add a warming slug of brandy or liqueur.

Index

Acknowledgements

My grateful thanks go firstly to Nan del Pozo, without whose enthusiasm this book would never have been written, and to Sue Macworth-Praed, who has shown such interest. So many people have helped, chief among them Manuel Carillo Díaz, Juan Díaz, Denyse Casuso, Beléta Child, Pilar Gernika, the family of Julián el Carnicero at Torrejas, Sarah and Alvaro Lozano Olivares, Jaime Manso Zubeldia, Janet Mendel Searl, Ampara Moreno, Vicente Muriel, Andres Núñez de Prado, Kristina and José Manuel Paredes Asencio, Maria-Angeles Pertierra, Angelina Portillo Giron, Alícia Rios-Ivars, Lola Ruiz de Javaloyes, Consuelo de Soto, Paloma-María Tomé Beamonte, Christina Venito and last, though very far from least, Gill Watling Ceballos.

My thanks are also due for support from Matilda Gladstone and Carmen Brieva at the Spanish Institute, Mercedes Reeves at Canning House and María José Sevilla and Janine Gilson at Foods from Spain in London.

I am also deeply grateful to the innumerable Spanish women who have answered my questions and my pointing finger, explained bits of recipes and family folklore to me, and guided me on my way.